The Political Economy of Inflation
in the United States

Paul Peretz

The Political Economy of Inflation in the United States

The University of Chicago Press
Chicago and London

Paul Peretz is assistant professor in the Department of
Political Science, University of Washington.

The University of Chicago Press, Chicago 60637
The University of Chicago Press, Ltd., London

Library of Congress Cataloging in Publication Data

Peretz, Paul.
   The political economy of inflation in the United States.

   Includes index.
   1. Inflation (Finance)—United States.   2. United
States—Economic policy—1981–   .   I. Title.
HG540.P47   1983   332.4′1′0973   82-24738
ISBN 0-226-65671-3
ISBN 0-226-65672-1 (pbk.)

To my Aunt Ann

Contents

Preface

This book is concerned with the relation between the effects of economic outcomes on the population and the process through which economic policy is made. It concerns itself primarily with the relation between inflation and economic policy making, but is also concerned with the degree to which changes in unemployment and income growth affect that relation.

This is a broad question and in order to answer it I have taken a broad approach. Most books either use original evidence culled from primary data or provide a reinterpretation of secondary material. This book intermixes the two modes. Likewise most works dealing with similar questions analyze aggregate data, or analyze public opinion data or analyze the actions and beliefs of those involved in the policy process. This book takes the approach that different parts of the overall question require different methods and as a result I do all three. Finally I have chosen to intermix both political and economic modes of analysis.

While I feel that this broad approach is necessary in order to deal with the questions I raise, it means that I have not been able to deal with many interesting questions in the depth that they deserve. It is my hope that some of the issues I raise will be explored by others in more detail.

Perhaps the most significant of the questions I ask, is whether the patterns of representation in this area best conforms to pluralist, Marxist or elitist models. It may be of some interest to the reader that my eventual answer was not the one that I had anticipated. I had expected that while none of the models would explain the data fully, the pluralist ones would be most successful. There is I think a natural tendency to try to make the data fit one's initial model, and my use of short-term correlations in chapter 3 might in part be prompted by such a tendency. This I feel gives added weight to my conclusion that pluralist models had little explanatory power and that the other models had a better fit.

In the first chapter of this book I outline the major questions dealt with. In the second, I introduce inflation theory, examine the debates in the economic literature over its causes and effects and look briefly at American economic policy in the past thirty years. In the third chapter, I examine the distributive effects of inflation, concentrating on the effects on the income of major factors of production. I also elaborate my study of distributive effects by breaking down major categories into politically interesting subcategories as well as by breaking down the time period to capture the effect of major political influences, acting on a non-continuous basis, on policy making. The fourth and fifth chapters examine public opinion toward inflation and seek to identify attitude trends as well as to reveal the differences in the opinions of relevant population subsets. The sixth chapter looks at the policy making system for macroeconomic policy and examines which actors are important and which are not. The seventh chapter introduces the attitudes of the major representative groups toward inflation. It shows changes in those opinions over time and compares the attitudes and actions of groups with both the "objective" effects of inflation on the population subsets that those groups supposedly represent and with the attitudes of those subsets toward inflation. An effort will be made to determine whether the attitudes and actions of the representative groups are most influenced by the attitudes of the constituents, the effects inflation actually has on their constituents, the desire of representative group members to maintain their power, influence or rewards, or by the desire to maintain or establish a class-based distribution system. In the final chapter, I explicitly relate my findings to the Marxist, elite, and pluralist-democratic models and attempt to establish which model is most isomorphic to the findings.

I would like to thank a number of people whose help, guidance and support aided me in the production of this book. Woody Kelly was particularly helpful in encouraging my theoretical focus and in sharpening my perception of methodological problems. Lloyd Rudolph read an early draft of this book and gave me much useful advice, as did the anonymous readers for the University of Chicago Press. Alan Robinson and Walter Murphy first introduced me to the questions that lie in the interstices of politics and economics and the problems they raise for political theory. Paul Peterson first interested me in the political aspects of inflation policy. My interactions with Ted Lowi and Adam Przeworski sharpened my awareness of the problems of modeling public policy. Philippe Schmitter clarified my understanding of pluralist theory while Jon Kraus improved my understanding of Marxist theory. I had useful discussions on aspects of the work with William Holt, Kristin Monroe, Ken Woodside, Lance Bennett and Don McCrone. Douglas Hibbs and Leon Lindberg included me in interesting projects that expanded my understanding of the area. My research assistants Craig Miley and Gary Spiegal helped in the collection and organization of data. Finally I would like to thank my parents and my sister and brother-in-law for their general aid and support.

1   The Problem

In the period since the Second World War inflation has become one of the major problems facing developed Western democracies. Though it has been less severe a problem in the United States than in countries like Italy, Japan and the United Kingdom, it has nonetheless been considered by policy makers as a problem of major proportions. In the hundred years before the second world war, inflation was essentially a cyclical phenomenon with periods of prosperity, particularly war periods, leading to demand inflation and the following recessionary periods being accompanied by a compensatory demand deflation. In the postwar period however, prices have increased fairly steadily, with some increase taking place, albeit at a lower rate, even during periods of recession.

This change has led to a vast literature from economists seeking to explain how inflation could take place in conditions where classical or Keynesian theory would have led one to expect stable or declining price levels. As this literature has developed, there has been an increasing tendency for economists to claim that the change is due in some part to the fact that political factors which they had assumed constant were in fact changing. Some pointed to the increasing power of the unions to prevent downward movements in monetary wages, some to the combination of an increasingly oligarchical corporate structure and an increasingly planned state in preventing downward movements in prices, while still others pointed to the role played by consumer expectations of government policy.

When these and other political variables have been employed by economists, there has been a tendency to see

1

these variables in the context of a polity that behaved as a pluralist democracy, a basically democratic state in which the major producer groups
wielded major amounts of power on behalf of their constituents.

The central purpose of this book is to find out whether policies affecting
inflation are made in the way that we would expect in a pluralist democracy, or whether other models, such as the Marxist and and elitist models,
provide a better description of the way such policy is made. Further,
because proponents of all three positions claim that economic policy making is particularly well described by their theory, this book can also be
seen as a critical test of the relative ability of the three theories to accurately describe the American political process.

The book has two secondary aims. First, it adds to our knowledge of
the effects of inflation, the patterns of opinion on the question of inflation,
and the positions of various governmental and quasi-governmental groups
on the inflation problem. Second, it aims to make a small contribution to
the solution of some particular problems arising from the economic literature, which involve political variables.

In this chapter I will first look at these two secondary aims. I will then
go on to look at the different models of the political process which this
book seeks to test and will spell out how I will use data derived from
examination of the inflation policy process to test them.

The descriptive aim falls into three parts. The first part is an investi-
gation of the effects of inflation on the incomes of various subgroups
within the population. The second deals with opinions regarding the effects of inflation and with shifts in those opinions. The last deals with
elite group attitudes toward inflation—particularly attitudes of those in
the state structure, parties and certain relevant pressure groups.

The effect of inflation on the population as a whole, and of subgroups
within it, has been the subject of innumerable a priori studies. Countless
economists have put forward models, not always consistent with one
another, aimed at demonstrating the effects of inflation under certain sets
of assumptions. But, somewhat surprisingly in view of the tremendous
political importance of the question, empirical research on the subject has
been somewhat sparse.[1] What work there has been tends to concentrate
on the effects of inflation on the income of the poor. Work by Hollister
and Palmer and Williamson does this most explicitly but works by Swan
and Phelps also deal primarily with effects on the poor.[2] There are also
articles by Bach and Stephenson and by Wolff dealing largely with effects
on wealth, and simulations of income effects by Budd and Seiders, Mirer,
Nordhaus and Minarik.[3] While the last four studies are more useful than
the rest, none of the material is entirely satisfactory and most of the results
rest on assumptions about the impact of inflation on individual income
types that lack extensive empirical support. The present work, though it

does not resolve the problems of this literature, does expand the current work by showing results based on different assumptions that are more politically plausible, and by looking at a somewhat wider range of factor incomes.

Work on the opinions held by the public toward inflation is meager, although there has been some expansion in recent years. Aside from various pieces by Katona and his successors at the Michigan Consumer Survey[4] and various newspaper and magazine reports, most of the work has concentrated on two topics. One, primarily the concern of economists, has been the degree to which expectations of inflation cause future inflation. Virtually all of this work however has used previous rates of inflation as the measure of current (rational) expectations, thereby measuring little more than auto-correlation in the inflation rate. The much smaller number of economists attempting to directly measure inflation expectations have almost invariably relied upon a bi-yearly survey of economists conducted by Joseph Livingston since 1947, which has obvious generalizability problems.[5] The other topic on which a literature has formed has been the relation between inflation and political popularity. This work, while useful and often informative, generally ignores the intermediate steps through which it is assumed inflation rates are translated into political support and hence avoids dealing with data on opinions toward inflation. My book presents a wide range of new opinion data, thus expanding our knowledge of consumer expectations and opinions about inflation and illuminating the process by which inflation is translated into political demands.

In seeking knowledge of elite attitudes toward inflation, I shall be concerned less with uncovering new material than with focusing on and interpreting that which already exists. Unlike the other two areas on which this work touches, there is a plethora of work on elite behavior—particularly within the state structure. In the United States the work of Bach on monetary policy, of Wildavsky, Pierce, and Manley on fiscal policy, of Weber, Sheahan and McConnell on wage-price policy, and of Mangum and Davidson on manpower policy, represent only the tip of an iceberg of literature related to elite behavior and economic policy.[6] All these works however deal chiefly with group and individual behavior in the policy making context, without endeavoring to trace particular policy positions to individual components of the economic matrix facing the respective policy makers. It will be the task of this work to extract from this and other material the attitudes of various elite groups toward inflation and toward the proper trade-offs between inflation and other goals, as well as to ascertain the degree to which those beliefs influence the actions of the groups and of the individuals composing those groups.

As well as describing the material, this book aims to test some middle-level generalizations arising out of the interaction between what are generally thought of as "economic" and "political" variables. Most of these will be described at the appropriate stage of the book. Here I will only mention three.

One of the most interesting problems arising out of the inflation phenomenon is the disparity between the real effects that economists judge inflation to have on people's incomes and the perceived salience of the inflation problem to the average citizen. As we shall see in chapter 3, even on the most pessimistic interpretation, the "welfare" costs of inflation are likely to amount to less than 1 percent of GNP at the generally moderate rates of inflation prevailing in the United States.[7] Under more optimistic interpretations these mildly negative effects would be more than offset by positive side-effects.[8] Although work on the distributional effects of inflation is both sparse and tentative, virtually all the writers have difficulty finding the adverse distributional effects on certain sections of the population postulated in some of the deductive models.[9] Indeed, even if there were such effects, they would have to be of the sort that take a lot from most of the population and redistribute it to a few for the effect on public opinion to be substantial. What evidence there is however implies that, if there is any effect, it is probably in the reverse direction.[10]

Despite the fact that economists have been unable to show substantial adverse effects, inflation is perceived as one of the most important problems facing the common man. Moreover, as we shall see in chapter 5, when one breaks down attitudes toward inflation by various groupings, they seem much the same for all groups. Inflation has been one of the top ten problems cited by most respondents and has been cited as the most important problem in the United States more than any other domestic problem during the postwar period.[11] I attack this problem from two angles, both of which shed some light on the apparent contradiction. One angle is to re-examine the economic impact data using the assumption that people will not see the real long-term effects of inflation on their total income but rather the short-term correlation between inflation and the change in their primary income source. The second angle is to question the implicit assumption that makes it a contradiction, that people base their view of inflation on their own experience of it.

An equally important topic upon which this book casts some new light is the validity of the rational expectations approach in economics, which yields the strong result that discretionary monetary and fiscal policy does not when systematically employed affect real variables or make possible a trade-off between inflation and unemployment.[12] "The analysis yielding this result presumes, as is well known, that the economy is entirely free of money illusion and that the public possesses the same information as the monetary authority concerning the structure of the economy, the past values of relevant variables and the policy rule in effect."[13] In this work I will present data which is inconsistent with the second of these assumptions and which casts some doubt on the short-term validity of the first.

A last question which this book confronts is whether there is, as is asserted by a large number of economists and political scientists, something approximating a political business cycle. This is generally seen as a situation where elected governments induce rapid growth in election years in order to insure re-election and deflate somewhat after elections. Used together with an expectations-augmented Phillips curve around a natural rate, or with institutional downward price rigidity, the political business cycle has been proposed as a central inflationary mechanism. I show that, when looked at carefully, the literature lends less support to the political business cycle theory than it first appears to. I also show that people do not have the sets of beliefs about economic matters that most versions of the theory explicitly or implicitly assume.

Alternative Models of the Policy Process

A major aim of this book is to use the material on inflation and policy developed in the bulk of the work to test certain key differences between the pluralist, elitist and Marxist models as accurate descriptions of political reality in the United States. My primary concern will be with the pluralist model—the most widely held among political scientists and the one most often claimed to apply directly to policy making. But I also want to make a preliminary attempt to assess the degree to which elite and the Marxist models yield behavioral predictions which fit the observed data. Brief decriptions of the models that I have developed from the full matrix of each of the three approaches follow. The reader should note that the accuracy of these models as representations of the theories for which they stand is open to question. In particular, in producing the Marxist and elitist models I have sometimes had to go beyond the original sources in order to derive a formulation that would enable them to be tested in this context. In doing so I have sought to extend the models in such a way that they are consistent with as many versions of the basic theories as possible, but it is inevitable that each of my more theoretically inclined readers will disagree with at least some of the particulars.

The Pluralist Models

Pluralist models, of which there are numerous variants, are principally identified by their emphasis on voluntaralism, individualism and group action, by their view of the political process as responsive to the demands of the citizenry and by their organic view of the political system. Here I examine a central pluralist-democratic model and two variants, the group model and the rational actor model, and apply them to the economic policy making process. These models all see macroeconomic policy as responsive to political demands emanating from the bulk of the adult population. All three visualize a process where people in different groups accurately feel the effects of inflation, form opinions toward inflation based on those effects, make demands upon political bodies in line with their opinions and find those demands answered, thereby restoring political equilibrium for the time being, or incompletely answered, thereby maintaining the flow of demands and responses. Further, all three assume that the mass of citizens can impose sanctions on non-responsive political entities, both individually and through representative groups themselves subject to sanctions.

More specifically the pluralist-democratic model, shown in figure 1, assumes that there is a state structure, of which the parties and interest groups are a part, which makes macroeconomic policy.[14] This policy embodies expected short- and long-term tradeoff points between inflation and other economic variables, of which growth and unemployment are the most important. When these policies are executed, changes take place which may affect the trade-off point. These policies then impact upon the economic system. After the policies have had time to work through the system, characteristic inflation rates, unemployment rates and rates of growth emerge. Changes in these three variables lead to changes in the real incomes of wage and salary earners, the self-employed, profit receivers and those on fixed incomes. These effects are then perceived by individual members of these groups, who decide whether changes in the three variables affected them favorably or unfavorably. If the effect is favorable it is assumed that they will support the policies causing this change. If the effect is unfavorable it is assumed that they will demand appropriate policy changes that will reverse this effect. These demands are made to the interest groups and parties that represent them, who work to obtain the policies demanded by their constituents. The figure as drawn shows only the predominant linkages and leaves open the possibility that interest groups and political parties may seek to represent groups other than those identified here when this does not conflict with the representation of their primary constituency.

The model leaves open the question of whether individuals have specific demand patterns for reacting to the effects of changes in each of the three variables, or whether the effects of changes in all three variables are combined to produce a single pattern of demands. It also leaves open the question of whether adverse effects will lead people to demand changes that would reduce the price level, or changes that would increase their monetary income, or some combination of these. It does not however leave open the question of consistency. For the pluralist-democratic model

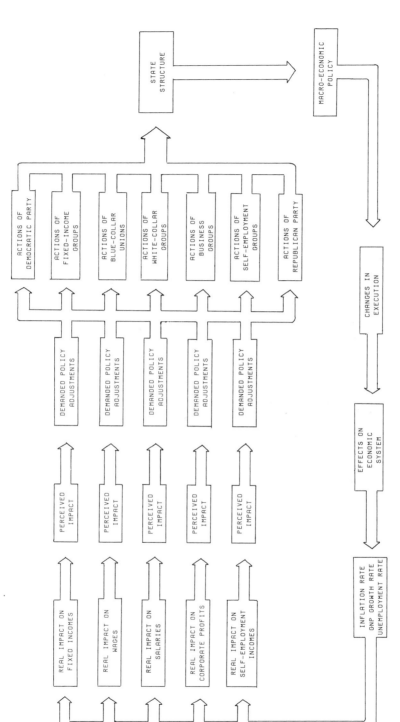

Figure 1   A simplified pluralist-democratic model of the inflation-policy-making process

to work it is necessary that the policy alterations demanded would have the intended effects and that those effects can be accurately perceived.

A few additional assumptions made by the model must be elucidated. One is that it assumes a semi-oligarchical political market oriented to producer interests. Barriers to entry are assumed to inhibit the emergence of new parties and interest groups. High information costs and a divergence between individual and group rational interest are seen as particularly hampering consumer groups.[15] The combination of these factors is assumed to reduce the chance that a consumer group aimed at reducing inflation would emerge. Despite these restrictions however the pluralist-democratic model assumes, as we have seen, that parties and interest groups act as if they were in a competitive market and must be highly responsive to constituent's demands. This responsiveness is meant to exist primarily because the constituents act as the owners of the interest groups and parties, imposing their demands on their representatives. The long-term threat that competing groups will be formed is also meant to keep groups responsive.

Another assumption is that the parties and groups perform different roles within the political system. The groups are seen as the representatives of particular bounded sections of the population. Although they are seen as primarily representing thier membership, they will also, wherever possible, represent non-members within their potential membership universe, hoping thereby to expand membership, prevent competition and increase their bargaining power vis-à-vis other sectors. Parties on the other hand, while seen as primarily representing a core coalition, are constrained both by the need to integrate the possibly incompatible views of different elements of their coalition and by the need to secure periodic electoral and frequent legislative majorities. These constraints lead them sometimes to propose policies that would not constitute the first preference of any single element of their coalition, and sometimes to sacrifice their constituents' policy preferences in order to attract sufficient people from the opposing coalition to form a majority.

One final assumption is that individualistic norm patterns underlie political demands. Pluralist-democratic thought assumes that people do not see themselves as primarily a part of some larger group and define their interest as being the same as that of this group, but that they arrive at a definition of their own needs in isolation and only then join with others. It is also generally assumed that individuals define their needs either by reference to an inner standard or by reference to their own past real incomes, but that they do not define their needs according to their relative standing vis-à-vis others.

While this pluralist-democratic model represents the mainstream among pluralists there are numerous variants stressing different aspects of the model. Of most interest here are what I call the group model and the rational actor model.

The group model varies from the main pluralist-democratic model in two major respects.[16] These are an intensification of the assumption that people view each problem separately and a relaxation of the assumption that barriers to entry and information costs make the formation of new groups prohibitively expensive.

The first of these changes means that people react to inflation separately from the way they react to other economic phenomena such as unemployment. A population that is previously undifferentiated with respect to inflation will thus look at it as an isolated phenomenon and ask what effect it has on their real income. People's demands will also be narrowed. Perceiving the effects of inflation on their real income separately from the effects of other economic variables they will seek to change or maintain their new real income through alterations in price levels rather than changes in their monetary incomes. It should be noted that a population that behaves in this fashion should find it hard to accept non-obvious inter-dependencies between economic variables.

The combination of lower barriers to entry and the multiplication of cross-cutting cleavages means both that people have an incentive to form pro- and anti-inflation groups, and that such groups would not find it hard to establish themselves. It will be these specialized interest groups, rather than general purpose groups, which will represent the interests of those affected by inflation. Such groups need not necessarily be formally or-ganized, and, at least initially, could appear as a coalition of interests or a joint ideological position. Over time however, formal special interest groups should emerge.

From the point of view of the pro- and anti-inflation interests, existing interest groups and government structures are free-floating resources. Acquiring a preponderance of these resources, either through coalitions or through persuasion from within, will be a major aim of the pro- and anti-inflation groups. This in turn means that the process of inflation policy making is more differentiated, more complex and less orderly than in the pluralist-democratic model, with groups, other than those representing the pro- and anti-inflation forces, rarely acting in a monolithic fashion in this area.

The second variant is the rational actor model. Where the group model stresses the role of interest groups, the rational actor model stresses the role of the electoral process in policy formation. In its pure form it re-sembles the market model in economics, with policy outcomes taking the place of products and votes the place of money. In this model individuals calculate their policy interests and vote into office those who represent those perceived interests. They can do this by voting for individual political entrepreneurs, but may choose to minimize information costs by voting for candidates of parties which generally represent their interests. If office holders fail to represent the policy views of voters, weighted by salience, they will be voted out of office. This forces office holders, whose major goal is assumed to be the retention of their office, to adjust policy to fit voters' desires, in order to assure re-election.

Because of its normative attractiveness and ease of measurement, this model, which had fallen into disuse during the 1950s and 1960s, has undergone a rebirth at the hands of public choice theorists such as Buchanan, Tulloch, Frolich, Oppenheimer, Riker, Ordeshook, and Downs, and has been partially adopted by the new rational voting school, including people such as Key, Pomper and Page.[17] It has also come to be the dominant model in the new political economy subliterature, and can be found, in one form or another, in the work of such writers as Kramer, Tufte, and Nordhaus.[18]

The Marxist Models

Marxism provides the major descriptive alternative to the pluralist explanation of economic policy making. As was true for pluralism, construction of a testable Marxist model is complicated by the many varieties of Marxist theory. Here I will focus on the two predominant strains seriously concerned with providing accurate descriptions of the workings of American society that could be tested empirically. The reader should be clear that this criterion excludes the bulk of current Marxist literature.[19]

The first and more traditional current, of which Milliband is the most recent major exponent, sees political power in capitalist societies as residing in a ruling class which derives its power from the ownership of the means of production.[20] Policy is made either by members of the ruling class or their "lackeys" with the aim of maintaining the ruling class in power and protecting its privileges. Power is maintained by the use of money in the "democratic" process, by the direct suppression of organized opposition that seriously challenges the status quo and through socialization mechanisms which foster the internalization and legitimation of capitalist norms in the working class.

The traditional model shown in figure 2 views profit receivers and a working class made up of wage and salary earners as the only relevant groups for policy purposes, with the former being vastly more important than the latter. Profit receivers who are seen as both owning and controlling the means of production, are assumed to form a self-conscious class, aware of its own economic interests and able to successfully guide state policy to realize those interests. Their primary aim is to maintain their dominance vis-à-vis the working class, with lesser but closely allied interests being the maintenance of profits and prestige. The working

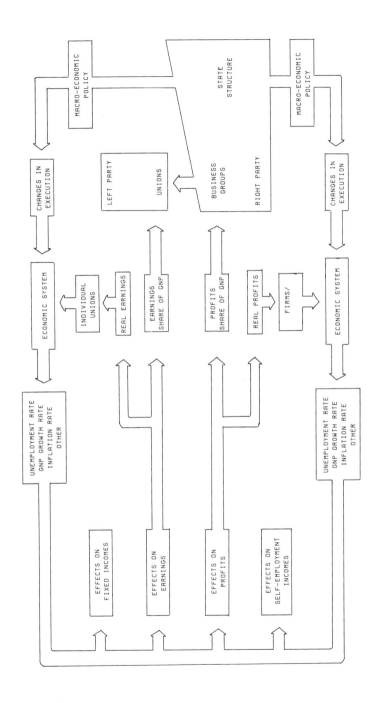

Figure 2   A simplified Marxist model of the inflation-policy-making process

class is seen as being generally subject to false consciousness and both misled as to their real economic interests and unable to combine effectively. Working class representatives are assumed to be weak and their leaders subject to co-option.

More recently a structuralist approach, expounded in various forms by Poulantzas, Offe and O'Connor, has arisen, which sees social and political entities as possessing more independent power than traditional Marxism allowed.[21] While these writers see policy makers as acting in the long-term interests of the ruling class, they also credit them with the short-term political flexibility needed to maintain the legitimacy of the political system. In addition these writers place more stress on division within the capitalist class and generally see the last two decades as a period of gathering crisis in which the increasing class-consciousness of the working class and the internal contradictions of capitalism have led to short-term policy expedients that further destabilize in the long run.

The revisionist model differs from the traditional one in two major respects, both of which move it closer to pluralist models. First it is assumed that the working class is more class-conscious, able to organize to some degree and to demand economic policy in accord with its real interest in improving its relative position vis-à-vis the ruling class, thus making the maintainance of legitimacy a continual concern of the ruling class. Because of this it is assumed that on occasion the ruling class will have to make real concessions to working class interests as well as delivering a stream of symbolic concessions.[22] Second it is assumed that the state structure has some independent power vis-à-vis the ruling class in the short term and hence that not all policy makers are from that class and not all economic policy reflects the short-term interests of that class. Indeed some writers in this vein see this independence as necessary if the long-term interests of the ruling class are to prevail over the individual short-term and sometimes shortsighted interests of members of that class. Needless to say this second version is harder to test than the first because it can explain away seemingly contrary outcomes.

The Elite Models

Elite theory is even more divided than Marxist or pluralist theory. One division is between those such as C. Wright Mills or Domhoff, who view elites as an evil and those such as Pareto, Mosca or Bell who regard them as morally neutral or good.[23] Another is between those such as C. Wright Mills who see a single power elite, those such as Mosca or Bell who see a main and a challenging elite at any given time and those such as Keller, Manelescu and the corporatists who perceive many functionally based elites.[24] A last division is between self-conscious elitists, such as Michels or Domhoff and those, such as Mancur Olson, who, while writing elitist work, do not see themselves as being in the elitist tradition.[25]

Nonetheless sufficient overlap obtains that we can construct two crude models illustrating the way that macroeconomic policy should be made that would not be inconsistent with most elite theory. It should be noted that both these models have obvious similarities with the Marxist models. This is not because the theories are the same, but because at the current stage of historical development they have similar implications for behavior in economic policy making.[26]

The institutional elite model is based primarily on the work of C. Wright Mills and disciples such as Dye.[27] Those occupying the leadership positions in the major corporate, military and political institutions are (somewhat tautologically) identified as the elite, with the corporate leaders being most influential. It is assumed that the leaders of these three functional bases cooperate both because they are interdependent and because of personal and social ties that link them with each other and separate them from the broad mass of the population. The primary aim of this power elite is to maintain themselves in power and they do so by manipulating the perceptions and actions of a misinformed and generally apathetic population.

In figure 3, which follows this outline, it is assumed that income receivers, with the possible exception of profit receivers, are unlikely to see their economic needs as soluble through political means and are even less likely to combine to demand policy change. We would expect this misinformed public to have contradictory and confused views on matters important to them that could threaten elite power. We should expect their representatives to be weak, to be easy to co-opt and to seek to control rather than represent their constituencies.

The competitive elite model, resting loosely on work by Mosca, Burnham and Bell, and best exemplified in public policy work by Alford, sees a dominant elite whose functional base lies in ownership of the means of production, being challenged by a technocratic and professional counter-elite whose functional base lies in their control of the information necessary to run an increasingly complex industrial society.[28] Policy making is a struggle between the two elites with the latter gaining at the expense of the former over time. Each elite might seek allies, and it seems reasonable to view such institutions as the Democratic Party, the unions, white-collar and consumer groups and research organizations as bastions of the new class, and business groups and the Republican Party as bastions of the old elite. Their basic struggle is over the speed with which society moves from the market economy where money is the basic resource to the planned society where information is more crucial, a struggle for which macroeconomic policy has obvious relevance.

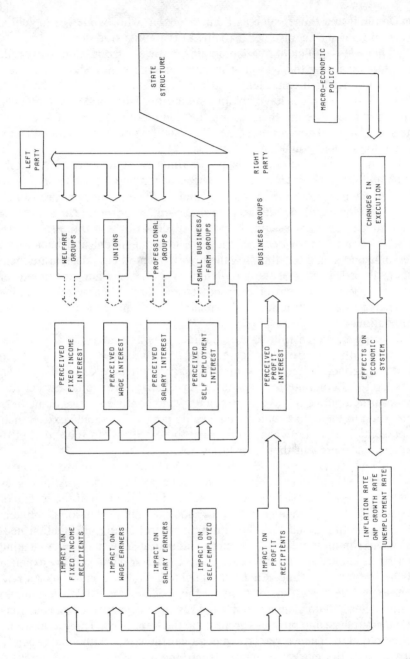

Figure 3   A simplified elitist model of the inflation-policy-making process

Points of Difference

As the primary object of this work is to test between the theories outlined above, it is important to firmly identify the phenomena in the policy process that would tend to support one theory and reduce the credibility of others. While the detailed differences will be presented later, it should prove helpful at this stage to lay out the major linkage points and show briefly what patterns of activity each theory would lead us to expect at each of the points.

The first of these points is the relation between the actual effects of inflation and other economic conditions on the five groups we have identified and their perceptions of that impact. Pluralist theory is most consistent with a process where all groups clearly perceive the effects of economic policy on them, at least in the short term, and seek to maximize their absolute level of benefits. The most reasonable prediction from elite theory is that all groups, with the possible exception of profit receivers, should have a muddled understanding which de-emphasizes political causes for individual economic distress. Marxist theory seems to demand a clear perception of interest by profit receivers, with emphasis on relative rather than absolute economic rewards, and with the working class in the traditional model suffering from false consciousness, but perceiving their real interest more clearly in the structuralist variant.

The second linkage point is the translation of felt effects into efficacious demands. The pluralist models predict that individuals can and do translate salient concerns on economic matters into effective political demands. The elite models and the traditional Marxist model predict an inability or unwillingness on the part of all non-elite members except profit receivers to translate their economic needs into effective demands. The structuralist model predicts similarly, except that the working class should also be able to translate economic needs into effective demands.

The third linkage point is the relation between the demands of those in the different groups and the actions of their representatives. Here it seems reasonable to view the pluralist model as predicting similar aims on the part of the groups and their representatives, with the direction of influence being from below. Elite theory would predict co-option and hence beliefs of leaders that more closely resembled those of the power elite than those of constituents. Traditional Marxism would predict a similar outcome except that only capitalists form the ruling group and the actions of leaders should reflect those of profit receivers. The structuralist model would lead us to similar conclusions but with more consistency between the views of the working class and the actions of their representatives, and more activism on the part of the latter.

The last linkage point in the process is the relation between the economic outcomes and the real interest of the different groups in society.

Pluralist theory clearly implies that economic policies should benefit the majority of the population, or, at a minimum, a majority of the participating population, and becomes less and less plausible as the benefits are restricted to smaller and smaller groups. Elite theory implies that the results of economic policy should benefit the elite and the functional group from which they spring and should benefit other groups only if that helps maintain elite political dominance or by fortuitous accident. Marxist theory seems most consistent with outcomes that preserve the power and wealth of the capitalist class, except at periods of crisis, when the structuralist variant might allow short-term concessions that improved the position of the working class. It is worth noting that none of the theories would predict gains for the fixed income receivers except possibly as the result of charitable impulses in the pluralist model and class identification in the Marxist one.

Perhaps as important as these differences in linkage are the differences in the views of man's nature and his relation to institutions held by subscribers to the three theories. Pluralists generally view the citizen as active, self-interested, rational and, at least in Western countries, capable of altering the institutional structure of society in order to better achieve his ends. Thus it would be consistent with pluralist views if citizens identified and acted to contain the major economic problems facing them, while giving little time or attention to those that did not affect them greatly. The Marxist view of man is more optimistic in judging what men are capable of but is more pessimistic about the ability of the average citizen in capitalist societies to stand against or control the major institutions of society. Thus it would be consistent with Marxist views if people were manipulated into supporting an economic structure that was in the interest of the ruling class rather than themselves and if they were led to misperceive their real economic problems. The elitist view is possibly the most pessimistic. Elitists tend to see as normal a state of affairs where a small elite is able to control the masses through its domination of the major institutions of society, though they vary on the desirability of this state of affairs. In societies where there was only a single ruling elite we would expect the economic beliefs of the population to be easily manipulated to support elite dominance. Where there was also a challenging elite we might expect perceptions of problems to be defined not by the interest of the individual but by those of one or the other elite.

A Defense of the Models

I have thus far presented my models as generally unproblematic. We will now look at some possible objections to both the presentation of the models and to the broader approach. I will also indicate briefly my reasons for selecting the outlined positions. We will look successively at problems surrounding the representativeness of the models, the approach to modelling used here, the examination of only inflation policy and the limited degree of comparativeness.

Our first concern is the degree to which the models are successful representations of the bodies of theory. It is clear that the various theories cover a broad spectrum and that no two major authors within a given tradition are in complete agreement. In selecting mainstream traditions from this rich array, my primary considerations were the representativeness of a given point and whether it distinguished one theoretical tradition from the other being tested.

Though it is my hope that the central assumptions of these models would be subscribed to by the majority as representative, it should be noted that much of the more recent work in the three traditions has moved away from some of the differences outlined here, toward what can best be described as unsystematic convergence. Thus Marxists such as Piven and Cloward and Bowles and Gintis have moved closer to pluralism by giving credence to electoral considerations, non-economic groups and a more pluralist process at the local level; American elitists such as Domhoff have postulated a class model; and pluralist writers such as Edelman, Lowi and McConnell have given a role to economic determinism and elite manipulation.[29] In dealing with this I have tried to maintain a balance between incorporating more recent developments in theory and maintaining the boundaries between the theories that make meaningful tests between them possible.

A second set of objections could be advanced over putting the various theories into a relatively precise systems model. Such objections could take one of three forms. First it could be argued that each of the theories is complex and that by translating them into a few precise relationships I am distorting and over-simplifying. Second it could be argued that, even if there is to be an attempt to model the theories, a systems model of the form I have chosen is the wrong type of model. This is a particularly important objection from the point of view of the dialectical-Marxist and cyclical-elitist theories. Last it could be objected that even if a systems model were suitable, the categorization of real-life phenomena is such that important relationships are obscured. Again this would be particularly important for the Marxist and elitist theories.

Although none of these objections is completely without foundation, these problems are the necessary concomitants of the effort to avoid even worse problems—as is so often the case in the social sciences. Thus, although it is true that modelling the theories oversimplifies them to some degree, it also makes it clear exactly what is being claimed, avoids internal contradiction, establishes what is essential, and makes it possible to bring to bear numerical data in a methodologically respectable fashion.

The other two objections also have some validity, but again the course chosen has compensating advantages. If one is to compare theories and subject them to meaningful tests, it is necessary to standardize the categories and linking mechanisms to the greatest degree possible. Given a choice of standardization criteria, I was guided chiefly by whether, in my opinion, something exists in the real world that fits the description of the phenomenon named and by whether the categories and linkages used enabled meaningful tests between the models. Where choice still existed I was guided by the fact that my major aim is to test the pluralist-democratic model and thus chose categories that would make this easier. My major regret is that these criteria forced me to use an essentially static form of analysis. It would however be my contention that it is useful and meaningful to test the theories even in a form that does not permit long-term changes to be fully explored.

A third, more general, set of objections cluster around the problems involved in looking at only one policy area. The artificial analytical separation of one policy from the wider policy matrix is one of the most persistent objections to policy studies. Is it possible to make such a separation without introducing damaging distortions? Even if this were possible, is not inflation, bound up as it is in a complex process of macroeconomic policy making, a particularly unsuitable choice?

Another objection under the same general heading relates to the choice of only one policy as a testing ground. Would it not have been better to take key aspects of a number of policies and to have used the state of given indicators as tests of the models?

One last objection under this rubric is the question of representativeness. Is it not true that inflation is not very representative of the mass of public policy? Does not its importance, its complexity and its macroeconomic character make it very different from the less important, simpler and more mundane policies that make up the bulk of public policy?

These objections are by no means trivial. In each case the path chosen represents a trade-off between competing problems rather than an ideal solution. Here I will indicate only the compensating advantages that I anticipate from concentrating on inflation policy.

The disadvantage of analytic separation is compensated for by the fact that it enables connected study of a complex and poorly documented policy. Thus it is possible to relate impact to demands and easier to separate various goals of policy makers—goals often intermixed in a given bill or law. It is also my general position that various policy arenas can be distinguished in the real world and the mapping of these areas for comparative study is part of the job of political scientists.

The disadvantage of looking only at one policy is offset by the advantages of in-depth policy analysis that may uncover underlying patterns of behavior that a superficial study of numerous policies may overlook. If a wealth of comparable studies existed, and if there were agreement on what constituted the key differences and similarities between them, a test utilizing material from only one policy area would be indefensible. But, given the paucity of such research, particularly in the area of economic policy, as well as the complete lack of agreement on how such studies should be compared or aggregated, examination of just one policy seemed the most fruitful approach.

The question of representativeness is to some degree a bogus issue. All policy areas are different to some degree, and hence the idea of a single representative policy is a mirage. This does not imply however that it is equally useful to look at all policies. Inflation policy offers many advantages. It is an important policy of interest for its own sake. It is a policy with considerable externalities in other policy areas. It is nearly an "ideal type" of the sort of complex high impact policies that are becoming increasingly important in modern industrial states. It is in an area—macroeconomic policy—that lacks substantial political science research.

More important however, inflation policy is a good testing ground for the theories we are interested in. One reason is that it is possible to make quantitative estimates of both the impact and the reaction to that impact of a given policy choice. In addition, as Prewitt and Stone point out,[30] many previous attempts have lacked conviction because they deal with exactly those non-central issues that Marxist and elitist writers would claim are exceptions to, or special cases of, their theories. Inflation policy, on the other hand, is precisely the sort of central policy that all the theories would claim as their province. Thus, although inflation might not be "representative," it is a good choice for our purposes.

2 Economic Theory and Inflation

For much of the postwar period inflation has been seen by both policy makers and the general public as one of the major problems facing the government in its attempts to guide the economy. In recent years, with the increase in the rate of inflation, the problem has loomed ever larger in the minds of both policy makers and the public. In this chapter, we will look at various theories that attempt to show why we have inflation, what the trade-offs between inflation and other goals are, and which policies are available to deal with inflation.[1]

In this book we are primarily concerned with policies used to affect the rate of inflation and with the political motivations behind such policies. Our analysis is complicated however both by the fact that the basic mechanism or mechanisms causing inflation are the subject of much current dispute among economists, with consequent controversy over the relative efficacy of alternative policies, and by the fact that the theories and policies most in favor have changed several times over the last thirty years.

Because these theories have different policy consequences and because these consequences affect relevant groups differentially, they have become intertwined with the policies advocated by different groups.[2] Often, as dissonance theory would lead us to expect, groups have adopted a theory that seemed to suit their interests and have come to believe in it sincerely, although, as Streeten points out with regard to the proponents of cost-push and demand-pull inflation, there are cases where groups have adopted theories contrary to their objective interests.[3] In the remainder of this chapter, we will examine the major theories and their policy implications.

Inflation is not an independent problem, but one that interacts with other economic goals in such a way that trade-offs are involved. Low inflation is generally regarded by economic planners as one part of an equation that also involves the goals of economic growth, low unemployment and a healthy balance of payments. There is little dispute among economists that low or even zero inflation could be achieved if the government were prepared to pay large enough costs in terms of the other goals. There is however considerable dispute over the size and nature of the trade-offs involved, as well as a normative dispute as to the optimum trade-off position. Most important for a majority of economists has been the trade-off between the rate of inflation and the rate or level of unemployment, though it should be noted that, under normal circumstances, the fact that such a trade-off exists has implications for other goals.

For our purposes it is useful to think of the raw inflation figure as being divided into internationally and domestically induced components even though, in practice, there are substantial interdependencies.

Looking first at the international component, it is generally accepted that under a system of fixed or "dirty" floating exchange rates four mechanisms can transmit inflation. It can be increased directly by rises in the price of imported goods (the price effect). It can be increased indirectly by increased worldwide demand leading to increased exports, thereby increasing home demand and demand inflation (the demand effect). It can be increased because an undervalued currency attracts foreign money, increasing the money supply and thus prices, at least in the absence of deliberate balance of payments deficits (the liquidity effect). More speculatively inflation can be increased through international demonstration of either government policy or actions of subnational actors (the expectations effect).[4]

Under the system of freely floating rates approximated since 1973, the transmission of inflation could, in theory, be less automatic. While "a rise in the price of a price inelastic import such as oil can still cause inflation,"[5] the transmission of inflationary impulses through demand mechanisms becomes more difficult. "However while it [a floating exchange rate] permits a country to protect its national price level against changes in the world price level, it does not ensure that the country will do so."[6]

The change to floating rates might have been expected to allow less inflation-prone countries such as West Germany and the United States to cut their inflation rates, while possibly increasing it in countries such as Great Britain where previous price restraint had been linked to recessions induced by exchange rate crises. In fact, although the standard deviation of the inflation rate of developed Western nations has increased, as theory would lead us to expect, so has the mean rate. This latter phenomenon is sufficiently obvious that most economists are inclined to ascribe part

of the increased U.S. inflation rate to international factors, even while
there is little consensus on the mechanism or mechanisms.

Turning to the domestic component, it is useful to briefly examine the
development of economic thought on the trade-offs implied by inflation,
before going on to look at current schools of thought. Early post-Keynesian analysis showed the price level and wage level as more or less static
up to the point where only frictional unemployment remained—commonly
called full employment. At this point, further increases in demand would
act to raise prices. It was soon realized however that prices and wages
had a tendency to increase even when some unemployment remained.
Phillips, in a pathbreaking 1958 article, found a fairly stable trade-off
between the rate of wage increase and the level of unemployment—a
trade-off that fitted pre-1958 British data fairly well.[7] This was later ex-
tended by Lipsey and Samuelson and Solow among others and applied
to American data, with the emphasis switching to the trade-off between
inflation and unemployment rather than that between wages and unemployment.[8] This early literature postulated a trade-off curve with a static
equilibrium. Within a certain range a policy maker could trade-off inflation
for lower unemployment. Beyond a certain point however the trade-off
curve becomes nearly vertical, indicating a hard core of unemployed. In
the 1970s, faced with instability in the short-term trade-offs, most economists came to view the original Phillips curve as a momentary short-run
curve and to see the long-term Phillips curve as being considerably steeper,
as shown in figure 4. It is generally agreed that this occurs because people
come to expect a higher inflation rate and reflect this in their decisions
on how to price their labor and products. The slope of this long-run,
expectations-augmented Phillips curve remains however in dispute, as
does the mechanism through which expectations become embedded in
pricing decisions.[9]

Monetarists generally argue that the long-term curve is vertical, like
AA in figure 4, implying no long-term trade-off between inflation and
unemployment. They argue that at a given level of efficiency in the labor
market, the unemployed are unemployed because they choose to remain
so at the prevailing wage rate to search for jobs at a higher expected real
wage rate. Therefore it is possible to move up the short-term Phillips
curve BB beyond the natural rate set by the structure of the labor market
only because workers perceive their monetary wage offers to be higher
than they actually are in real terms. Once expectations adjust to the new
inflation rate they will accept positions only at even higher monetary
wages, shifting the short-term Phillips curve to CC and moving back to
the natural rate along pathway D. At this point the government has the
option of maintaining the new rate of inflation at the natural rate of unemployment, of further increasing inflation (the accelerationist option

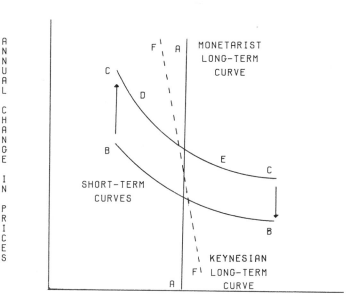

Figure 4   Long- and short-term Phillips curves on monetarist and Keynesian assumptions

or of trying to move back to curve BB along pathway E, by increasing unemployment above the natural rate. This obviously has strong implications for policy makers' freedom of action.[10] Instead of being able to permanently exchange higher inflation for lower unemployment, they can at best exchange a temporary reduction in unemployment for a permanent increase in the rate of inflation. Further, if over the long-term they wish to maintain a steady rate of inflation, any reduction below the natural rate at one time point must be balanced with an increase above it at another.

Reacting to this view, mainstream Keynesians have concluded that the long-run Phillips curve is steeper than the short-run curve but tend to deny the proposition that there is no long-term trade-off at all.[11] Instead many see a long-run curve more like FF in figure 4. In addition they tend to discount in part or whole the monetarist view that the process is generated through the expectations of voluntarily unemployed job searchers, stressing instead the role of unions and other institutions[12] and market failure.[13]

Schools of thought on inflation are less monolithic than the above accounts would indicate and important divisions exist within both main streams of thought. It seems worthwhile to briefly describe the most important of these. In so doing it will be helpful to look separately at views on the causes of base-level unemployment and views on which trade-offs are possible above that level.

Theory on Causes of Base-Level Unemployment

There is general agreement among all schools of thought that there exists some degree of unemployment which is impervious to peacetime macroeconomic policy, regardless of the rate of inflation a policy maker is prepared to endure. There is however considerable dispute as to the size and composition of this base unemployment. Economists who stress the voluntary nature of such unemployment generally assume a higher figure than those who see it as involuntary. Economists posit four major explanations of base unemployment. Two see it largely as a voluntary phenomenon and two see it as primarily involuntary.

A majority of economists agree that some part of base unemployment is structural in nature.[14] It is argued that, even when sufficient aggregate demand exists, there are people who will not be employed because jobs generated by that demand do not match the qualifications of the people available to fill them. Three types of mismatching are generally cited—mismatching of skills, mismatching of region and mismatching of personal qualities. Structuralists usually place most emphasis on mismatched skills. In societies subject to rapid technological change, some skills become obsolescent, leaving little demand for workers who possess them. In addition, with the general decline in demand for unskilled labor, that portion of the labor force with no special skills, poor education and low adaptability faces reduced demand for its services. Regional problems are also seen as important. Because certain industries account for a large proportion of the employment in some areas, a decline in the demand for labor in those industries can result in pockets of heavy regional unemployment. Imperfect labor mobility and sunk overhead capital may cause these pockets to persist even when there is excess demand in other areas. The importance of personal qualities is also cited. Even where there are job openings the employer or union may reject applicants with certain personal characteristics even if such applicants would be prepared to accept lower pay. Teenagers, females, blacks and recent immigrants are the groups most commonly cited, but there are others.

A second type of unemployment results from restrictive rules. Though exclusive rules made by unions and employer groups are sometimes cited, most attention in this area has been focused on minimum wage laws and welfare rules. Minimum wage laws—often blamed for excess teenage unemployment—are said to prevent employment of workers with comparative disadvantages in the market because the marginal return from employing them is less than the minimum wage.[15] Welfare rules have also been seen as a cause of unemployment. Rules that penalize welfare recipients by taking away most of their welfare money when they accept employment are viewed as distortions of the incentive structure which result in people avoiding employment and its associated costs.[16]

A major reason for voluntary unemployment was posited by early Keynesians. They argued that the primary form of base unemployment is frictional unemployment—that caused by people changing jobs—near the full employment level. This refrain has since been taken up and expanded by Chicago school economists as well as others. Pointing to the fact that long-term unemployment accounts for only a small portion of total unemployment, economists such as Mortensen, Holt and Salop have produced models postulating base unemployment as the result of rational maximization of income in a labor market characterized by imperfect information flows.[17] Assuming that the individual can more efficiently pursue higher-paying employment while unemployed, they argue that the natural rate of unemployment is that point where the utility of searching while holding a job is balanced by the utility of searching while unemployed. Another version of this model does not depend on job search but simply assumes that the worker supplies more labor at higher prices and that in the short term he mistakes nominal for real increases with results similar to those above, generating a short-term Phillips curve.[18] Finally a recent version of the same model postulates some permanent involuntary unemployment as a result of frictions generated by having to pay similar wages to new and old workers.[19]

Much of the empirical force behind the newer view that unemployment was primarily voluntary rather than structural came from a series of articles in the early 1970s that showed the average unemployment spell was around five weeks.[20] This finding cast into doubt the appropriateness of the retraining and temporary employment programs that account for the bulk of current manpower funding. However, more careful recent work has undermined the original finding and it now appears likely that in fact the average unemployed person remains unemployed for between eleven and eighteen weeks.[21]

Another reason for remaining unemployed is that leisure is a good, the utility of which must be balanced against goods obtainable by working. A certain number of people at any one time, it is argued, will choose leisure and hence appear unemployed. This argument appears more convincing when applied to those, mainly housewives, who enter the labor force during booms and leave it during recessions, but it may account for some of the unemployment in the permanent labor force, particularly where unemployment benefits exist.[22] Finally factors that affect the expected cost benefit ratios of job search and work versus leisure can lengthen or shorten unemployment. The most important of these factors is the ratio of unemployment compensation to offered wages and the length of time for which it is paid.[23]

Each of these views has certain policy implications for policy makers trying to lower unemployment whle leaving the rate of inflation unchanged. On the whole, Chicago school economists stress the voluntary component of base unemployment and propose policies on this assumption, while mainstream economists either stress the structural nature of base unemployment or argue that increased general demand, rather than any specific measure, is the best solution.

Those who stress the structural component usually stress three types of compensatory policy.[24] To deal with the problem of mismatched skills, they advocate extensive retraining of workers, both to equip them with skills which are in demand and to provide them with remedial basic education. The Manpower Development and Training Act of 1962 and the Comprehensive Employment and Training Act of 1973 are examples of this kind of policy. The regional problem sparked two main policy responses. The less important, in terms of resources expended, was the encouragement of worker mobility through such means as travel allowances, moving allowances and finding workers jobs in other areas. More important were policies such as the 1961 Area Redevelopment Act which were intended to provide jobs in depressed areas by building a government financed infrastructure, supporting declining industries and providing financial incentives for industries to relocate in these areas. Finally, to deal with discrimination in employment, the simple banning of such discrimination has been advocated. Examples are the American affirmative action policies of the early 1970s.

Those who point to inefficient social rules naturally urge changes in those rules to undo their evils. Restrictive trade union practices have sometimes been attacked on these grounds. However, given the lack of unity and the limited penetration of unions, these practices are probably more important in the allocation of employment than in determining absolute magnitudes. A variety of welfare reform proposals have also been advanced with the aim of increasing the incentive to work. The best known is probably Friedman's proposal for a negative income tax.[25] Lastly, minimum wage laws have been attacked by economists. Believing in the virtues of competitive labor markets, they argue that such laws prevent willing workers from finding jobs.

Economists who believe that much or most unemployment is voluntary do not necessarily think that nothing can be done to reduce it. Those who lean toward the job-seeking explanation point out that although spending some time unemployed may be rational given existing structural constraints on the job market, there is nothing sacred about those constraints. Policies aimed at improving the worker's knowledge of alternative job oportunities and at providing knowledge that would enable him to better assess the costs and benefits of alternative choices could do much to improve the efficiency of the market and reduce the time that needs be spent unemployed.[26]

Only the tiny minority who argue that unemployment is a way of obtaining leisure, or time to do non-market labor such as home repairs, do not seek remedial policies. They argue instead for a more comprehensive definition of employment.

The Inflation-Unemployment Trade-Off

There is, as we have seen, considerable controversy over the causes of, and solutions for, base unemployment. There is also controversy over the possibility of trade-offs above this line, although in recent years there has been sufficient convergence that "most economists now more or less agree that aggregate demand policy should not permit unemployment to fall below its natural, or non-accelerating-inflation, rate for any length of time" in the absence of supply shocks.[27]

Although there is little disagreement on this point, or on the existence of a short-term trade-off between inflation and unemployment, monetarists and Keynesians still differ on whether a long-term trade-off of some sort exists and on whether discrete government intervention in the economy is likely to be stabilizing or destabilizing.

The major division in modern macroeconomics is between neo-Keynesians and monetarists. Keynesians are split between those believing in demand pull, cost push and other institutional theories, and mixed models; while monetarists are split into those stressing adaptive and rational expectations.

The oldest and probably most agreed-upon mechanism of inflation is demand-pull. Following Keynes, demand-pull economists hold that, by utilizing an appropriate mix of monetary and fiscal policy, demand can be increased. This increase in demand, usually accompanied by increases in the money supply, is seen as leading to increases in the amount of goods produced, while excess capacity prevents aggregate increases in the price level. Once demand moves above the full employment level however, shown as U in figure 5, it outstrips the capacity of the economy to provide goods to satisfy it. Assuming permissive monetary policies on the part of government, there will be a competitive bidding up of prices as people compete for scarce goods, and a secondary bidding up of wages as industries compete for scarce workers. This demand-pull inflation will

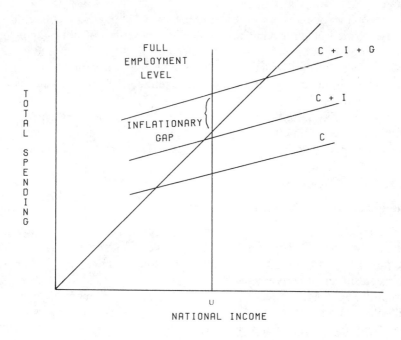

Figure 5   Keynesian national income diagram showing inflationary gap
                  Legend: C = Consumption expenditure
                            I = Investment expenditure
                            G = Government expenditure

continue unless demand is depressed by an increased propensity to save, a lower rate of investment, or restrictive government policies.

In early versions of the theory there was a tendency to see full employment as something like Beveridge's point where vacancies equalled the number of unemployed.[28] But this was quickly seen to be empirically dubious. Most of the work done after 1950 viewed the full employment point as being in a range somewhat higher than Beveridge would have claimed, with things such as bottlenecks in supply and the non-homogenous character of the labor force leading to something like the Phillips curve. More recently still it has been defined as that point or series of points on the long-term Phillips curve where inflation and unemployment are in equilibrium. Until recently the "full employment" level of demand was thought to imply around 4 percent of the work force unemployed but more recent estimates range between 5.5 percent and 7 percent.[29]

In the late 1940s an alternative to the demand-pull mechanism began to be advanced. Called variously cost-push, wage-push or sellers' inflation, the theory held that inflation could take place even in the absence of excess demand, if unions and/or oligopolists were able to exploit market imperfections to increase wages and/or prices.[30] The early emphasis was on wage-push inflation. It was argued that industry-wide unions could demand wage increases higher than the increase in productivity and employers could grant the increases because they knew that all their competitors would have to pay the same wage rate. Given union power, the rational response by employers to union demands would be to increase prices, possibly with some accompanying decrease in employment. In the absence of government action, such price increases would lead to unemployment and falling sales and profits. But postwar democratic governments, under strong pressure to maintain full employment, would have little choice but to sanction the higher prices by creating the demand to absorb them. And, as employers became more certain the governments would increase demand, there would be less and less pressure on them to fight cost increases or keep down prices.

As time went on and it became clear that, in some cases, wages were rising as fast in non-unionized as in unionized industries, there was some change in the theory. Greater emphasis was given to the causal role of sellers rather than unions, and a number of theories emerged which assumed the existence of independently powerful sectors each trying to increase their share of gross national product.[31] There were changes too in the time structure of the theory, with increased emphasis on lagged models and on the role played by the changing expectations of different actors. But the basis of the theory, the argument that prices increased because of a combination of oligopoly and monopoly in the goods market with monopsony and oligopsony in the labor market, remained unchanged.

In addition to the pure cost-push and demand-pull models there are a number of models that combine elements from both. The most influential in the United States has probably been that of Charles Schultze, first developed in 1959.[32] In a purely competitive economy, as demand for one product increased, its price would rise, production would increase, more workers would be needed and a higher wage would be offered to attract them. Likewise in declining industries prices would fall and decreases in production would lead to declining wages. Schultze postulated that although the first part of the mechanism worked fairly well, the development of unions and oligopolistic practices meant that wages and prices tended to exhibit downward rigidity. Given this, the only way the economy could reallocate consumption and labor to expanding industries was to have a steady positive rate of inflation which would reduce real wages in declining industries while leaving their money levels unchanged. A corollary of this theory was that if the rate of growth is greater than the maximum adjustment required, there is no necessity for inflation. Reallocation of labor and consumption could be achieved by distributing the gains from the increase in productivity disproportionately to the workers and profit receivers in the growing industries. This is not the case in the so-called structural models which, while following similar reasoning, focused on relative rather than absolute levels of wages. "They attribute the long run trend of a rising price level to (i) differences in the rate of growth of productivity in the industrial and service sector (with slower productivity growth in the latter); (ii) differences in the price and income elasticities between the two sectors; (iii) a uniform growth of nominal wages in both sectors, whereby the pace of money wage increase is determined by the faster growing sector; (iv) price and wage rigidities (downward inflexibility of prices and money wages)."[33] There are variants on this basic model. The Scandinavian model focuses on the difference between an efficient sector exposed to the world market and a less efficient sheltered sector.[34] The Jones model talks in terms of efficient and inefficient industries generally.[35] But all share the basic characteristic of demand-induced wage growth in the more efficient sector, spreading to a less efficient sector through rigidities in the labor market.

Whereas the Schultze and structural models focus on differences in industry characteristics, the Post-Keynesians focus on labor market rigidities. They perceive the economy as characterized by business cycles. At periods of high demand oligopolistic unions become stronger and are able to successfully demand wages higher than the marginal productivity of their members would warrant. These are then passed on by oligopolistic firms. This process over time becomes a struggle between capital and labor in which inflation is generated because the total claims exceed the rate of productivity increase.[36] This struggle becomes worse if productivity worsens.[37] The solution is some form of pluralistic social contract in which labor and capital agree to equitably share productivity gains.

Marxist models form a variant on this. They see inflation as a defensive move by capital in the face of strong unions. Unable to prevent unions from gaining higher wages, oligopolistic capitalists protect profits by raising prices. If and when they become unable to offset the entire wage increase, and real profits fall, they induce a recession, not with the aim of reducing inflation per se, but primarily to weaken the power of the working class to obtain higher real wages.[38]

Keynesian analysis—the root for both demand-pull and cost-push arguments—replaced earlier classical theories which had focused much more on liquidity, interest rates and the money supply than on aggregate demand and the quantity of goods. In recent years there has been a revival of interest in monetary analysis, particularly in sophisticated versions of the quantity theory under the auspices of the Chicago school. Arguments advanced by the Chicago school resemble those of the demand-pull economists. However, unlike these latter, the Chicago school economists hold that in the long term there can be no trade-off between inflation and unemployment.

The new approach begins with the classical quantity theory tautology— $MV = PT$—where M = money, V = velocity of money, P = prices and T = transactions or the quantity of goods sold. As with classical theory it focuses on the relation between M and P. Like the classical economists, but unlike the Keynesians, the Chicago school tends to see V as fairly constant at least over the long run. However, unlike the classical economists, they do see increases in M as leading to increases in T, but only up to the point where demand equals the natural rate of unemployment, a rate set by the factors discussed earlier. In the short term an expansion in the money supply may enable the policy maker to reduce unemployment below the natural rate with only minimal inflation, because workers who would otherwise choose to remain unemployed are under the illusion that the wages they are offered are worth more than they really are and because people mistake a nominal for a real change in interest rates. But eventually people will revise their opinions as to the real present and future value of monetary offers, and employment as well as the quantity of production will decrease in the manner described earlier. Because of this the long-term trade-off is between a given rate of unemployment with inflation and the same rate without it. Thus the only long-term effect of expanding the money supply is to increase prices.[39]

This initial monetarist position rests upon the notion that expectations are adaptive and that current expectations of inflation are a weighted sum of past expectations. More recently this view has been challenged by the rational expectations group who think that expectations are formed in response to all relevant information including current policy changes, with the degree of relevance being guided by the best available economic theory. An implication of this view is that expectations as well as inflation will change when the money supply changes and hence that systematic policy cannot have even a short-term effect on real variables such as unemployment.[40]

These different views of the causes of inflation have different policy implications. Thus the various schools recommend very different combinations of monetary policy, fiscal policy and wage-price policy, the major policy alternatives. Economists who stress demand-pull generally recommend a balance of monetary and fiscal measures, with the emphasis normally on the latter. Those who stress cost-push forces point to the necessity of wage-price policy in addition to more general demand management, and often place emphasis on curbing ripple effects from key sectors. Those who see both demand-pull and cost-push forces as operating often stress the importance of increasing productivity and removing bottlenecks, as well as recommending some suitable balance between monetary and fiscal policy and wage-price policy. The adaptive monetarists look chiefly to the expansion of the money supply, normally arguing that this should increase no faster than productivity.[41] Finally those stressing rational expectations generally hold that non-random policy changes are powerless to affect real variables but can affect inflation negatively. Periods when one or another of the policy alternatives achieved prominence are shown in figure 6. In the rest of this section we will examine in more detail the policy options and attempt to assess their advantages and disadvantages.

The two major policy tools are fiscal and monetary policy. Over the last thirty years there has been much controversy over the degree of reliance to place on each, with consequent periodic shifts in policy emphasis. However for most of the period there has been a general consensus that both tools are necessary and that monetary policy is more suitable for effecting small but frequent changes while fiscal policy is more suitable for large but infrequent changes.[42] Despite increasing acceptance of monetarist views that the efficaciousness of fiscal policy is dependent on the mode of financing and/or that fiscal policy is simply unable to affect demand at all, the older view does not seem to have been displaced among most policy makers.

Of the three main types of fiscal policy, probably the most common is change in the level of taxation. By lowering tax levels the government can increase demand in the private sector of the economy. Likewise by increasing taxes it can take excess purchasing power out of the economy. Moreover, by shifting the incidence of taxation a government can stimulate a lagging sector or change the relative levels of consumption and investment. A second means of affecting demand is through changes in government expenditure. Viewed as a purely economic proposition, this is the most certain method of affecting aggregate demand. However, as we

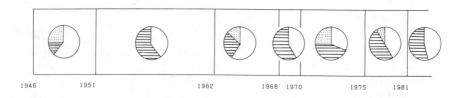

| 1946 | 1951 | | 1962 | 1968 | 1970 | 1975 | 1981 |

Figure 6   Change in policy emphasis, 1946–1983. The diagram is not meant to be a precise expression of the weight given to the three policy tools in the different periods, but rather a necessarily subjective rough guide.
Legend: ⊖ Monetary policy emphasis
          ○ Fiscal policy emphasis
          ⊕ Wage-price policy emphasis

shall see later, there are both political and economic reasons for not relying on changes in government expenditure, and it is not generally favored by administration economists. An increasingly popular third type of fiscal policy is changes in government economic regulations governing investment and consumer spending. Changes in depreciation procedure, housing financing and credit controls are the most important of these, but there are many others.

Economists often speak in terms of an "inside lag"—the length of time between the point when a policy is proposed by the executive and the point when it becomes law—and an "outside lag"—the time elapsing between the execution of a policy and the realization of intended effects. Changes in expenditure tend to have the greatest outside lag, changes in regulations the smallest and tax changes somewhere in between. Changes in regulations have the smallest inside lag and tax changes tend to have a greater lag than changes in expenditure.

Monetary policy tends to have a much shorter inside and, at least for small changes, outside lag. Doubts about monetary policy are concentrated not so much on the length of time before policy changes take effect as on what the limits of effectiveness are. Generally speaking there are three major monetary policy tools: altering the reserve requirements— the percentage of its deposits that a bank must hold in liquid form; changing the discount rate at which the central bank will lend to other banks when their liquid reserves are too low; and selling government securities. The selling of securities has been the major tool in the United States with changes in reserve requirement being less frequently used and changes in the discount rate used only rarely.

The major controversy regarding monetary policy has not been over which tool should be utilized, but rather on which indicator should be watched. Since the early 1950s some economists have been placing primary emphasis on the rate of increase of the quantity of money, while others have placed primary emphasis on the level of the market interest rate.[43] The monetarists and their predecessors in the 1950s, for reasons examined earlier, see steady expansion in the money supply as a long-term cure for inflation and consider overly high interest rates at a given time point a temporary phenomenon which will be cured by changes in expectations. The generally more Keynesian exponents of watching the interest rate have argued that if the quantity of money is held down to the extent advocated by monetarists, interest rates could reach levels where investment would be strongly discouraged, thus leading through accelerator-multiplier processes to a premature downturn in the economy. Although this would indeed lower inflation, the costs of doing so in terms of growth and employment would be too high. By concentrating instead on keeping the interest rate at its proper level, an optimal investment policy that would provide a more advantageous trade-off between inflation and other goals would be encouraged.

Because fiscal and monetary policy are different ways of operating on the same force—the amount of demand in the economy—they have often been seen as alternatives. Proponents of the fiscal path have sometimes held that the proper way to manipulate the economy was to rely primarily on fiscal policy and follow a permissive monetary policy. Proponents of monetary policy, on the other hand, have argued that Keynesian economists reacted too strongly to the prewar experience, and that monetary policy, operating through the interest rate and the quantity of money, offers a highly effective method of controlling the economy which produces fewer distortions than fiscal policy.[44] Over time, as mentioned previously, the necessity for both types of policy has come to be generally accepted, but the relative emphasis to be placed on each is still the subject of considerable debate.

Wage-price policy is far more controversial. Based primarily on structuralist and Post-Keynesian theories that stress rigidities and imperfections in labor and product markets, and cost-push through autonomous unions, wage-price policy seeks to use public powers to overcome the private advantage accruing to unions and firms from inflationary wage settlements and pricing policies.

The basic way of distinguishing one type of wage-price policy from another is by the degree of compulsion involved. At the lower end of the scale is the issuance of guidelines, by the executive or by some consultative body, giving the rate of wage and price increase consistent with the desired level of prices and criteria to be employed in individual cases to judge whether their particular rate of increase should be greater or less than the guideline. The criteria laid down by the Council of Economic Advisers in 1962 were of this type, relying on pressure from the executive branch generally referred to as "jawboning."[45] At the next level is some sort of "voluntary" wage policy. Here typically an agreement is reached between some subset of the elements comprising the state structure, the union structure and the business structure, to restrict wage and price increases to a given amount. Though very common in European countries such as Britain and the Netherlands this has only been used in the United States during the Second World War and to some extent in the aftermath of the Nixon price freeze. The strongest version is that of central administration compulsion, typically resorted to after the more voluntary options have broken down. Here the government usually lays down a norm and creates a body or bodies to decide individual cases. Compulsory policies split in turn into two types, total freezes on prices and wages, and restricting wage and price increase to some specified rate, often that rate consistent with allowing increases equal to the rate of increase of productivity. Examples of both versions are found during the Nixon wage/ price controls in the 1971–1974 period.[46]

It is helpful to think of the different policy instruments as hierarchically related.[47] At the peak of the hierarchy is foreign policy. As long as the exchange rate remains fixed in terms of other currencies, it becomes difficult, as Flemming points out, for the rate of inflation in a given country to depart greatly from that of the average of its trading partners, unless it has radically different inflation rates in the export and non-export sector. Monetary or fiscal policies that lead to high rates of inflation will lower exports and raise imports, promoting a balance of payments crisis which in turn forces more restrictive monetary and fiscal policy. If however the fixed exchange rate is exchanged for a flexible one, this constraint is removed, allowing the option of a more rapid rate of inflation accompanied by a declining currency value.

At the next level of the hierarchy is monetary policy. In the long run restrictive monetary policy is able to control the inflationary potential of fiscal and labor market policies. Given reasonably constant velocity and production near the full-employment level, refusal to increase the stock of money faster than the long-term growth in production makes it difficult for budget deficits to cause inflation, as government spending will merely crowd out private investment, giving no overall inflationary impetus. Likewise, with a constant money supply, large wage increases would reduce profits, lowering investment and increasing unemployment, rather than causing inflation. When however the rate of increase of the money supply exceeds the rate of increase of production it becomes possible for budget deficits to be financed through increases in the money supply, creating an inflationary implicit tax.

At the third level of the hierarchy is fiscal policy. Fiscal policy offers a more immediate way of curbing labor market pressure or expanding demand than is offered by monetary policy. Budget surpluses, with a constant money supply, can reduce demand and drive up unemployment, making workers less able to risk strikes and more willing to settle for low increases in wages. Likewise budget deficits stimulate demand and increase employment, strengthening the position of the worker and the union and making wage demands more difficult to resist.

Finally those policies primarily intended to affect the labor market, such as wage-price and manpower policies, are at the bottom of the hierarchy. Given restrictive monetary and fiscal policy, bidding up of wage labor by unions will either move capital and labor to the non-unionized part of the economy or, in the presence of short-term mobility rigidities, increase unemployment, putting further pressure on unions to moderate wage demands.

The hierarchical system described above is of course a considerable simplification of the real world. Although the long-term effect of policy measures may be as described, in the shorter term lags and short-term adaptations make the picture much more uncertain. Thus it makes a difference for example at the first stage how open the economy is, whether or not one's currency is a reserve currency, and what the relative inflation rates are of export and other goods. At the second stage it is important how long it takes for monetary policy changes to affect the economy, whether one includes or excludes near money and whether there are short-term adjustments in velocity. And at the third stage inflationary expectations and the degree of monopoly in the labor market are clearly important in determining what level of unemployment "controls" the labor market. These factors, which often act to lengthen the lag between policy changes in the upper levels of the economic hierarchy and the effects at the subsidiary levels, have important political implications in that they permit obfuscation and make possible seemingly rational short-run moves which may worsen the inflation rate in the longer term. Nonetheless it is important to bear in mind the generally hierarchical relation of the different policy measures.

In summary then we can say that for an economy that has reached an equilibrium in its balance of payments position, four types of policy can be used to attack inflation. These are manpower policy, monetary policy, fiscal policy and wage/price policy. Unfortunately there is considerable disagreement as to the efficacy of the different policies, as well as the parameters within which the theories behind the policies are supposed to hold true. There does seem considerable agreement that if a nation is prepared to pay a heavy enough price in terms of such competing goals as employment and growth it can achieve a low rate of inflation through monetary and fiscal policy. But "it has been estimated that to reduce inflation by 1 percentage point—say from 10 to 9 per cent annually—costs $150 billion in lost output."[48] Many economists feel that this Thatcher style remedy may well prove worse than the disease.

There also seems considerable agreement that changes in expectations have increased the underlying inflation rate at the full employment point, especially after 1967. The reasons for this however remain in dispute. The uncertainty as to the cause of inflation has widened the number of policy options put forward, even though some of these, like the Laffer curve with its optimistic psychology and TIPS with its optimistic administrative assumptions, seem unlikely to be helpful.[49] It has also increased the temptation to pursue symbolic policies to make it appear as though something is being done,[50] and has increased the pace of policy change.

The United States Economy, 1947–1980

I have examined the major theories seeking to explain the high rates of inflation in the postwar period and the policy alternatives that are emphasized by the different theories. I will now briefly outline the economic history of the United States in the postwar period, focusing on changes in macroeconomic policy and their effect on the economy.

Secular Trends

The outstanding feature of U.S. macroeconomic behavior in the period was the relatively poor performance of the economy compared with the economies of other developed Western nations. Figure 7 shows the rate of growth of GNP in the United States and a number of other countries.

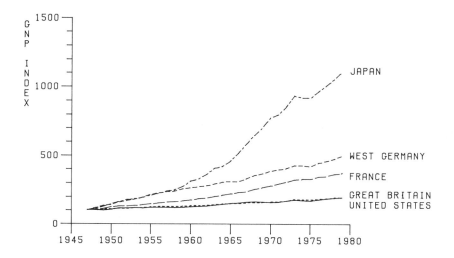

Figure 7   Growth of real per capita GNP in selected countries, 1949–1979. Source: United Nations Statistical Office, *Statistical Yearbook* (New York: United Nations), various issues.

Although the level of per capita GNP was higher in the U.S. than in the other countries throughout the period looked at, the rate of change lagged behind that of all the countries except the United Kingdom, itself generally regarded as an unhealthy economy. Part of the difference can be explained by the relatively low postwar economic base of some other countries, the fact that other countries could use existing U.S. technological and managerial advances in knowledge to greatly shorten the lag between potential and actual technology and the fact that there was more room for growth-inducing occupational shifts in other countries. But the slow growth seemed also to be partly caused by the tendency of American administrations to leave considerable unused capacity, by the large, erratic business cycles and by the lack of central planning.

These latter features can be also seen in the trends in inflation and unemployment. Figures 8 and 9 show the postwar trends in these two variables in selected developed Western countries. Figure 8 confirms the lesson learned from the growth rates. United States unemployment figures were relatively high throughout the period, reflecting unused capacity, and there were relatively wide swings in unemployment as the business cycles waxed and waned. As we might expect, the combination of low growth and high unemployment has kept the inflation rate below that of almost all the developed nations. This combination seems to have been deliberate rather than accidental, with successive American administrations placing a higher emphasis on controlling inflation and a lower emphasis on increasing growth and employment than their non-American counterparts.

As well as these overall differences from other countries there are also differences in the behavior of the various economic magnitudes across time. Growth in per capita GNP was lower in the 1950s and 1970s than in the 1960s. As we can see in figure 10, unemployment showed a tendency to edge up in absolute terms over the period, though part of the increase can be attributed to changes in the demographic composition of the work

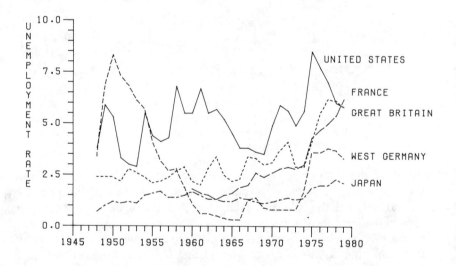

Figure 8   Unemployment figures for selected countries corrected to United States definitions, 1948–1979. Source: United Nations Statistical Office, *Statistical Yearbook* (New York: United Nations), various issues.

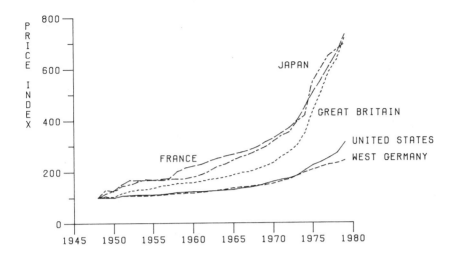

Figure 9   Retail price index in selected countries, 1948–1979. Source: United Nations Statistical Office, *Statistical Yearbook* (New York: United Nations), various issues.

Figure 10   Changes in prices and unemployment in the United States, 1950–1980.
Source: Council of Economic Advisers, *Economic Report of the President 1982* (Washington, D.C.: Government Printing Office, 1982).

force.[51] Inflation showed little variation, with the exception of the Korean war period, until 1965. Thereafter it began to steadily increase, echoing a tendency found in other Western democracies. This movement led to a considerable worsening of the trade-off between inflation and unemployment after 1969.

Cyclical Behavior

The postwar period was marked by a series of expansions interrupted by recessionary periods. Over the postwar period, as we can see in figure 11, there have been eight recessions, in 1949, in 1953–54, in 1957–58, in 1960–61, in 1970, in 1974, in 1980 and in 1981–82 with each except the 1957–58 and 1980 recessions being followed by periods of rapid growth.

The number of recessionary periods was greater than in other industrial states in the period. Furthermore the fluctuations brought about by this cyclical pattern were unusually severe, with periods of negative growth during the downturns and growth rates often over 5 percent in the upturns.

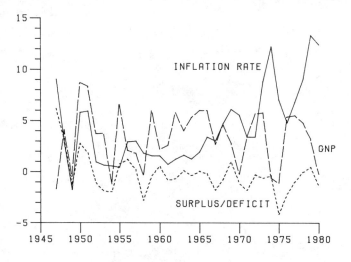

Figure 11   Annual change in GNP, prices and budget surplus as a percentage of GNP in the United States, 1947–1980.

This cyclical pattern was not the result of natural forces, but was clearly policy-related. To a large extent policy changes aimed at balancing the budget or at reducing the rate of inflation were responsible for sparking off recessions,[52] with miscalculations on the timing of counter cyclical policy often a facilitating force.[53]

During the Republican regimes during which six of the eight recessions occurred, the dominant ideology among policy makers was one that extolled the virtues of free competition, lack of government interference in the economy, low inflation, high "natural" rates of unemployment and balanced budgets. To the extent that these objectives were translated into policy—something that was more common under Eisenhower and Reagan than under Nixon or Ford—they tended to result in an economy run below full capacity and subject to the vagaries of the business cycle.[54]

Though this was the main explanation for the cycles there are other less important reasons. One was the structure of government in the United States, which made it more difficult for administrations to enact policies at the correct time.[55] Others were the low rate of capital formation, the deteriorating balance of payments, postwar adjustment problems, the effects of the Korean and Vietnam wars, and oil and food price rises.

Economic Policy

American economic policy varied considerably under the various postwar administrations, partly in response to changing economic fashion and advancing knowledge, partly in response to a changing political environment in Congress and partly in response to an evolution of economic ideology within the main parties.

The Truman administration placed major reliance on fiscal policy with some reliance on direct wage and price controls. Monetary policy was in abeyance until 1951 with the Federal Reserve directed to issue money to support Treasury policy. Though the administration had a somewhat activist orientation, the economic sophistication of its policy makers was not high and from 1947 to 1949 it faced a highly conservative Republican Congress. As a result it blundered into a recession in 1949, from which it was saved by the outbreak of the Korean war.

The two Eisenhower administrations saw the virtual abandonment of fiscal policy and direct controls in favor of monetary policy, with a tax cut in 1956, passed for reasons having little to do with macroeconomic stability, being the only major fiscal measure to have a significant impact in this era. Monetary policy mainly concentrated on the interest rate rather than the supply of money and used open market sales of short-term government bonds as a primary instrument. The Eisenhower regime had an essentially passive economic posture and, together with an economically conservative Congress, saw its task as one of making the naturally functioning economy work. It accepted business cycles as a natural phenomenon, believed in the virtues of balancing the budget and considered inflation as a more important problem than unemployment. Partly as a result, three of the eight postwar recessions occurred during the Eisenhower administration. Automatic stabilizers built into the fiscal structure, together with a proper, if somewhat tardy, application of monetary stimulus, and the fortuitous 1956 tax cut, brought the economy out of these recessions before they could develop into something worse. Nonetheless the years 1953–1961 are marked by a wide gap between actual and potential growth.[56]

The Kennedy and Johnson administrations were both marked by an expansionary, activist attitude toward economic policy making. They used the full range of policy tools, including monetary and fiscal measures, direct controls and manpower policies, but fiscal policy tended to predominate. Using the concept of the full employment surplus,[57] they aimed at continuous growth and were willing to risk some inflation in order to maintain the unemployment rate around 4 percent. Informal institutional arrangements, such as the Troika,[58] improved communications between the bodies responsible for formulating policy, with some consequent improvement in the coordination of fiscal and monetary policy. The greatest policy success of the period was the tax cut of 1964, which maintained non-inflationary growth. The greatest failure was the inability of the Johnson administration to persuade Congress of the necessity of a tax increase to offset Vietnam war expenditures until 1969, three years late, and the consequent buildup in inflationary pressure.[59]

The Nixon and Ford administrations were marked by a tension between a belief in Republican economic principles such as a balanced budget and low inflation and a desire to keep a healthy economy, partly to improve re-election chances. The dominating motif however was what Herbert Stein called ''the old time religion,'' a tendency to aim for long-term stability of the inflation rate at the expense of short-term growth. There was a re-emphasis on monetary policy, with the supply of money rather than the interest rate being the key indicator, and an accompanying de-emphasis of the role of fiscal policy. Manpower policy fell into disfavor, but direct controls did not, and under Nixon firm wage-price controls were applied in the 1971–72 period and milder controls were applied in the 1973–1976 period. The period was marked by a rapid acceleration in the rate of inflation accompanied by a marked worsening of the trade-off between inflation and unemployment, a combination that can be seen in figure 10. Attempts to control the rate of inflation led to recession in 1970 and in 1974–75, the latter the most severe postwar recession to that time.

The Carter administration was also marked by a conflict in principles, this time by the traditional Democratic desire to maintain growth and reduce unemployment and the growing belief among its economic advisers that traditional expansionist policies served only to raise inflation without achieving faster growth or a long-term reduction in unemployment. This dilemma was resolved by expansionary fiscal (and monetary) policy in the first two years followed by a gradual shift to more restrictive policy in the next two years. The general aim in this latter period was to cause a mild recession in 1979 and to be on an upturn by mid-1980. However, declines in the propensity to save, seemingly linked to inflation expectations, served to postpone the recession a year. In terms of policy tools the Carter administration largely eschewed wage-price policy, aside from some symbolic jawboning, and gave more emphasis to monetary policy and less to fiscal policy than any previous Democratic administration.

In the first two years of the Reagan administration a contradictory belief in both supply-side economics and monetarism led to a somewhat bizzare attempt to stimulate the economy through fiscal policy while restricting it through monetary policy. This, combined with earlier deregulation of mortgage and interest rates, led to the highest real interest rates on record, maintained in the short term by government deficit financing with a restricted money supply, and in the long term by the inflation expectations that forecast future government deficits seemed to imply. The result has been the most severe economic recession since the great depression, which, at the time of writing, is expected to give way to a slow and halting recovery.

Finally it is important to note that despite these changes in policy direction there was a steady increase in the role of government in the period before 1981. Total government expenditure as a percent of GNP increase from 20 percent in 1947 and 24.5 percent in 1955 to 31.5 percent by 1970 and 33 percent by 1980. The bulk of this increase was in transfer payments, with defense expenditures dropping from 10.9 percent of GNP in 1955 to 4.9 percent in 1980. It seems possible that this expansion was aided by inflation. Although short-term regressions tend to show inflation reduces real spending more than it increases real revenue, even at the federal level, a reasonable argument can be made that in the longer term the fact that inflation reduced the need for explicit tax rate increases may have made it somewhat less difficult to raise government spending.

Conclusion

The overall impression one comes away with after looking at American economic policy making in the postwar period is the importance given by successive administrations to the control of inflation. Even Democratic administrations, though less inclined to emphasize stable prices than their Republican counterparts, were prepared to trade-off higher rates of unemployment to secure low inflation in the short term than were most European governments. As Haveman puts it, "Even though substantial changes in the constraints imposed on workers enterprises and markets have occurred, and some structural imbalances have developed, it is difficult to conclude—especially in the case of the . . . United States—that a lack of aggregate demand is a trivial cause of the current unemployment problem.''[60] The question then arises as to whether this was rational be-havior. Are people in the United States severely hurt by inflation and do they generally support the government's emphasis on anti-inflationary policies? The next chapter will deal with the first of these questions and chapters 4 and 5 with the second.

3   The Distributional Effects of Inflation

Inflation does not have the same effect on everyone's income. Indeed there seems excellent reason, whatever the criteria chosen, to expect its effects to differ widely. The greatest differential, as with most variables, occurs between individuals. During the 1970s and early 1980s it was virtually impossible to pick up a newspaper without reading about some individual who was being harmed, or thought he was being harmed, by inflation. Nor is the differential impact on individuals the only sort of difference. It is fairly easy to specify subgroups, such as pensioners primarily dependent on private pensions, or borrowers immediately before an unanticipated inflationary surge, whose income in real terms was strongly affected by inflation.

Our primary concern in this chapter however will not be with individuals, or with subgroups such as those mentioned above. Rather we will be interested in the impact on a number of broad aggregates. This will enable us at a later stage to examine the relationship between such large groupings of people and the interest groups and politicians that are commonly thought to represent them. The reader should be reminded, before we go on to examine these aggregates, that dealing with such large and often diverse groupings inevitably has the effect of diluting the relationships involved. Therefore a finding that inflation has a small effect on the grouping does not imply that inflation has no effect on every member of that grouping.

In terms of the models outlined in chapter 1, the purpose of this chapter is to give content to the first stage of the models—that linking inflation to the impact on the real income of various catagories of income receiver.

Approaches to Determining the Impact of Inflation

At first sight nothing would seem more conceptually straightforward than determining the effects of inflation on the income of a given group of income receivers. One would find out the incomes of the group one is interested in and see how those incomes vary with the rate of inflation. Unfortunately, things are not this simple. One reason is that it is extraordinarily difficult, given available data and techniques, to determine what the long-term effects of inflation on the distribution of income actually are. The other is that even if it were easier to determine that impact, there are good reasons to suppose that the average citizen might perceive the effect on his income rather differently.

Why is it so difficult to determine the real effects of inflation on incomes? First, in order to properly analyze those effects, it would be necessary to have a model that included each of the determinants of each kind of income and showed the complex interactions between these determinants, so that one could factor out the changes due to inflation alone. Second, one would have to determine the appropriate distributed lag, in order to know the period over which a change in inflation would have effects on incomes. Last, the resulting model should have a theory of behavior underlying it.

This ideal analysis is virtually impossible for a number of reasons. One, as we saw in chapter 2, is that there is little theoretical agreement on the causes of inflation, with the various theories positing rather different relations between changes in inflation and changes in factor incomes. Another is that data for many of the variables we might like to include in such a model is unavailable, and data for other variables is obtainable only for yearly periods or only for recent years. A last reason is that there are some technical problems such as auto-correlation, multi-collinearity and the determination of the proper shape of the equations, which make it hard to determine the percent of the variance in incomes due to inflation alone. For these reasons and others, actual attempts to estimate the long-term effects of inflation, such as those we will look at later, are less than ideal. They usually contain simplifying assumptions that are open to objection and hence the results are not universally acceptable.

Even if they were however, another problem would remain. People in the real world live with a large number of demands upon their attention span and there may be a multitude of possible explanations for any given set of phenomena. Even if we assume that they act rationally it is not necessarily in their interest to uncover the causal patterns underlying all aspects of their lives, and it becomes less so the more complex and contradictory are the stimuli that must be decoded.

Where the links between a phenomenon and its cause are simple, we would expect that people would have beliefs that are fairly accurate. Where the links are complex, as they are with regard to the relation between inflation and income growth and distribution, we would expect people either to develop rough rules of thumb or to rely heavily on other people's opinions. Whether the citizen's view of the causal patterns is accurate in these cases will depend on the accuracy and unbiased nature of the information source, or on the degree to which the picture that first presents itself to the individual is a reasonable representation of reality.

It is important for our purposes both what the actual distributional effects of inflation are and which distributional effects it might be reasonable to expect the average citizen to perceive. The actual distributional effects are important for straightforward reasons. If we know what they are, it is possible to compare them with people's conscious perceptions of the distributional effects and with the fervor with which they support anti-inflationary policies.

It is also important however to look at the data on distributional effects that might be expected to be perceived by the citizen, because each of the models outlined in chapter 1 carries with it different expectations of how the citizen gathers the information upon which he bases his actions. The clear implication of the elite model is that a ruling group or groups will seek to manipulate the information available to the average man, and that this manipulation will be successful. We would therefore expect the individual to form his views of the distributional effects of inflation not from his own personal experience, but from the political leaders and media, sources which would emphasize the message that best served the interests of the elite.

In the Marxist model we would expect a capitalist class to manipulate information and a working class characterized by false consciousness to accept it. In the structuralist variant we would expect significant sections of the working class to obtain their information from more "reliable" sources, such as unions, or to work it out for themselves. One would expect this portion of the working class to assess this information in light of a Marxist model that would lay heaviest stress on variables such as unemployment, real wages and the share of GNP going to wages and profits.

The pluralist models on the other hand assume that the citizen's primary source of information is his own experience. Given this, media should compete to provide the most accurate information, lest they lose credibility. But in any case media information on personally experienced matters that directly affect the citizen should be accepted only if it corresponds with his life experience. The sort of real life data relevant to the formation of expectations about the distributional effects of inflation would however be expected to differ for citizens acting in accord with different pluralist theories.

The pure group model would lead one to expect the citizen to focus on short-term changes in the cost of living and, given the multitude of roles the model expects of individuals, one would expect the citizen to view the changes in isolation, not directly connecting the cost-of-living changes with changes either in his wage or other income or in other economic variables such as unemployment.

The pluralist-democratic and rational actor models, on the other hand, assume a citizen who is a rational balancer, one who does not rely upon an invisible hand to assure optimal outcomes. One would therefore expect him both to look at the effects of inflation on his real income and to roughly filter out the confusing effects of other major variables such as changes in demand and unemployment. But one would not expect either version of pluralist man to look at the long-term effects of inflation. Because he reacts to events rather than to analyses of events, and because he will connect changes in present income with recent rather than distant changes in the rate of inflation, we would expect him to react to the short-term rather than the long-term effects of inflation.

As we noted earlier, the primary emphasis in this book is upon testing the pluralist-democratic model. I will therefore present both what economists consider the "real" effects of inflation, and the effects that we would expect to be perceived by pluralist-democratic man.

In pursuit of the first of these goals I will examine some theoretical and some empirical work by economists seeking to estimate the long-term distributive effects of inflation. In pursuit of the second I will look at the short-term distributive effects as they should be perceived by a citizen acting in accord with pluralist-democratic assumptions, making some alternative assumptions as to the variables other than inflation that he might consider in the process of isolating those distributive effects.

Inflation: Distributive Theory

Generally speaking, economists see two charactaristics that make inflation a problem. One is the so-called "welfare effect"—the degree to which reductions in cash balances occurring under inflation make the economy less efficient and lead to possible reductions in real gross national product. The other is the redistributive effect, the claim that inflation redistributes resource claims from some individuals to others in a suboptimal manner. Let us look at these two postulated effects in turn.

Welfare costs of inflation arise because inflation can be seen as a tax on cash balances. In terms of the liquidity preference schedule shown in figure 12 the effect of anticipated inflation is to cause people to move from M_0 to M_1, thereby increasing their non-monetary assets and reducing their cash balances. On the assumption that people's cash holdings at M_0 were optimal in terms of utility and economic efficiency, we can assume, following Bailey, that the shaded area shows the loss of utility and decrease in efficiency resulting from this reduction in cash balances.[1] For reasons given by Kessel and Alchian, the desire to switch from monetary to non-monetary assets should also make investment in capital goods relatively more attractive than the employment of labor, thus lowering real wages and using factors less efficiently.[2]

How important are these welfare losses? During hyperinflations, as Cagan and Kessel and Alchian show, these effects can be moderately important.[3] But during the moderate inflation experienced in postwar America, these effects, as Phelps points out, are likely to be small—amounting at best to some fraction of one percent of GNP.[4] Indeed recent studies that have tried to find the expected cash balance reduction that should flow from the welfare effect have not been very successful.

The welfare effect does not represent the only possible loss from inflation. Where the government or private business operates on the basis of rules or contracts that assume that the price level will remain fixed, unanticipated inflation may induce market inefficiencies.[5] Probably the most

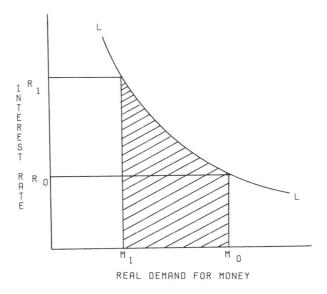

REAL DEMAND FOR MONEY

Figure 12   A liquidity preference curve showing the demand for money before and after anticipated inflation. Source: Adapted from Martin J. Bailey, "The Welfare Cost of Inflationary Finance," *Journal of Political Economy*, April 1956, p. 95.

commonly mentioned of these is the possibility that depreciation and inventory accounting rules might lead to overtaxing of profits and hence to a decline in capital accumulation and future growth.[6] Such effects however rely on both a lack of compensatory effects of inflation and continued failure of the institutional structure to adjust. For example the profit effect mentioned above may well be outweighed in practice by such things as inflation-induced gains arising from the net debtor status of corporations, the switching of accounting systems from FIFO to LIFO and compensatory accelerated depreciation rule changes by government.[7]

Although, to an economist, the welfare costs may seem the most important real cost of inflation, most people would emphasize the negative redistributional effects of inflation. Of these there are three types which follow from the definition of inflation and others about which there is more doubt.

The first effect is the redistribution from the private to the government sector of the economy. This comes aboout through two mechanisms. The issue of money, in and of itself, acts as a tax on cash balances. If we can assume constant velocity and that the quantity of goods produced fully utilizes capacity, the issuance of money means that those who hold non-interest-bearing forms of money will see their asset lose value over time. Thus holders of cash pay a tax to the government for the privilege of holding assets in this form. A second redistribution to government occurs where income taxes are, on average, progressive. With income taxed according to its nominal rather than its real value, inflation will result in a higher proportion of real income going into taxes, the so-called "bracket creep" effect, with a consequent transfer of real buying power to government. Another redistribution is from creditors to debtors. With a debt fixed in nominal terms, creditors will repay less in real terms than was borrowed whenever the interest rate fails to take into account future inflation. Lastly there is the redistribution from those on fixed incomes to those whose incomes can be increased relatively easily and to those whose incomes automatically increase with inflation.

It should be noted that all of these, except the tax on cash balances, occur only to the extent that the institutional structure is not adjusted as anticipations of inflation change and/or that inflation is unanticipated. It is worth remembering that in the United States federal income tax rates have been periodically lowered, roughly in line with inflation, that interest rates have risen in line with expected inflation and that many of the most important fixed incomes, including social security, have been effectively indexed.[8]

A number of other redistributional effects have also been claimed at one time or another, many of them mutually contradictory.[9] Thus it has been claimed that there is a redistribution from non-union to union workers, from wage and salary earners to profit receivers, from salary earners to wage earners and from uneducated income receivers, supposedly more subject to money illusion, to educated ones. In addition, there have been claims both that inflation benefits producers of consumption goods at the expense of those producing investment goods and vice versa. Perhaps most important is the assertion, derived from various combinations of the above, that poor people, for whom the utility of an extra dollar is presumably higher, lose to the better off, with a consequent net loss of utility for the community as a whole.

Given the political and economic importance of such effects there is a paucity of empirical research aimed at confirming or discounting them. What research there is tends to show that, except in the very short term, most of the probable effects of inflation outlined above are not very important.[10] Moreover, with respect to the most important of the claimed redistributional effects—the claim that inflation redistributes from the poor to the rich—the available evidence does not seem to support the assertion. This seems basically to result from compensatory mechanisms that reduce and in some cases reverse the unfettered effects of inflation. The most convincing case can be made for a redistribution in favor of government, but even here it must be noted that the tax system is not very progressive, that governments can and do reduce tax rates, and that government spending may contribute just as much as private spending to the welfare of most individuals.

Nor is this the end of the story. It is likely both that inflation confers some real benefits and that successful attempts to reduce inflation may be more costly than maintaining it at current underlying rates. If we view inflation as a mechanism for accommodating demands, the total of which is greater than the available real product, then one benefit is that it reduces costs attached to alternative means of resolving the same conflict—for example, continual strikes with their attendant loss of real output. More speculatively, in an era when government is subject to increasing demands, inflation provides more revenue to satisfy those demands in a relatively invisible form. This reduces conflict and increases government stability. Further, if there is, as some analysts claim, a systematic tendency in democracies to undersupply public goods, then inflation helps to solve the problem.

Even if one thinks that the pains of inflation outweigh the pleasures, it does not follow that a reduction of the current underlying rate is desirable, even if it could be achieved without the heavy costs in terms of unemployment and growth that we know are attendant on such attempts. This is because most of the plausible costs associated with unanticipated inflation are also associated with unanticipated deflation. For example, at the time of writing, mortgage rates are averaging around 14 percent while inflation is around 11 percent, yielding a real expected mortgage rate of around 3 percent. If inflation dropped to zero, mortgages taken out today would cost 14 percent in real terms, with a consequent massive unanticipated redistribution. It follows that even if inflation does carry redistributive costs, the optimal inflation rate is likely to be not zero but the expected rate to which society is currently adjusted.

Given that the above discussion leads one to suspect that aggregate and distributional costs are not very high for most of the population, why has inflation come to be seen as such an important problem? Four answers initially suggest themselves. The first reason I would advance is a preference for continuous over discontinuous income. The inflation process is typically marked by fairly steady price increases, accompanied by sharper increases in individual incomes. Hence the real income of most individuals tends to lead the average at some points of time and lag it at others. If, as Ricardo thought, people give a higher weighting to a dollar lost than a dollar gained, the result is a net loss of utility over time.[11] The second reason is that there may be a preference for stable prices over unstable prices, irrespective of what is happening to income. If one assumes that increases in uncertainty involve planning costs, and that there are significant information costs attached to rising prices, then there will be a net loss of utility attached to inflation even if real income remains the same. The third possible reason is what I term "income illusion." This posits that people realize that they have both increasing income and increasing prices, but do not connect the two. Thus when there is inflation, but an individual's real income is constant, he may believe that although his income is rising, price increases are cheating him out of his gains. A secondary form of the same phenomenon is the failure to connect increasing public benefits, arising through inflationary redistribution to government, with the reduction in post-tax income. A final possible reason is what I term "demand transference." This posits that when people receive less income than they had expected, for reasons such as a fall in the demand for their services, a general international redistribution of resources, or a recession, they blame inflation rather than the actual cause.

Determining "Real" Distributive Effects

There have been a number of attempts to estimate the distributive effects of inflation. They fall into two major classes. One set of writers sees inflation as standing in a more or less permanent relation to other economic variables and attempts to estimate the net distributional effects of the total process of which inflation is a part. The other set attempts to separate out the distributional effects of inflation by controlling for the effects of other economic variables. Generally economists have preferred the first approach, mainly because the technical difficulties involved, although great, are far smaller than those involved in attempting to separate out the effects from one of a number of highly collinear variables. Given the tendency of modern macroeconomic theory to move away from assuming long-term trade-offs between inflation and other variables, the results from this mode of analysis must now be regarded cautiously.

There have been two major foci in the works that seek to determine the effects of a number of mutually interactive variables. One, deriving from a definition of the Phillips curve which allows trade-offs between inflation and unemployment, has attempted to estimate the net benefits and costs involved in different trade-off points. Generally speaking this is the approach of Bodkin, Thurow, Metcalf, Phelps and Hibbs.[12] Most of this work has assumed stable long-term Phillips curves and hence must now be regarded with suspicion. Generally the work argues that the effects of inflation are neutral or mildly negative with respect to redistribution toward the poor, while reduced unemployment and/or increased demand have strong positive effects on the incomes of wage-earners and the poor. Therefore, it is agreed, the combination of low unemployment and inflation has a net redistributive effect toward lower-paid workers and the poor.

In a somewhat less empirical variant on this general conclusion, Phelps has assumed a vertical Phillips curve at the "natural rate" of unemployment and argued that, even when this was the case, net distributional effects should benefit the poor, owing largely to the training of otherwise hard core unemployed during inflationary periods.[13]

The other major multivariate approach focuses on the business cycle rather than the Phillips curve. Schultz, Metcalf, Kuh, Mirer, and Boddy and Crotty generally take this approach.[14] The tendency here is to focus on productivity rather than on inflation or unemployment and to look at the effects of the different rates of increase of productivity at the various stages of the business cycle on profits, wages and the wage-profit ratio. Sometimes this is generalized to assess the effects on the distribution of income defined more broadly. Those taking the business cycle approach, with the possible exception of Boddy and Crotty, have seen the early part of the business cycle as one where both wages and profits increase rapidly, owing to productivity spurts attendant upon employment of underutilized labor and capital. The increase in this early stage is greater for profits than for wages, leading to an increase in the profit-wage ratio. In the second half of the cycle, with productivity increases declining in the face of capacity shortages and the employment of more marginal capital and labor, the rate of increase of both wages and profits declines. Since the economy is nearing the full employment point however, wages will increase in order to attract scarce labor and because trade unions have an improved bargaining position. The profit/wage ratio therefore falls and the distribution of incomes becomes more equal. This trend continues into the ensuing recession due to the greater downward elasticity of profits, particularly in the face of long-term labor contracts.

The business-cycle-approach writers generally agree with those taking the Phillips curve approach that a configuration of low unemployment and high inflation will be correlated with an increase in income equality. They would generally argue however, that this comes about more as the result of productivity changes at the different stages of the business cycle than as the result of changes in unemployment and inflation themselves.

A variation on this general conclusion is found in the work by Mirer. He simulates the effects of different business conditions on the factor income of families, using the 1962 Federal Reserve Survey of Financial Characteristics as his data base. While he agrees with the other writers that the poor and blacks suffer during recessions, he also finds, as one might expect, that the well-off also do relatively badly during recessionary periods.

The other major approach to the determination of the distributional effects of inflation, and the one that is of most relevance to this work, is to seek to control for the effects of other variables and to then attempt to estimate the distributional effects of inflation considered in isolation. There are four main lines of cleavage in the work taking this approach. It can look at the effects of differential inflation on those with different kinds of income, or on those who buy different combinations of goods. It can look at wealth effects or income effects. It can look at actual changes, or it can simulate the effects of inflation on units with given wealth, income and debt positions. Or, lastly, it can look at the effects of anticipated or unanticipated inflation.

Hollister and Palmer look first at the effects of differing rates of price change for different goods.[15] They construct price indexes for poor people and the elderly, and compare rises in these price indexes with rises in the standard price index. Their major finding is that the cost of living for the 1947–1967 period which they examined seemed to have risen more slowly for the poor and aged than for the population in general. This was primarily due to the importance of food costs in poor people's budgets in a period when food costs were rising slowly.

In addition they look briefly at the wage income, transfer income and wealth of the poor. They conclude that the wealth effects are negligible for the poor, that transfer payments rise in step with inflation and that the tight labor markets associated with inflation benefit the poor. Overall therefore, they conclude that inflation benefits the poor.

A later more sophisticated piece by Williamson generally confirmed Hollister and Palmer's results for the 1947–1967 period by showing that there was little change in the relative price of necessities and luxuries.[16]

However, he also showed that this was not true for the 1967–1974 period, primarily because a rapid increase in food prices raised the price of necessities relative to luxuries. Reworking his calculations using more recent data I found necessities increased more rapidly than luxuries in the 1967–1980 period taken as a whole, though most of this increase was in the earlier part of the period. Additionally, in the latter part of this period the fact that housing is calculated into the index as the price of a new house, rather than as rent, combined with the fact that social security has been indexed, has almost certainly led to the elderly gaining from inflation.

The approach of Fountain and Brimmer is to look at the income data from periods with and without inflation and try to roughly estimate the effect of inflation.[17] Fountain uses Michigan Consumer Survey data from the 1966–1969 period and compares it with similar data from the 1959–1961 period. Her overall conclusion is that people at all levels fared rather better in the latter period and that there were negligible redistributional effects. But she is careful to point out that her data do not allow her to distinguish between the effects of inflation and some other variables.

Brimmer tries a similar approach using aggregate economic data. In an attempt to control for demand factors he compares the 1961–1964 period with the 1964–1968 period. He finds a significant trend toward greater income equality in the latter period, but tends to attribute this largely to other factors such as the increase in the percentage of the population at work and real growth. Much of his analysis suffers however from not considering some of the points raised by the business cycle theorists.

Swan uses aggregate data from the 1947–1967 period in an attempt to determine the effects of inflation on income distribution measured in deciles of the population.[18] He concentrates on income effects and looks at the distribution of income during periods of low and high inflation. He concludes that the distributional effects of inflation are likely to be small and that there is little evidence that they will increase inequality. Indeed, in the most interesting part of his dissertation he reinforces Hollister and Palmer by showing that, well before social security was indexed in 1973, transfer incomes, long assumed to be the income source most vulnerable to inflation, had little vulnerability in the medium and long term, due to congressional sensitivity to inflationary effects on welfare payments.

Bach and Stephenson, following the earlier work of Stephenson, are primarily concerned with the effect of inflation on the distribution of wealth.[19] Looking at the distribution between wage earners and profit receivers they find that the former tend to gain at the expense of the latter, though their method of analyzing raw aggregate data does not exclude the business cycle reasons advanced by Kuh. Looking at net creditor-debtor effects they estimate inflation to have caused redistribution of between four and six hundred billion dollars, mainly from households toward government and corporations. Looking at the effects of inflation through the net asset/debt position of different kinds of household, they estimate some losses by lower- and upper-income households and aged and retired households to the middle-income employed population. They noted however that the effects should be minor for most of the groups studied.

Similar work for a more recent period has been performed by Wolff.[20] Using a subsample of the 1970 census, he compares changes in the asset bundles held by different population groups in the 1969–1975 period, under the assumption that each population group kept the same mix of assets over the whole period. Given this assumption he finds that inflation increased wealth equality over the period, because the prices of assets primarily held by lower income groups increased more rapidly than those primarily owned by upper income groups.

Despite the obvious problems of income simulations, the most methodologically convincing of the various studies are those of Budd and Seiders, Nordhaus, and Minarik.[21] Budd and Seiders use a variety of methods, particularly regressions employing Almond distributed lags, to estimate adjustment coefficients for a wide variety of income and wealth sources. They then apply these price elasticities to the income from all sources received by various income classes, using the 1962 Federal Reserve Survey, and simulate inflations of 2 and 5 percent. Their overall conclusion is that the middle-income groups gain at the expense of the lowest 40 percent and the top 5 percent of income earners, with the greatest losses being incurred by the bottom 10 percent and the top 0.25 percent. They use four different income concepts, and the degree of redistribution, though not the direction, varies according to the income concept used. With a simulated inflation of 5 percent the reduction in the share of the bottom 40 percent ranged from 0.4 percent to 2.5 percent, the reduction in the share of the top 3 percent varied from 0.5 percent to 1.8 percent and the increase in the share of the middle-income group varied from 0.25 percent to 0.9 percent. They do however show a drop of 8 percent in the share of the bottom decile, 5 percent in the share of the second decile and 5 percent in the share of the top 0.25 percent when they use their most inclusive income definition, mainly because of the low price elasticities of welfare payments and some assets. On the whole, they conclude that the redistributional effects of inflation are moderate, at least in the short term, and that "if the rather mild effects noted here for income are deemed to be undesirable ones they can be mitigated by modifications of existing tax and transfer policies."[22]

Nordhaus's article is in many respects the most ambitious of the attempts to uncover the redistributive effects of inflation. This too is a simulation, but it differs from the Budd and Seiders study in a number of respects. Most important is the use of estimated lifetime income rather than momentary income, although his data base is the same 1962 Federal Reserve Study used by Budd and Seiders and by Mirer. He simulates the effects of inflation under what he calls classical, neo-classical and Keynesian assumptions. Under the first two, income effects are assumed to anticipated and hence zero, with only wealth effects important. Under the Keynesian assumption an income effect deriving largely from the trade-off between inflation and unemployment is added to the wealth effect. Despite the very different form of analysis and the different income concepts, his conclusions parallel those of Budd and Seiders. For all three simulations he finds the redistributive effects of inflation to be very mild, with a slight tendency to redistribute from the lowest quintile and the upper 5 percent of the tail to the rest of the income distribution.

More recently Minarik, using a merged file compiled from a 1971 Current Population Survey and 1970 Internal Revenue Service data, simulated 2 percent and 5 percent increases in the annual inflation rate, using both the census income definition and a more comprehensive measure that includes payments in kind and accrued wealth. Using the census definition and simulating a 2 percent inflation increase he finds small losses for those earning less than $7,000, small gains for the 10 percent earning more than $25,000, offset by losses in suceeding years, and virtually no effect on the 50 percent of the population in the $7,000 to $25,000 range. Using the more comprehensive income concept he also finds small losses for the less well off and little effect on those in the middle income range, but the effect of a 2 percent inflation on the well off becomes drastically negative, with income loss in the first year rising from 2 percent for those earning $25,000 to 17 percent for those earning $200,000, then falling back to a 5 percent loss for those earning $2,000,000. These latter results, if true, are of major importance. However, not only do they seem contradicted by the data we will examine later in table 30, but I find the logical implications somewhat unbelievable, and would like to see more of Minarik's methodology than was revealed in his articles before placing heavy reliance on them.

We have examined a number of articles looking at the redistributive effects of inflation. Although their conclusions differ in some respects there is considerable agreement on a number of crucial points, agreement particularly surprising when one considers the wide variety of data examined, income concepts used, and methods adopted. First there is some agreement that the redistributive effects, insofar as they occur, tend to reduce the share of both the upper and lower parts of the income distribution while leaving unchanged or increasing the share of the middle. Second, with the exception of the upper 10 percent under Minarik's more comprehensive income definition, it is generally agreed that any redistributive effects of inflation per se are small, that they do not provide a very strong reason to oppose inflation and that such effects as there are could be and often have been mitigated by government tax and expenditure changes. Lastly it is generally agreed that the redistributive effects of other economic variables, particularly unemployment and productivity, are much more important than the effects of inflation.

Short-Term Effects of Inflation

It should be clear from the work just surveyed that there are a number of ways in which citizens could plausibly attempt to take account of the effects of inflation. They could see it as part of the business cycle, as something in a trade-off relation with unemployment or as a variable with independent effects. They could see it as something to be compared with the sum of changes in all their sources of income or as something to be compared only with changes in their major sources of income. They could see it as affecting their lifetime income, their current income configuration in the long run or their current short-term income.

It is my position, for reasons that will become clearer as we examine the public opinion results, that most of the approaches discussed above, while defensible as attempts to uncover underlying redistributional effects of inflation in the face of severe data and methodological problems, are not plausible as simulations of how the citizen acting according to pluralist assumptions might reasonably be expected to view inflation. Furthermore the groups that have been looked at are often not those that are most important from the point of view of the political system.

In this section therefore I will look at the distributional effects for some politically relevant groups. I will look at short-term rather than long-term effects, will assume that citizens focus on their chief source of income in assessing the real effects of inflation, that they see inflation as separate from other economic variables and are able to roughly factor out the simultaneous effects of changes in demand and unemployment on their incomes. It is not assumed however that this is a conscious process, but only that, after possibly unconscious calculations have been made, people can reach a conscious position on inflation consistent with these calculations.

In what follows I will first look at the short-term effects of inflation on a number of politically relevant factor incomes, controlling for the simultaneous effects of unemployment and GNP change. Following this I will briefly examine some complications of the basic model.

Some Technical Problems

Even when we confine ourselves to the relatively simple task of determining how pluralist man could reasonably be expected to feel the effects of inflation, a number of technical difficulties intervene.

The first and most important problem is that the available data has a number of weaknesses for the purpose of estimating the relation between inflation and income. This is particularly true of the data on per capita incomes. The major problems are summarized where I deal with the individual results. Because of these problems, I have recalculated many of my results using alternative data and techniques that have different strengths and weaknesses from those reported. I have not shown the results as they generally supported the reported findings. But it should be noted that what is probably the most intractable of these problems, the fact that much of the income data is pre-tax rather than post-tax, remains generally unsolved by this strategy.

A second problem, common to much econometric analysis, is the restricted time period over which the data has been run. For a number of reasons, most of which are fairly obvious, I am of the opinion that the post-1947 period is likely to have substantially different relations obtaining among relevant economic variables than those obtaining in earlier periods. In addition much of the data is obtainable in a reliable form only for the postwar period. The number of observations has been further reduced by the fact that in general I use yearly rather than monthly or quarterly data. This decision was again prompted largely by the desirability of using comparable data for a wide range of incomes, much of which was available only at yearly intervals. Though the yearly figures have some advantage in that they filter out some irrelevant short-term influences, they have the disadvantage of making causal inference more difficult and of making it more difficult to control for such things as the influence of the business cycle.

A third problem arises over the choice of lag. It must be re-emphasized that I am interested not in the period elapsing between a rise in prices and a price-induced rise in incomes, what might be referred to as the economic lag, but in the period that elapses between a rise in prices and the time that the income receiver feels the effect of that rise on his income—what I would refer to as the political lag. Monroe's work, using Almond lags to determine the relation between inflation and presidential popularity, found that the effect peaked after about four months and that there was virtually no addition to the coefficient after twelve months.[23] Working with a somewhat more direct measure, expectations of future inflation, I found a similar lag. Using the Almond technique on quarterly data from the 1971–1979 period and correcting for auto-correlation, I found virtually all the positive effect of inflation occurred in the first six months. Finally, running earlier scattered expectations data lagged successive months behind, I found the correlation to be highest when inflation was lagged between two and three months. Thus working with the yearly data I have chosen not to lag. It should be noted however that the use of unlagged regressions presents the problem of causal direction. Where possible I ran monthly and quarterly data to check direction and I do not feel it to be a major problem.

Auto-correlation does not appear to be a major problem in most of the runs. Examination of the Durbin-Watson statistics and inspection of the residual plots revealed few cases where auto-correlation was obviously a problem, although, as the reader can see, rather more cases fell into the doubtful range where it is not certain whether auto-correlation is present. Further, one should bear in mind that the Durbin-Watson is not very reliable for the small N that I use.

Because of the generally low correlations between the independent variables, there seems little problem with multi-collinearity. However the reader might note that one of the reasons for choosing the rate of unemployment, rather than the rate of change, as a control variable was the fact that the latter formulation led to major problems with multi-collinearity in the more recent part of our period.[24]

It should also be noted that the income figures have been deflated, using the consumer price index as the deflator. In addition, for technical and substantive reasons, all dependent variables have been converted into rates of change. The reader might also wish to note that although I present the t scores, I do not think that tests of statistical reliability are appropriate when the data represent the universe and no future inference is being made.

As well as presenting the raw b for inflation, I present the standardized beta weights for inflation, change in GNP and the unemployment rate, to better enable the reader to compare the relative short-term effect of each on the dependent variable. The beta can be interpreted as the degree to which a change of one standard deviation in the independent variable will change the standard deviation of the dependent variable. For example an inflation beta of .79 says that if inflation changed by one standard deviation, the dependent earnings variable would change by 79 percent of a standard deviation.

I chose an equation of the form shown in (1) where Δy is the annual rate of change of deflated incomes, Δg is the annual rate of change of deflated GNP, u is the annual rate of unemployment, and i is the annual rate of inflation.

(1) $$\Delta y = a + b_1 i + b_2 \Delta g + b_3 u + e$$

It should be mentioned in passing that this form was chosen despite the fact that an equation of the form shown in (2) would have provided a marginally better fit.

(2) $$\Delta y = a + e^{-b_1}i + e^{-b_2}\Delta g + e^{-b_3}u + e$$

Inspection of the scattergrams led me to the conclusion that, except for very large variable values, the linear equation would introduce little distortion. I thought that these marginal losses were outweighed by the gain in comparability and the likelihood that the public would view the impact of inflation on their incomes in linear terms. The reader should bear in mind however that the use of equation (1) rather than (2) will have a slight tendency to reduce the value of the beta weights and R^2s.

The reader should also note that the choice of equation (1), rather than a distributed lag equation and the choice of rates of change rather than rates, considerably lowers the R^2 and tends to understate the effect of the real variables, change in GNP and the unemployment rate. This should not be surprising when it is recalled that we are not trying to explain what causes incomes to vary, but rather to simulate the connections between inflation and incomes likely to be perceived by the average person.

Using equation (1) also assumes that the citizen roughly controls for the effects of changes in GNP and unemployment, when assessing the effects of inflation upon his income. Even given the linear shape of the equation, this could be too strong an assumption. I therefore reran the reported runs using

(3) $$\Delta y = a + bi + e$$
(4) $$\Delta y = a + b_1i + b_2\Delta g + e$$

In no case did this change the sign of the inflation coefficient and the almost invariable result was a slight increase in the coefficient as one moved from equation (1) to equation (4) to equation (3). Because the b value proved so stable, I have not reported the results of these reruns.

For some types of income, in particular profit income, the assumption that people will look only at the short-term effects might be considered false. Further it is of some interest to know what the longer-term effects of inflation might appear to be. In order to determine this I ran the same data with six-year lags, using equations (5) and (6), employing Almond lags and correcting where appropriate for auto-correlation.

(5) $$\Delta y = a + \sum_1^6 b_2i + e$$

(6) $$\Delta y = a + \sum_1^6 b_2i + \sum_1^6 b_2\Delta g + \sum_1^6 b_3u + e$$

Given the assumptions outlined earlier I consider the results less useful for the purposes of this book than the results of the runs using equation

(1), with the possible exception of the profit results. Hence I do not present the results in detail, but I do use them to give background and context to the short-term results.

Earnings from Employment
There is no properly adjusted series for wage and salary income together, as there is for wage income alone. The measure used here is based on national income data that, while the best available, contains some material that we would prefer not to have and omits some other income that we would like to have included. In addition, it is in the form of aggregate income, rather than being adjusted for either the number of income receivers in the category, or the time period over which the money was earned. I have adjusted the data to some extent to try and improve it. However these adjustments are necessarily crude. The pre-tax data has been adjusted by dividing by the number of wage and salary earners during the year concerned, and by deflating it. The post-tax data has been further adjusted by subtracting the total income tax and social security payments to all three levels of government.

These caveats having been voiced with respect to the data, what do the regressions show? As can be seen in table 1, there is a reasonably heavy short-term impact of inflation on earnings in the same year, something that makes sense when we remember that inflation erodes the real value of earnings continuously but that compensatory income adjustments occur only periodically. This pattern holds for both pre- and post-tax earnings. A percentage increase in inflation is associated with a 0.45 percent decrease in pre-tax earnings and a 0.45 percent decrease in post-tax earnings during the same year.

If we look at the standardized beta weights rather than the partial *b*'s, the picture is very similar. Further, inflation has an effect on earnings that is relatively as well as absolutely important. The unlagged beta weights for inflation are more important in the short term than changes in either GNP or unemployment for both pre- and post-tax earnings.

Overall then, whether the earner looks at the raw impact of inflation on his income or at the relative influence of inflation with respect to other causative variables, inflation has a major negative short-term effect on earnings. This effect is not continuous. Using the Almond technique one finds that inflation has a negative but steadily smaller effect on earnings in the second and third years, before beginning to have a positive effect in the fourth and succeeding years. However it is the initial negative effect in the first year that is politically relevant.

Table 1   Short-term Effects of Inflation, GNP Change and Unemployment on Change in Incomes, 1948–1979

Incomes	Mean	Inflation		GNP	Unemployment	R^2	D/W
		b	Beta	Beta	Beta		
Pre-tax earnings	1.69	−.45	−.79 (−10.66)	.37 (5.10)	−.07 (−0.95)	.85	1.28
Post-tax earnings	1.17	−.45	−.77 (−6.24)	.06 (0.49)	.10 (0.79)	.85	1.28
Pre-tax wages	1.64	−.46	−.80 (−8.70)	.18 (1.97)	−.15 (−1.66)	.78	1.31
Post-tax wages	1.32	−.44	−.73 (−5.65)	.13 (0.86)	.09 (0.71)	.55	1.51
Pre-tax profits	3.72	−.90	−.22 (−1.65)	.67 (5.08)	.26 (1.94)	.53	2.37
Post-tax profits	4.55	−1.43	−.25 (−1.47)	.32 (1.93)	.36 (2.13)	.25	2.04
Post-tax dividends	3.17	−.83	−.44 (−2.89)	.40 (2.65)	.22 (1.47)	.28	2.15
Pre-tax farm income	0.14	1.19	.21 (1.21)	.38 (2.19)	.10 (−0.59)	.18	2.15
Pre-tax small business income	1.28	−.51	−.40 (−3.00)	.56 (4.24)	.09 (0.66)	.51	1.54
Social Security payments	4.71	−1.23	−.30 (−1.69)	.18 (1.01)	.14 (0.77)	.13	2.29
AFDC payments	1.41	−.18	−.17 (−0.94)	−.17 (−0.94)	−.14 (−0.77)	.08	1.88

Wages

The wage data refers to hourly wages for non-agricultural blue-collar workers. The data is probably the most reliable of the various indicators of income used in this section.

The short-term negative impact of inflation on wages is roughly equivalent to the impact on total earnings. A percentage increase in inflation is associated with a 0.46 percent decrease in pre-tax wages and a 0.44 percent decrease in post-tax wages. As with earnings, rerunning the data using Almond lags shows an initial negative effect in the first year that fades over time then becomes positive, with the positive effect commencing three years later for pre-tax wages and two years later for post-tax wages.

It is worth noting that the gap between the size of the beta weights for earnings and the other variables is greater for wages than for earnings, which might be expected to make inflation appear relatively more important to wage-earners than to other earners, but the difference is not great.

Salaries

We should be aware of the short time span for which reasonably reliable salary figures are available, the fact that the figures are drawn from a sample which does not include all salaried occupations, the fact that the figures are for changes in wage rates at given job classification levels, hence discount grade inflation, the fact that salary earners move up over time and the fact that only pre-tax figures are available.

Table 2 compares the association between inflation and salaries with that between inflation and other kinds of income in the 1962–1977 period. The effect of inflation on salaries appears more negative than we found to be the case for pre-tax earnings and wages, though the difference is not great. A one percent increase in inflation in this period is associated with a 0.52 percent decrease in salaries, compared to a 0.36 percent decrease in wages in this period. However, as the beta weights indicate, salary rates are also more sensitive to changes in GNP and unemployment.

The pattern over time revealed by using the Almond lag is that the adjustment period has, as seems reasonable, shortened in the more recent period. The coefficients for both wages and salaries become positive by the second year after the inflation increase, although they become mildly negative again in the fourth and fifth years.

Profits

The profit data used here are aggregate profits, using the national income definition, corrected for the effects of inflation on inventory appreciation and depreciation. They were chosen in preference to dividend payments because a large proportion of stock owners' income comes from stock appreciation, owing partly to an increasing use of internal financing. They are not on a per income receiver basis, largely because of the difficulty of determining the relevant population. Though the data used is the best available, the reader should note that profit data is inherently unreliable. The fact that the figures are not on a per income receiver basis further weakens them.

Looking at table 1 we see that there is a large negative short-term relation between inflation and changes in profits. A percentage increase in inflation is associated with a 0.90 percent decrease in pre-tax profits and a 1.43 percent decrease in post-tax profits, both larger than the equivalent figures for earnings.

The Distributional Effects of Inflation

Table 2   Short-term Effects of Inflation, GNP Change and Unemployment on Change in Incomes, 1962–1977

	Mean	b	Inflation Beta	GNP Beta	Unemployment Beta	R^2	D/W
Pre-tax earnings	1.31	−.39	−.69 (−4.88)	.38 (2.92)	.11 (0.98)	.88	2.00
Post-tax earnings	0.65	−.75	−.99 (−3.76)	−.27 (−1.10)	.45 (2.16)	.58	2.98
Pre-tax wages	1.22	−.36	−.59 (−3.15)	.38 (2.19)	.01 (0.01)	.79	1.11
Post-tax wages	1.22	−.50	−.72 (−2.80)	.16 (−0.69)	.44 (2.18)	.60	1.61
Pre-tax salaries	0.70	−.52	−.96 (−4.81)	−.01 (0.07)	.33 (2.09)	.76	1.04
Pre-tax profits	3.77	−1.77	−.37 (−3.13)	.61 (5.59)	.63 (6.79)	.91	2.16
Post-tax profits	5.26	−4.20	−.62 (−3.07)	.29 (1.58)	.91 (5.74)	.80	2.43
Post-tax dividends	2.96	−.19	−.09 (−0.38)	.59 (2.76)	.18 (0.96)	.56	1.93
Pre-tax farm income	0.83	2.74	.34 (1.02)	.61 (1.99)	−.36 (−1.35)	.33	2.26
Pre-tax small business income	0.66	−.66	−.39 (−2.38)	.75 (4.43)	.34 (2.68)	.84	1.80
Pre-tax OASI	3.04	−.20	−.09 (0.22)	.04 (0.12)	.06 (0.19)	.00	2.36
Pre-tax AFDC	2.09	−.07	−.06 (−0.15)	−.13 (−0.37)	−.31 (−1.04)	.12	2.31
Pre-tax unemployment compensation	0.89	−.41	−.70 (−2.09)	−.34 (−1.09)	−.04 (−0.16)	.33	1.64
Pre-tax aggregate transfers	7.50	−.18	−.11 (−0.36)	−.71 (2.47)	−.12 (−0.47)	.41	1.71

However, these figures must be looked at in the context of the extreme volatility of profit income, and the fact that GNP change and unemployment have more important short-term effects on profits than on earnings and wages. The short-term negative beta for inflation and profits is considerably lower than the comparable betas for earnings and wages, while those for changes in GNP are higher. Nonetheless, taken at face value, there appears good reason for business to push for deflation, as the gains from higher unemployment and higher inflation taken together seem to outweigh those from a higher growth rate. However the relatively low R^2's, especially for post-tax profits, should induce caution in reading too much into the figures.

A second reason why the figures might be misleading is more problematic. The general assumption that people look only at short-term effects seems less plausible for profit receivers than other types of income recipient. One might reasonably expect some percentage of profit receivers to estimate the effect of inflation on profits over a longer period. Using equation (6) I reran with a six-year lag for inflation. I found that an initially large negative inflation coefficient became positive by the third year and that the sum of the lag coefficients was positive.

Self-employment Income

Self-employment income breaks down into two distinct categories— farm income and trade and professional income. I have measured these separately by using national income data, corrected by dividing by the number of self-employed people. The major weakness of the resulting data are that they are pre-tax only and that the corrections used to obtain figures on an individual basis are somewhat rough. I do not however think that the latter problem has much effect on the regressions, although it may have a marginal effect on the means.

Tables 1 and 2 show rather different effects of inflation on the two major kinds of self-employment income. Trade and professional income shows a moderately negative association with inflation both in the longer period and in the most recent period. Thus a one percent rise in prices is associated with a 0.51 percent income decrease in the longer period and a 0.66 percent decrease in the more recent period, in both cases approximating the absolute effect on pre-tax wages. As we might expect, trade and professional incomes are more volatile than wages, making the relative effect rather less.

The association between farm incomes and inflation is quite different from that between inflation and trade and professional incomes. There is an absolutely large (although relatively small) positive association. Thus a one percent rise in prices is associated with a 1.19 percent increase in farm incomes in the longer period and a 2.74 percent increase in the more recent period. However, this should be seen in the context of the year-to-year volatility of farm income. As we can see looking at the betas, the effect of inflation is much less than the effect of changes in GNP and the whole equation accounts for only around 20 percent of the variance in farm incomes in the longer period. Thus it would seem more reasonable for rational farmers looking at the short-term association to view inflation as a mildly beneficial force rather than as strongly benefitting them.

Transfer Payments

The data used for transfer payments is of two kinds. One is per capita payments to AFDC families, retired couples and the unemployed, the three major recipient groups. But these figures have two defects. First, people in these categories have become the beneficiaries over time of an ever increasing number of new cash and in-kind programs. Hence their real transfer income increase is not fully measured. In addition the percentage of those in poverty receiving government aid has increased over time, meaning more of the welfare pool receives aid. As a partial way of dealing with this I have also included the national income figures for transfers to persons, a figure that can be interpreted as the total increase going to the welfare-prone. This figure also has defects in that it is not on a per capita basis, includes some transfers such as bad debts and business and federal payments to non-profit institutions that we might wish to exclude, and does not allow for reductions in the welfare pool over time. However, taken together these two sets of figures give a reasonably full picture.

The relation between inflation and short-term change in the three types of transfer income varies, as we might expect. Looking at the largest category, the retired, we can see that while there was initially some tendency for old-age security income to be eroded by inflation, there is virtually no relation between the two variables in the more recent period. Looking at the relation between inflation and AFDC payment levels we can see a similar picture, with the erosion being absolutely and relatively less. In both cases economic variables have little direct short-term impact, as we can see by the low percentage of the variance in these transfer incomes that is explained.

Unemployment compensation, on the other hand, does appear to have been eroded by inflation, with a percent increase in inflation being associated with a 0.66 percent decrease in unemployment payments in the longer period and a 0.41 percent decrease in the more recent period. Further, in both periods inflation is a more important influence than the other economic variables on payment levels. Lastly, looking at aggregate transfers there appears to have been some negative correlation with inflation, but it is clearly lower in the more recent period.

Looking at transfers overall I would be inclined to discount the importance of the results for aggregate transfers and unemployment compensation and stress those for the retired and AFDC recipients. For unlike the unemployed and some other recipient groups, these latter receive transfers on a relatively long-term basis and are thus more likely to view transfers as their primary income source, and more likely to worry if general economic forces should reduce the growth in their transfer income.

Summary

In this section we have examined the short-term relation between inflation and a range of factor incomes. We did this primarily to provide an alternative short-term experiential basis for later tests of the relation between actual and perceived effects of inflation. We found, as seems reasonable, that the short-term relation between inflation and most factor incomes is negative. But the degree of negativity varied. The most negative relation, all things considered, appeared to be that between inflation and salary rates, with that between inflation and wages being only a little less negative. The relation with trade and professional incomes appeared mildly negative. The profit results were, as we saw, unstable, but on balance seemed mildly to moderately negative. The two most important transfer incomes had a mildly negative association with inflation over the period as a whole, but virtually no relation in the more recent period. Farm incomes had a mildly positive relation in both periods. Finally it seems worth noting that the strength of the short-term negative relation seems lower for almost all incomes in the 1962–1977 period than in the 1948–1979 period, something consistent with the greater use of indexing.

Some More Detailed Short-term Results

As well as performing the overall tests to assess the short-term relation between inflation and factor incomes reported in the previous section, I also performed four more detailed tests to assess the effects of differences in the environments of those receiving given factor incomes. These have been reported in more detail elsewhere.[25] Here I wish only to report the most important findings.

For three different reasons it seemed worthwhile to break down the most important of the factor incomes, wages and profits, by industry. First, it would provide a test of the robustness of the aggregated figures. Second, it would test whether workers and profit receivers in different industries might see different short-term relations between inflation and their income. Last, a lack of differentation would reinforce our confidence in the factor income classification used in the models, by denying differentation according to an alternative functional income classification.

In order to carry out the test I reran equation (1) using wage and profit data from nineteen separate industrial sectors. The basic finding was that there was little variation by industry. The sign of the b relating inflation to wage and profit income remained the same in seventeen of the nineteen industries (the exceptions were leather manufacturing for both wages and profits and petroleum products for profits). Further, the variance was fairly restricted, with twelve of the nineteen wage betas in the −.50 to −.70 range and twelve of the profit betas in the −.10 to −.30 range. Thus it seemed fair to conclude that the factor income classification was the apppropriate one and that the aggregated figures were a fair representation of the experience of the bulk of wage and profit receivers.

A second more detailed test attempted to see whether the relation between inflation and wages and profits was different in industries charactarized by different levels of unionization and concentration. The major finding was that inflation seemed less correlated in the short term with both wages and profits in those low concentration, low unionization industries which are often referred to as the competitive sector. However, the difference in the betas and b's between these industries and the others was not great.

A third detailed test reran equation (1) for the same factor incomes as in the previous section, but broke down the 1948–1979 period into years when there were Democratic and Republican administrations, with the aim of finding out whether people might perceive a different short-term relation between inflation and their income under administrations of the different parties. The basic finding was that the short-term relation between inflation and the bulk of the different factor incomes seemed much the same under administrations of both parties, but that profits seemed to have a mildly positive relation to inflation in periods when the Democrats were in power and a mildly negative one in periods when the Republicans were in power.

A last test examined the proposition that inflation aids the expansion of the federal government in the short term because it expands revenues. I found in common with other work that the negative short-term effects on real expenditures are greater than the positive short-term effects on real revenues, something that does not support at least the short-term version of the argument.

Conclusion

In this chapter we have looked at some studies that attempt to estimate the "real" underlying long-term effects of inflation. We have also attempted to show the effects of inflation as they should appear to a pluralist citizen who bases his actions on the short-term effects of inflation on his major source of income.

Our examination of the studies attempting to calculate the long-term effects of inflation indicated that inflation has few aggregate effects and rather minor long-term distributional effects. Insofar as there were effects, these appeared to indicate some redistribution away from the bottom 20 percent and the top 5 percent toward the rest of the income distribution, but some of the studies questioned whether even these minor redistributional effects took place. Thus the predominant emphasis of the studies was that the reader should be skeptical toward claims that inflation has major negative long-term redistributive effects on incomes.

Our examination of the short-term effects that we expected would be most visible to a citizen acting on current pluralist assumptions led us to quite different conclusions. We found that the short-term effects on most incomes were negative, with the effect being strongest for salaries and wages, but also quite negative for trade and professional income and (more debatably) profits. We also found little negative relation with transfer incomes or farm incomes.

Overall then we seem to have established that the effects of inflation on most people are very small, especially when compared to the effects of other economic variables. However, we have also established that if people look primarily at the short-term effects on their primary income source, most people see a negative relation of varying proportions. In the next chapter I will examine the attitudes of those in these various income receiver catagories toward inflation, in order to see whether their "subjective" interests resemble the "objective" interests we have looked at in this chapter.

4   Public Perceptions
of Inflation

In the last chapter we looked at the available evidence on the real effects of inflation and showed the short-term correlation between inflation and various factor incomes. In this chapter we shall examine how people perceive and evaluate inflation. In order to do this we will sequentially examine the public's perception of past and future inflation rates, their overall evaluation of inflation, why they view inflation so negatively and how salient inflation is compared to other problems that face the public. In the course of doing all this we will also see whether people in different occupational classes perceive inflation in different ways.

In terms of the models illustrated in chapter 1 this chapter examines the second point in the linkage, the perceived effects of inflation and the degree to which they are consistent with the real effects examined in the last chapter. Figure 13 shows the mechanisms through which inflation could be perceived and converted to policy demands. It is immediately apparent that whether the individual forms his opinions on his own or as the result of guidance by leaders and reference groups, there are three primary pathways through which the evaluation of inflation can take place. The first is through the perceived effect of inflation on the individual's income. The second is through perceived non-income effects on the individual. The last is through the perceived effects on valued groups or persons. As these pathways combine, the individual would form an overall evaluation of inflation which would then be ranked relative to evaluations of other potential problems competing for his attention. The individual can then make demands on society with the aim of mitigating the problems inflation is seen as causing, through direct economic actions or through some form of political action.

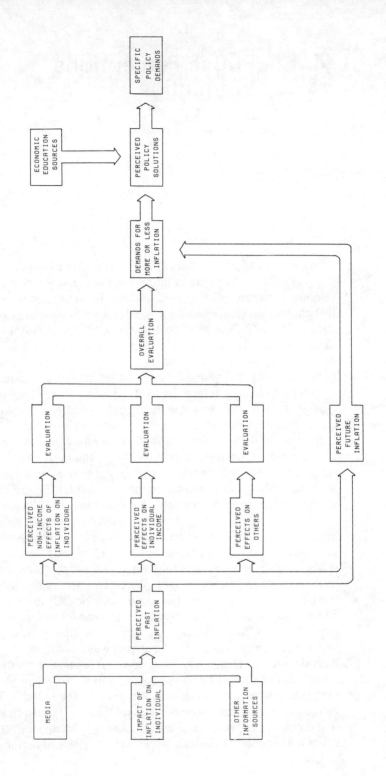

Figure 13   Mechanisms for converting inflation impacts into policy demands

In the remainder of this chapter and in the next, we follow this progression. Before we do so, a brief digression on methodological problems associated with the data is in order.

Some Methodological Problems

Ideally we would like to have time series covering the entire postwar period at regular intervals for each of the questions we will use in this chapter. What we in fact have is less satisfactory. Several questions have been asked at irregular intervals for most of the period, some questions have been asked a few times and some only once. There is also considerable bias in the period covered, with more of the questions coming from the last fifteen years or so, when inflation has been higher than in the earlier period. This means that one must be wary in interpreting the results. Often attitudes that obtain during periods of high inflation would not obtain when inflation was lower. In addition, where I have used questions that were only asked once, it is possible that particularistic influences may have affected the result.

I have attempted to cope with these problems in two ways. First, whenever suitable data is available, I have used answers from more than one time point and have indicated where opinion has changed over the period. Second, for my cross-sectional analysis I have primarily relied on data from the 1960s, which is midway in the period studied and has inflation rates between the low rates of the 1950s and the high ones of the 1970s. Even if one believes, as many economists and others do, that rates below 6 percent are unlikely to be seen in the next decade, these years are better than more recent ones with higher inflation rates for distinguishing between the attitudes of different population groups toward inflation, because at high rates of inflation unanimity in answering tends to prevail, washing out differences in intensity of feeling by the several groups. In particular for some of the questions asked by the Michigan Survey of Consumer Finances, I have been able to present answers for the fall of 1962, when inflation was 1.13 percent, for summer 1966, when inflation was 3.49 percent and for fall 1969, when inflation was 5.75 percent. If we were to take inflation in all postwar years as our universe, these years would fall on the 25th, 56th and 72d percentiles respectively. Further, to allow for the reasonable possibility that inflation has become built in at rates nearer 9 or 10 percent, I have supplemented this earlier data with data from the 1970s. Despite this, many of the presented results may not be fully generalizable. They do however represent our best information on attitudes at present.

Another methodological problem with the results in this chapter is that it has sometimes been impossible to apply appropriate controls. One reason is that much of the data is nominal or ordinal, limiting the techniques that may be applied to the data. Another is that I have had in many cases to work with published data rather than the original files. For both these reasons I have primarily relied on contingency tables and measures of association based on these. While it has been occasionally possible to control for one or two variables, it has not usually been possible to control for all possibly relevant independent variables simultaneously. Fortunately much of the analysis in this chapter is more concerned with finding out the positions of specified groups than in directly uncovering the causes of these opinions. For this purpose the available data is usually adequate. Lastly the reader should note that the numerous simple regressions discussed later in this chapter are all, unless otherwise indicated, based on the simple linear equation $y = a + bi + e$ where y is the dependent variable in question, and i is the rate of inflation.

Perceiving Inflation

In this section we are primarily concerned with the preliminary question of the accuracy with which people perceive the amount and direction of inflation and the degree to which they are prone to convert present experience of inflation into expectations of future inflation. Though all three theories are consistent with reasonably accurate perceptions of inflation it seems reasonable to suppose that pluralist man is the most likely to accurately note what is happening in the economic arena and that the masses in elite theories are the least likely to have accurate perceptions.

Past Inflation

Looking first at the question of whether people perceive inflation, the answer would seem to be that they do. Figure 14 shows the relation between people's answers to a question on whether prices have increased in the past year and the rate of inflation in the previous twelve months over the 1957–1966 period. This is a particularly interesting period becuase for most of it inflation was below the 2 percent level. Thus the data in figure 14, showing that even at these low rates between 40 and 60 percent of the population thought prices had risen, is quite impressive. Further, the data also shows that as the rate of inflation increased, the percentage of the population feeling the prices of things they had bought had gone up also increased.

However, it is evident that the relationship is far from perfect. To give but one example, in November 1957, when the annual rate of inflation stood at 3.27 percent, 34 percent of the population thought that prices had not changed over the past year, 3 percent thought they had decreased and 9 percent did not know.[1] Further, although the sensitivity to inflation

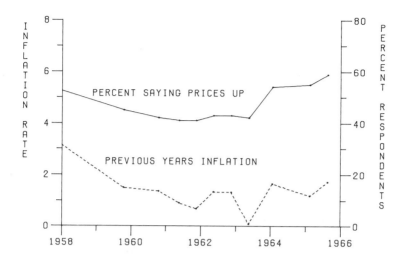

Figure 14   Actual and perceived inflation rates, 1957–1965. The question was, "We'd
like to know what happened to prices on household items and clothing here
in (community name) during the past year. Have they stayed the same,
gone up or gone down?" Sources: U.S. Department of Commerce, *Handbook of Cyclical Indicators* (Washington D.C.: Government Printing Office,
1977), p. 109. George Katona et al., *Survey of Consumer Finances* (Ann
Arbor: University of Michigan), various issues.

increased somewhat over the period, inflation explained only about one
third of the variance in the responses to the survey question.

Additional evidence on the question of sensitivity to past inflation is
available from a Harris Poll series, asked in the 1971–1980 period, which
attempts to measure not just whether people perceive higher prices, but
whether they can perceive changes in the rate of inflation. Respondents
were asked, "Do you feel that the prices of most things you buy are rising
more rapidly than a year ago; about as rapidly as they were then; rising,
but less rapidly than a year ago; staying the same; or are prices going
down?" The data from this question confirms the real but limited sensitivity shown by the earlier figures. During the period 1974–1979, when
inflation averaged 8.6 percent, the question was asked 49 times. Less than
1 percent of respondents thought that prices had decreased and only
around 7.4 percent thought prices had stayed the same.

Figure 15 shows the percentage responding that prices were increasing
more rapidly than a year ago, plotted against the actual rate of change in
the quarterly inflation rate from that in the previous year. In addition,
although I do not show it on the figure, I ran the series against the yearly
rate of inflation. I found a relationship both with the rate of inflation and

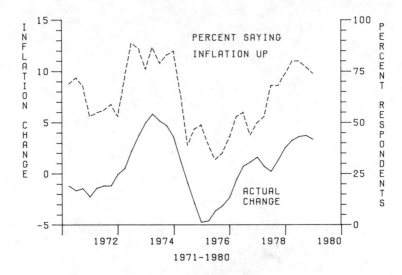

Figure 15   Actual and perceived changes in inflation rate; quarterly figures, 1971–
               1979. The question was, "Do you feel that the prices of most things you
               buy are rising more rapidly than a year ago, about as rapidly as they
               were then, rising but less rapidly than a year ago, staying the same, or
               are prices going down?" Sources: U.S. Department of Commerce,
               Handbook of Cyclical Indicators (Washington, D.C.: Government Print-
               ing Office, 1977), p. 109; Council of Economic Advisers, *Economic Re-
               port of the President* (Washington, D.C.: Government Printing Office,
               1979 and 1981); Data supplied to author by Harris Polls.

with the rate of change of inflation. Inflation during the previous year
accounted for around 18 percent of the variance in the series. And the
rate of change of inflation plotted in figure 15 accounted for 52 percent
of the variance in the perceived rate of change.

    Thus overall it seems reasonable to assert that most people have been
able to perceive inflation, that they are more likely to do so at higher
rates of inflation and that they are sensitive to changes in the rate of
inflation.

Future Inflation

    The fact that people can perceive past inflation does not necessarily
imply anything about their expectations of future inflation. Yet it seems
reasonable to suppose that experience of inflation in the near past might
be a major determinant of future expectations. The data we shall examine
here tends to confirm this supposition to some degree. But it also shows
that there is a systematic tendency to expect future inflation to be less

than the rate of inflation actually experienced in the past and that the population becomes less and less likely to agree on future inflation rates as the rate of inflation increases.

Figure 16 shows a series on the expected future rate of inflation over the 1947–1975 period, constructed from questions on future price expectations asked by the quarterly Michigan Survey of Consumer Finances. This has been plotted against quarterly inflation at the annual rate over the same period. As can be seen, there is a relation between the two series, with inflation in the same quarter explaining 44 percent of the variance in future price expectations. Moreover there is reason to think that the relation is higher than appears here. Later Michigan data, giving responses of people who were asked more directly what rate of inflation they expected, is considerably more highly correlated with quarterly inflation.[2] Using data from the 1961–1978 period reconstructed on the basis of these later results, the variance explained improved to 82 percent, with the Durbin Watson statistic, at 1.7, indicating little auto-correlation.

Thus there seems considerable correlation between inflation and expectations. However, it seems worth noting that as inflation increased people seemed to show less unanimity in predicting future rates. Thus in the 1954-1963 period the variance for the 36 means shown in figure 16 varied between 2.78 and 3.75, with a mean value of 3.29. In the 1964 to mid-1973 period the variance for the 38 means varied between 2.85 and 13.24, with a mean value of 7.36 and other data indicates that variance was even higher in the post-1973 period.

Moreover it is apparent from figure 16 that despite the relation between the two series and despite the tendency for expectations to rise when inflation rises, the expected rate of inflation usually remains below the actual rate. Given the rather complex way the mean figure is constructed from semi-ordinal data, particularly prior to 1966, we should be cautious about accepting this result uncritically. However, this is an important finding if other data should confirm it, as it indicates that to the degree that future inflation depends on the expectations of the general public there should be a systematic downward pressure from this source.

Finally, it seems worth noting that this lower expectation figure does not come as the result of people optimistically expecting the future to be better than the past. On the contrary the limited evidence available indicates that people are generally more pessimistic about the future. Figure 17 shows data taken from a period when the yearly inflation rate was virtually constant at around 0.5 percent to 1.5 percent. As can be seen, there is a persistent tendency for a higher percentage of the population to think future prices will increase than to think prices increased in the past year.

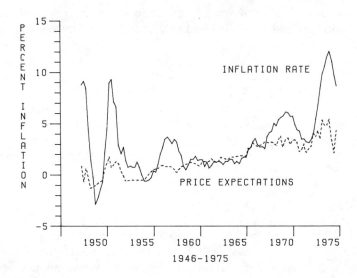

Figure 16   Future price expectations and yearly inflation, 1948–1975. Source: U.S.
Department of Commerce, *Handbook of Cyclical Indicators* (Washing-
ton, D.C.: Government Printing Office, 1977), p. 109; Council of Economic Advisers, *Economic Report of the President* (Washington, D.C.:
Government Printing Office, 1979 and 1981); F. Thomas Juster, "Uncertainty, Price Expectations and the Personal Savings Rate," in Burkhard
Strumpel et al., *Surveys of Consumers 1972–73* (Ann Arbor: University
of Michigan, 1975), pp. 25–30; Richard Curtin, ed., *Surveys of Consumers 1974–75* (Ann Arbor: University of Michigan, 1976), p. 193.

Where do People Acquire Information about Inflation?

A final question related to the perception of inflation is the source of
information about inflation rates and their interpretation. Although multiple sources of information are compatible with all three of the major
political approaches we are considering, it should be apparent that if
information comes from people's direct experiences in the market, it
would be harder for any elite to manipulate their perceptions than if it
comes from the media. Short of asking people, something which, to the
best of my knowledge, has not been done, and which has its own problems,
it is difficult to disentangle the source of information.

One possible approach is afforded by the fact that media information
about inflation usually comes a month or so after the fact. Thus we would
expect perceptions of inflation to be correlated more strongly with inflation
in the preceding than in the same month if the primary source was the
media. As we can see in table 3, there is a mild tendency for this to be

the case when questions on perceptions of past inflation, asked at irregular intervals, are correlated with inflation in the same and in the preceding

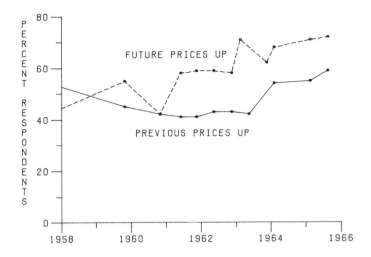

Figure 17   Past and future perceived price change. The question for past prices was, "We'd like to know what happened to prices on household items and clothing here in (community name) during the past year. Have they stayed the same, gone up or gone down?" For future expectations the question, between 1957 and 1960, was, "What do you expect prices of household items and clothing will do during the next year or so? Stay where they are, go up or go down?" Between 1961 and 1965 it was, "Speaking of prices in general, I mean the prices of the things you buy—do you think they will go up in the next year or go down, or stay where they are now?" Sources: *Survey of Consumer Finances* (Ann Arbor: University of Michigan), various issues; F. Thomas Juster, "Uncertainty, Price Expectations and the Personal Savings Rate," in Burkhard Strumpel et al., *Surveys of Consumers 1972–73* (Ann Arbor: University of Michigan, 1975), pp. 25–26.

month. But the difference is not great and, because it was not possible to control for auto-correlation, not too much should be read into either the difference or the fairly high correlation with inflation in the same month.

Lastly we should note that if people do indeed get all their information about inflation from the media, we would expect information on the amount of inflation to be more accurate than information on its effects on different groups. And even if people perceive the amount of inflation directly, as some must do, it is plausible that they would use media information in interpreting its meaning for them.

Table 3   Inflation Rate Lag versus Prediction of Rising Prices

Inflation rate lag	Correlation with % predicting rise in inflation
1 month previous	.63
2 months previous	.71
3 months previous	.66
6 months previous	.51
9 months previous	.48
12 months previous	.42

The number of data points is only 25 and hence the results should be treated cautiously. The data are from various irregular time points in the 1947–1971 period.

Sources: Council of Economic Advisers, *Economic Report of the President* (Washington, D.C.: Government Printing Office, various issues); G. Katona et al., *Survey of Consumer Finances* (Ann Arbor: University of Michigan), various issues.

Evaluating Inflation

Although, prima facie, it would seem reasonable for people to pay more attention to phenomena that are important to them, there is an obvious difference between perceiving inflation and evaluating it. In this section we shall look at whether people favor or oppose inflation, how strongly they feel about it, who they feel to be most affected by it, why they feel the way they do about it and how bad they think it is in relation to other problems.

These questions are of obvious relevance to our central concerns. Given the findings in the previous chapter, the pluralist models would lead us to expect that if people were sensitive to the real effects they would not feel very strongly about inflation and that the upper and lower parts of the income distribution should mildly oppose it while the middle classes together with other beneficiaries, such as borrowers and those paying off mortgages, should mildly support it. If instead we felt it more reasonable to see pluralist man as reacting to the short-term effects on his income, we would expect most people to be opposed to inflation, with some support from farmers and with the welfare receivers, especially the aged, being essentially neutral. In either case we would expect groups that benefit in both the short and long-term, such as mortgage holders, to favor inflation, or at the least oppose it much less strongly than others. We would expect primary attention to be paid to effects on the respondent and less attention to be paid to effects on groups, including reference groups. Finally, we would expect inflation to be seen as less important than other problems such as lack of income, unemployment, social problems or war, especially among those groups who are most prone to suffer from such problems.

It is harder to make predictions about the state of public opinion from elite and Marxist theories, as both sets tend to see public opinion as dependent rather than as independent. However, some tentative predictions can be identified. Both Marxist and elite theories would lead us to expect a ruling group that would systematically try to sway the general public to downgrade the importance of those real problems that can only be solved at some cost to the ruling group and to upgrade the importance of more peripheral problems that pose no threat to the ruling group, with all except possibly the structural variant of Marxism expecting the attempt to be successful in our period. This would lead us to expect attempts to downgrade "real" problems such as unemployment, slow wage income growth, poverty and lack of income redistribution and to upgrade inflation to the status of a major problem. Further, if this attempt were successful, we might even find groups that benefitted from inflation believing it harmed them.

In the structural version of Marxism we should find some evidence of of a class-conscious working class. In the present context this implies that this group would be less likely than others to swallow the "myths" about inflation and more likely to rate "real" problems such as unemployment or income distribution as more important. One might also expect a more group-centered basis for concern about inflation, with inflation being evaluated more for its effects on the working class as a whole than for its effects on the individual.

Attitude toward Inflation

Given these different possibilities, how do people regard inflation? To test this I use answers to a question asked in the 1957-1966 period of those who thought inflation would increase in the next year. They were asked, "Would you say that these rising prices would be to the good or to the bad, or what?" The responses to this question are presented in figure 18. Of primary interest is the fact that most people consider inflation harmful. Of those who thought prices went up in the last year, between 67 and 84 percent of respondents thought inflation harmful. It is interesting to note, however, that not all respondents are of this opinion, with around 9 percent saying that it makes no difference and between 7 and 16 percent saying that higher prices are actually beneficial.

A question that naturally occurs is whether opinions on the desirability of inflation become more adverse when inflation rises. This might happen because people become more aware of what inflation is as the rate increases, or because strong inflation is regarded as a different phenomenon than weak inflation. Using the data illustrated above, I tested for this by running the annual rate of inflation against the percentage who thought that prices had gone up. This showed that people's opinion of inflation is

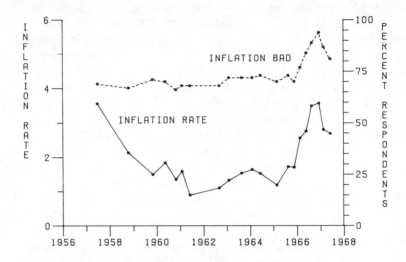

Figure 18   Normative perceptions of price increases. Sources: George Katona, et al.,
                 Survey of Consumer Finances (Ann Arbor: University of Michigan), var-
                 ious issues; Council of Economic Advisers, *Economic Report of the Pres-
                 ident* (Washington, D.C.: Government Printing Office), various issues.

not constant or independent of the rate. The run yielded a value of 58.78
for the intercept and 7.19 for the slope, indicating that, when there was
no inflation, around 59 percent of the population thought inflation to be
a bad thing, and that every time inflation increased one percent an extra
7 percent thought it harmful. The run accounted for 56 percent of the
variance and the inflation coefficient was significant at the .01 level.

A second test of the sub-hypothesis is to run the opinion figures on the
goodness or badness of inflation against the differing perceived rates at
a given time point. Table 4 drawn from the fall 1966 survey, when inflation
was 3.5 percent, shows people's opinions of inflation broken down by the
rate of inflation that they thought existed. These figures also confirm the
view that the degree of inflation affects the opinion of it, with Tau *C*
significant at the 0.01 level. As can be seen from both table 4 and figure
18, there is a strong tendency for everyone to oppose inflation as the rate
increases. There is little doubt that were the same question asked today
there would be virtual unanimity that inflation was a bad thing.

Having looked at aggregated figures we now break them down by different population catagories. Table 5, taken from the 1962 Survey of Consumer Finances, shows the breakdowns at a period of low inflation with
Tau *C* significant at the 0.01 level for all variables and chi-square significant
at the 0.02 level for all variables except occupation, where it was signif-

Table 4   Normative Attitude toward Price Increases in 1966

Attitude toward price increase	Perceived price change next year				
	1-2%	3-4%	5%	6-8%	10% or more
Bad	80.1%	81.8%	84.7%	87.8%	90.3%
No difference/ depends	12.1	8.0	7.5	9.8	6.9
Good	7.8	10.2	7.8	2.4	2.8
N	(372)	(137)	(294)	(41)	(72)

The questions were, "How large a price increase do you expect? Of course nobody can know for sure, but would you say that a year from now prices will be about 1 or 2 percent higher, or 5 percent, or closer to 10 percent higher than now, or what?" and "Would you say that these rising prices would be good or bad or what?" Both questions were asked only of those who had previously said they expected prices to increase next year.

Source: *Survey of Consumer Finances* (Ann Arbor: University of Michigan), Summer 1966.

icant at the 0.12 level. The most obvious fact about the data presented in table 5 is that no group appears to have a generally favorable attitude toward inflation. In addition it is worth noting that although the differences between the different ascribed groups are statistically significant, they are not large in an absolute sense. As we shall see later, this echoes the findings on the effect the different groups perceive inflation has on their income.

Despite the relatively small differences in attitude between members of different groups, what differences there are prove interesting. Looking first at sex, we find men more likely than women to perceive inflation favorably, with 22 percent of men thinking inflation was good compared with only 13 percent of women. Turning to age, we find a positive monotonic relation between age and dislike of inflation, with 69 percent of the under 35 group and 85 percent of the over-sixty-five group regarding it unfavorably. The income and education breakdowns are consistent with that for age, with the less educated and lower-income respondents being more likely than their better educated, higher-income brethren to perceive inflation as an evil. Lastly, factor incomes move in the same direction, with fixed income recipients more likely than wage earners to dislike inflation and wage earners more likely than salary earners. The self-employed however—particularly farmers—are somewhat more likely than salary earners to perceive inflation as an evil. Overall then, one can say that people in all groups see inflation as bad, but that the lower classes are more likely than the higher ones to regard inflation as bad.

This data should not be read as if the same differences in attitude would obtain at higher inflation rates. As early as fall 1966 the increasing unanimity on the badness of inflation had made the differences between the different sex, education and income groups insignificant. It does however

84   Chapter Four

Table 5   Attitude in 1962 toward Inflation among Those Who Thought Prices
                 Would Increase During the Next Year

| | Attitude toward price increase | | | |
	Good	No difference	Bad	N
All respondents	17.0%	7.8%	75.2%	(613)
Sex of respondents				
Male	21.9	9.6	68.9	(278)
Female	12.8	7.8	79.4	(335)
Age of head				
18–34	21.6	9.6	68.9	(167)
35–44	25.6	2.3	72.1	(129)
45–64	11.5	11.0	77.5	(218)
65 plus	10.3	5.2	84.5	(97)
Education of head				
0–8 grades	11.7	6.1	82.2	(180)
9–12 grades	13.3	8.2	78.6	(196)
High school plus	23.0	8.1	68.9	(148)
B.A. or more	24.7	10.6	64.7	(85)
Family income				
Under $5000	15.2	5.4	79.4	(257)
$5000–7499	15.7	7.0	77.3	(172)
$7500–9999	17.1	9.8	73.2	(82)
$10,000 and over	26.6	16.5	57.0	(79)
Occupation of head				
Fixed income	10.5	7.3	82.3	(124)
Wage earner	14.3	7.4	78.3	(203)
Salary earner	21.8	9.3	68.9	(193)
Self-employed	16.9	4.6	78.5	(65)

Those who thought prices would increase during the coming year were asked, "Would you
say that these rising prices would be to the good, or to the bad, or what?"

In all cases Kendall's Tau C was significant at the .01 level.

Source: *Survey of Consumer Finances* (Ann Arbor: University of Michigan), Fall 1962.

provide a reasonable indicator of the degree to which different sex, age,
education, income and occupational groups are worried about inflation,
and is broadly consistent with more recent evidence on the perceived
effects of inflation, which we will examine later.

It should be noted that the strong agreement that inflation is a problem
at a period when it was very low, together with the failure of upper-income
groups to consider it worse than middle-income groups, does not fit the
pluralist model well. Even if one disbelieves the admittedly weak economic work on the real effects of inflation presented in the previous
chapter and thinks that inflation has important redistributive effects, the
unanimity of the results makes little sense in the pluralist model, as one

would expect the winners to be as strongly for it as the losers are against it, and for the difference to increase, not decrease, as inflation gets larger.

Nor is there any evidence for a class-conscious working class thinking inflation less important than other groups, as might be claimed by some structuralists. Examination of the income, education and occupation breakdowns in table 5 clearly give this notion little support. Thus the first set of evidence appears to fit the elitist and traditional Marxist models better than the others.

Inflation and Other Problems

It is clear that looking at inflation in isolation it is almost universally evaluated in a negative fashion. But many problems face the public and it is clearly of central importance how salient inflation is when compared with other problems. In addition we are particularly concerned whether inflation is rated more negatively than related problems such as unemployment and economic growth, the solution to which might require policies that would increase inflation.

The primary evidence on the relative importance of inflation comes from a question asked periodically by the Gallup Poll in the period from 1939 to the present. The question has normally been "What do you think is the most important problem facing the country today?" but there have been occasional minor variations in the wording. As might be expected with an open-ended question the coding of the responses is not completely consistent over time. Nevertheless I have attempted to recode the responses to the sixty-six polls in which it was possible to distinguish inflation from other problems, into broad categories that enable comparison.

There are three major categories of problem: foreign affairs, including wars, domestic social problems and domestic economic problems. Over the whole period foreign affairs was seen as the major national problem for a majority of the period, with the economy following closely behind and social problems a poor third. Over time the pattern was for foreign affairs problems to dominate the national consciousness during the late forties, the fifties and the sixties, especially during the Korean, Vietnam and Cold wars. Economic problems, always important, came to dominate public concern during the seventies. Social problems were seen as most important only in the early and late sixties.[3]

Let us turn now to the individual issues. Figure 19 compares the percentage of the population who saw inflation as the major problem facing the nation with the percentage who saw the other most commonly cited domestic problems, race/civil rights and unemployment, as most important. The results are interesting in a number of ways. First it is clear that even before inflation rates took off in the mid-1960s and early 1970s inflation was regarded as one of the most important domestic problems.

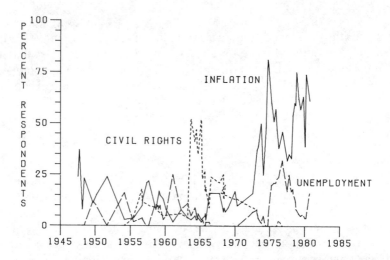

Figure 19   Perceptions of worst domestic problems facing the country. The question
has usually been "What do you think is the most important problem facing the country today?" but sometimes the wording has varied a little
from this. Sources: George Gallup, *The Gallup Poll*, 3 vols. (New York,
Random House, 1972); *The Gallup Opinion Index*, various issues.

For example, in September 1949, 11 percent of the population saw inflation
as the most important problem at a time when prices had actually declined
2.6 percent in the preceding year. Similar results hold for other years in
the 1940s and 1950s.

Second it is evident, as might be expected, that the percentage thinking
inflation is the most important problem varies with the rate of inflation.
Regressing the percentage citing inflation on the rate of inflation in the
previous year yielded an intercept value of 4.49 and a *b* value of 4.67,
with the inflation coefficient significant at the .001 level and the equation
accounting for 55 percent of the variance. This says that around 4 percent
of the population thinks inflation is the most important problem facing
the nation even when inflation is zero, and that each time the inflation
rate increases 1 percent another 5 percent come to think it is the most
important problem.

Third, the regularity with which inflation is perceived as an important
problem is impressive. Over the 1947–1980 period it was mentioned more
often than any other domestic problem, and as figure 18 makes clear, it
is almost always considered more important than the other major domestic
problems.

Finally it is worth noting that these figures, impressive as they are, probably understate the relative importance of inflation to individuals. As we will see later in table 7, there seems good reason to think that people consider inflation even more important for them and their families than for the nation as a whole.

In view of our discussion in chapter 3, the magnitude of worry about inflation seems extraordinary. It seems even more so when we focus on purely economic problems. Perhaps most remarkable is what is not in the figures. Throughout the post-1947 period the United States had the slowest rate of per capita income growth of any major developed nation except Britain, well behind that of its major rival the USSR. This already slow growth slowed further in the 1970s and, when combined with growth in the government sector, led to gross weekly earnings falling from $104.38 in 1969 to $101.02 in 1979. Despite this, respondents have rarely if ever volunteered slow income growth or slow GNP growth as a major problem facing the United States, and the problem of poverty and welfare has only occasionally been mentioned and never by more than 6 percent of the population.

Almost as remarkable is the relative emphasis given to inflation and unemployment. We saw in chapter 2 that the United States has, by international standards, high unemployment rates and low inflation rates. Further, as we saw in the last chapter, the ill effects of inflation do not seem to be large, while psychologists rate unemployment as a traumatic event on a par with deaths in the family. Yet, as we saw in figure 19, people almost always consider inflation a greater problem than unemployment when asked to name the most important national problem.

There also seems a tendency for people to consider inflation a worse problem than unemployment when asked to directly compare the two problems, although evidence is only available for the 1970s, when both inflation and unemployment exceeded their postwar averages. Figure 20 shows responses to a Michigan Survey of Consumer Finances question, "Which of the two problems—unemployment or inflation—do you think will cause the more serious hardship for people during the next year or so?" and to a Harris Poll question, "As far as you personally are concerned, which is a more serious problem for you and your family today— rising prices or unemployment?" The figure shows that, as was the case when people were allowed to choose their own problems, most see inflation as the more serious problem for the country and even more see it as the major problem for them and their family.

However there are also two interesting differences. It is clear that when directly asked to choose between the two problems people are much more likely to see unemployment as the major problem than they are when they

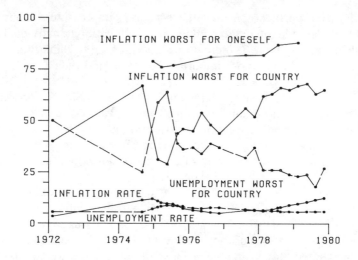

Figure 20   Perceptions of inflation or unemployment as the worst problem. The Michigan Consumer Survey question was "Which of the two problems—unemployment or inflation—do you think will cause the more serious economic
hardship for people during the next year or so?" The Harris question was
"As far as you personally are concerned, which is a more serious problem
for you and your family today—rising prices or high unemployment?"
Sources: Richard Curtin, ed., *Surveys of Consumers 1974–75* (Ann Arbor,
University of Michigan, 1976), p. 202; data supplied to author by Harris
Polls; data supplied to author by Michigan Consumer Survey; Council of
Economic Advisers, *Economic Report of the President 1981* (Washington,
D.C., Government Printing Office, 1981).

have to provide their own problem list, indicating that many people normally suppress unemployment in favor of inflation but, when reminded,
consider unemployment the greater problem. In addition, when asked
directly to compare the two, lower-income and blue-collar workers are
more likely than higher-income and white-collar employees to see unemployment as the more serious problem, something that makes sense
in view of the higher incidence of unemployment among blue-collar workers. But no such relation exists for the open-ended Gallup question, indicating that the tendency to suppress the importance of unemployment
may be greater in the less well educated blue-collar workers.[4]

How does this relate to our models? It is clear that the pluralist models
leave us with many puzzles. While it is possible to partly explain the
unemployment-versus-inflation results from this perspective by pointing
out that at a given time inflation affects a lot more people directly than
unemployment, this does not explain the difference between the open- and

closed-ended results, the failure to mention slow income growth or income redistribution, or the tendency to rank inflation so far above such problems as crime, health, race, poverty, housing and energy. The data is clearly somewhat more consistent with the elitist and Marxist view that the masses are encouraged to misperceive their real problems. This would explain why people in general, and blue-collar workers in particular, are likely to suppress unemployment as a problem. It is also consistent with their failure to mention slow income growth, redistribution and poverty in the open-ended questions as well as with the tendency to overestimate the relative importance of inflation.

Who Is Seen as Most Hurt

It is clear that inflation is regarded as a serious problem by an over-whelming majority of the public. A problem, however, may have different consequences for different groups, and we saw earlier that there has been much speculation among economists on the distributional consequences of inflation. In this section I will look at who the public thinks is most and least hurt by inflation. While the implications of this question for our basic models are not major, it would clearly help the pluralist argument if the public perceived accurately which groups were most and least hurt, if they saw only small differences in impact between the different groups and if their primary concern about the effects of inflation was focused on its effects on themselves, rather than on classes of which they might be a part or groups they felt sorry for. Likewise findings that people had been persuaded that the primary losers were those who had the most to gain from redistribution and higher employment and evidence that people evaluated inflation in terms of its effects on their class rather than on themselves would be consistent with most versions of the Marxist and elitist models.

Table 6 shows responses in the December 1969 Michigan Survey of Consumer Finances to questions on who is most hurt and who is least hurt by inflation. This table reveals a clear tendency to perceive inflation as differentially hurting such groups as the poor, the old and retired, those on fixed incomes, and average working people—those groups that tend to be sympathetically perceived by most people. Likewise the groups perceived as being least hurt by inflation are primarily those with high incomes and businessmen—groups that are not traditional recipients of sympathy from the general population.

Interestingly these results hold for all income groups studied, although there is some evidence of a normal tendency to bias perceptions toward one's own group. Just as interesting is the fact that there was little attempt on the part of respondents to claim that all groups were equally affected, with only around 4 percent making this claim.

Table 6   Who People in Different Income Groups Thought Were Most and Least Hurt by Inflation, in 1969

	All families	Less than $3,000	$3,000 −4,999	$5,000 −7,499	$7,500 −9,999	$10,000 or more
Hurt most						
Poor/little man	50%	61%	56%	49%	50%	43%
Old/retired	18	14	12	18	16	24
Fixed incomes	21	13	11	20	15	32
Ave. working man	27	21	29	29	35	25
Everybody	2	2	2	2	2	1
Other[a]	10	11	10	10	13	9
Hurt least						
Well-to-do/rich	70	75	79	73	65	65
Businessmen	11	10	8	9	15	13
Rising incomes	6	2	2	5	5	11
Working people	2	2	2	3	2	2
Nobody	4	4	5	2	4	6
Other[b]	9	7	4	10	8	12

The questions asked were, "What kind of people, would you say, are hurt most by inflation?" and "What kind of people are hurt least, or not at all, by inflation?" Totals exceed 100 percent because two answers were tabulated if given.

[a]Mainly businessmen, farmers, large families, those who need to borrow.

[b]Mainly speculators, "wise spenders," government people.

Source: Jan Schmiedeskamp et al., *1969 Survey of Consumer Finances* (Ann Arbor: University of Michigan, 1970), p.241.

These results, while only of minor importance for our main concerns, again seem to lend a little more support to Marxist and elitist than to pluralist arguments. While the identification of the old, those on fixed incomes and the poor as among the worst hurt is consistent with the "real" results in the previous chapter—though not the short-term simulations—the identification of the average working man as among the worst hurt and the well-to-do as the least hurt clearly does not fit the real facts and only loosely at best fits the short-term simulations. Thus to the extent that the pluralist models require accurate perceptions, it does not fit well. The same inconsistency between reality and perceptions, on the other hand, fits Marxist and pluralist predictions. More importantly so does the direction of the bias. Those who would gain most from redistribution and stimulation are seen as worst hurt and those who would lose from redistribution are seen as benefitting from inflation. There is also some evidence of group consciousness in people's tendency to see both their own group and groups they sympathize with as being harmed more than others by inflation.

A possible alternative interpretation of the above data might be along the lines put forward by Kiewiet and Kinder.[5] They argue that there is a departure from strict consistency with personal effects in people's evaluation of inflation and other economic variables, but that this occurs because people are more concerned about the effect on the country taken as a whole than on themselves. It would seem consistent with this view for people to be more concerned about the effects on those they sympathized with than on themselves. However this does not seem to be the case for inflation, although it may for other economic variables such as unemployment. Indeed the data we have appears to support the proposition that people are more worried about its effects on them and their families than on others.

An example is the data presented in table 7. This compares answers to three polls in which people were asked, "What do you consider the most urgent problem facing you and your family today?" with answers to three taken at the same times in which people were asked, "What do you consider the most urgent problem facing the nation today?"

As can be seen, inflation in all three periods was perceived as a relatively more important problem on the personal than on the national level, a

Table 7   Perceived Problems Facing the Family and The Nation

	Mar.–Sept. 1951		June 1955		October 1967	
	Family	Nation	Family	Nation	Family	Nation
High cost of living/ inflation	67%		35%		60%	16%
Jobs			9		3	
Economy/inflation/ taxes/govt. spending		54%		10%		
Health	5		10		8	
Housing	4		4			
Family/morals/old age	4		10		3	
Race/civil rights				4	4	21
Internal communism				6		
Draft/Vietnam/ foreign policy	4	56		48	5	50

The questions were, "What do you consider the most urgent problem facing you and your family today?" and "What do you consider the most urgent problem facing the nation today?" In 1951 the family question was asked in March and the nation question was asked in September.

Source: George Gallup, *The Gallup Poll*, 3 vols. (New York: Random House, 1972).

result consistent with the findings on inflation and unemployment reported in figure 20. In June 1955, with the annual rate of inflation at −0.7 percent, less than 5 percent of the population saw the cost of living or inflation as the most important problem facing the government in Washington, but fully 35 percent saw the cost of living or inflation as the most important problem facing them or their family. Likewise, in October 1967, with the annual inflation rate at 2.9 percent, 16 percent of the population thought the cost of living or inflation was the most important problem facing the nation, but fully 60 percent thought it the most important problem facing them and their families. Finally in November 1982, when unemployment was at a postwar high and inflation at its lowest level in years, 51 percent of the population perceived inflation to be the major problem facing them and their family compared to 41 percent citing unemployment. Indeed it seems likely, from the somewhat fragmentary evidence, particularly the 1955 survey taken when inflation was near its postwar low, that while many problems compete for attention at the national level, Americans almost always see inflation as the most important problem facing them and their families.

Why Is Inflation a Problem?

Even more important than the question of who the public perceives as most hurt by inflation is the question of why they think inflation is such a major problem. Why do people have such a negative view of inflation? One way of approaching this problem is to focus on what people perceive as being harmed by inflation.

The most obvious answer, and the one most in accord with pluralist views, is that people feel the effects of inflation on their real income. Thus they would see inflation as both increasing the costs of the goods they buy and increasing their monetary income. Given the highly negative view most people have of inflation, this implies that people see inflation as raising the costs of the goods they buy much more than it raises their monetary income. While this view has the virtue of simplicity, it has the problem that it is not obvious why such a way of evaluating inflation, if done accurately, should lead to such universally negative evaluations.

Two variants of this approach, both most in accord with what I have termed group-pluralism, imply that people focus exclusively on one or the other side of the real-income equation. Money illusion implies that people see inflation increasing their incomes, but fail to realize that rises in the prices of goods mean that there is no increase in their real income. What I term income illusion implies that people perceive the effect of inflation on their expenditures, without perceiving that it also raises their monetary incomes by roughly equivalent amounts. This latter variant has the virtue of explaining the highly negative evaluation of inflation. Both variants, seen as pluralist explanations, have the problem of explaining why individuals consistently ignore readily available information on a matter of high salience.

A second type of answer, more in accord with Marxist and elitist models, is what I term demand transference. People whose financial situation is getting worse for reasons unrelated to inflation, such as a decline in demand for their occupational skills, or a reduction in overall demand due to recession, can come to blame their misfortune on inflation rather than on its real cause. Such a transference is much more plausible if one postulates guidance by external forces such as the media. The advantage of this view is that it explains why aversion to inflation is so much greater than we would expect from its real-income effects. Its drawback is that it does not seem to explain why the more fortunate also dislike inflation.

A third type of answer is that people dislike inflation for its non-income effects. There are three variants of this view. One, in accord with the rational man variant of pluralism, which emphasizes the costs of political activity, stresses that even if inflation does not change individuals' real income in the final analysis, it does force them to undertake costly actions to protect their income which would not otherwise be necessary. While this is consistent with the negative evaluation of inflation, it seems to imply more activity than at first sight would seem plausible. A second variant, more consistent with Marxist and elitist models, would stress pure uncertainty costs. According to this view, people dislike inflation because it makes them fear what the future will bring, and makes it harder to plan their future finances. This variant is consistent with the highly negative evaluation of inflation in the face of low actual real-income effects. But it seems to require external influence on the individual if we are to explain both why inflation causes so much more uncertainty than unemployment, low income growth, crime and health problems, and why the uncertainty persists in the face of continued experience of mild effects. A last variant, more diffuse than the other two, and most consistent with elitist models, would see the evaluation of inflation as largely divorced from any real world effects on individuals, or attached to extremely implausible ones such as alienation or decline of the nation's moral fiber. Inflation in this view is negatively evaluated because people are told that it is bad, and only for that reason. While this variant explains the negative evaluation of inflation, it seems to require an extreme dearth of analytical ability on the part of the public.

Testing between these different ways of perceiving inflation's effects is difficult. Clearly it is possible for different individuals to have different ways of perceiving inflation's effects and it is also possible for a given individual to dislike inflation for more than one of these reasons. However, we can test for the existence and extent of these different ways of viewing inflation and attempt a rough judgment on which are more important.

The most obvious reason why people might negatively evaluate inflation, the presumption upon which most of chapter 3 was based, is that people see inflation as lowering their real income. But do they? Examination of a wide variety of poll results reveals a rather complex set of attitudes toward what is harmed by inflation. While some connections are clear, others are less so.

One thing that seems reasonably clear is that people do not suffer from substantial money illusion. Most perceive inflation as lowering their real income. The Michigan Survey of Consumer Finances has been asking people since 1946 whether their financial situation has improved or worsened over the previous year and why. Generally, fewer than 2 percent of those whose situation improved credited inflation. However, many of those whose financial situation, worsened blamed inflation, with the percentage of those doing so rising with the rate of inflation. Table 8 shows the results. When inflation is negative, only 2 percent of all families and 8 percent of worse-off families claim that higher prices lowered their real income. This increases to 14 percent of all families when inflation was between 0 and 4 percent, 21 percent of all families when it was between 4 and 6 percent and 31 percent when it was over 6 percent. These findings are reinforced by answers to a rather more direct question asked by NBC News in December 1978, when the annual rate of inflation stood at 9 percent. Asked "Has the inflation of the last few years reduced your standard of living? (If yes) Would you say it has reduced your standard of living by a great deal, some or only a little?" 48 percent did not think it had reduced their standard of living, 13 percent said it had reduced it a little, 24 percent said it had reduced it some and 14 percent said it had reduced it a great deal.[6]

Table 8   Families Claiming To Be Worse off Due to Higher Prices

Yearly inflation rate	Mean % of all families	Mean % of worse-off families	Number of surveys averaged[a]
Negative	2%	8%	1
0–4%	14	38	10
4–6%	21	49	11
Over 6%	31	81	15

[a]I took 37 survey results showing the numbers of families blaming inflation, found the yearly rate of inflation at the time and averaged the results from the surveys in each inflation category.

Source: *Survey of Consumer Finances* (Ann Arbor: University of Michigan), various issues.

Nor is this merely an unthinking visceral response to the word inflation. When people are asked separately whether their financial situation has improved, and whether their money income has increased, they show an unconscious ability to distinguish between the two and to feel that their money income is increasing faster than their real income. Moreover this tendency increases as the rate of inflation goes up. Figure 21 shows the percentage of those who thought their money income had increased who thought their financial situation was the same or worse. This makes it clear that even at low rates of inflation some could perceive the difference between money and real income and also shows that the percentage perceiving a difference increased markedly as inflation increased.

However, somewhat confusingly, the fact that people can distinguish between real and monetary increases and the fact that they tend to blame inflation for falls in their real income when asked, does not mean that they are more likely to feel worse off in real terms when inflation rises. Figure 22 charts responses to the question asking people if their financial situation had improved or worsened, asked in the first quarter of every

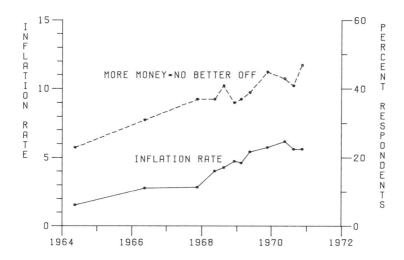

Figure 21   Perceptions of increased income without improved financial situation. The questions were, "We are interested in how people are getting along *financially* these days. Would you say that you and your family are better or worse off financially than you were *a year ago?*" and "Are you people making as much money as you were *a year ago,* or more, or less?" Sources: George Katona, Jay Schmiedeskamp, et al., *Survey of Consumer Finances* (Ann Arbor: University of Michigan), various issues; Council of Economic Advisers, *Economic Report of the President* (Washington, D.C.: Government Printing Office), various issues.

year since 1946, together with the rate of inflation for the year preceding. The figure appears at first glance to show that there is a mild correlation between inflation and the percentage of the population thinking its financial situation is worse. This is supported by the results of equation (1) which yielded an R^2 of .24. Closer inspection of the figure however raises the possibility that this apparent correlation may be due to the fact that both inflation and perceptions of financial ill health are high during the early part of recessions. To test for this I reran, controlling for personal income and using the Cochrane-Orcutt technique to remove auto-correlation. This produced . . .

$$y = 32.38 - 0.03i + 0.73p + e$$
$$(21.33) \ (-0.14) \ (3.65)$$

where y is the percentage of the population that thinks its financial position has worsened, i is inflation, p is change in personal income and the figures

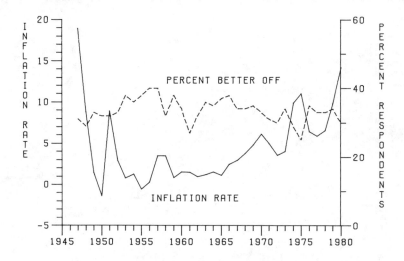

Figure 22   Inflation and recession versus people's perception that they are financially better off. The question was "We are interested in how people are getting along financially these days. Would you say that you and your family are better off or worse off financially than you were a year ago?" Sources: U.S. Department of Commerce, *Handbook of Cyclical Indicators* (Washington, D.C.: Government Printing Office, 1977); Council of Economic Advisers, *Economic Report of the President* (Washington, D.C.: Government Printing Office), various issues; George Katona et al., Survey of Consumer Finances (Ann Arbor: University of Michigan), various issues; data supplied by Michigan Consumer Survey.

in brackets are *t* scores. As is evident, once we control for personal income, inflation becomes an insignificant predictor.

The contrast with the earlier results suggests that, while people may see some connection between inflation and reduced real income, this comes about primarily because they blame inflation for decreases in income caused by other factors such as reductions in demand. This is consistent both with the fact that people form their opinion of their financial situation in response to "real" factors such as unemployment and with the fact that they attribute any decrease, when asked, to inflation.

This conclusion is supported by additional data. Inflation in reality has a very similar effect (or lack of effect) on different people's real incomes and expenditures, something that follows both from its definition as a universal rise in prices and from results presented in chapter 3. We would expect therefore, if people were looking either at its effects on their real incomes or on expenditures, that people in different financial situations would tend to think it equally harmful. If, on the other hand, it was being blamed for problems caused by other phenomena we would expect those who had fared worse to be considerably more likely to see themselves as harmed by inflation.

Table 9, utilizing data from a 1969 Michigan Survey of Consumer Finances, shows that it is this latter interpretation that best fits the facts. Whereas only 20 percent of those whose financial situation had improved over the past year saw themselves or their families as seriously harmed by inflation, 47 percent of those whose financial situation had deteriorated saw themselves or their families as seriously harmed. Nor, as one might at first suppose, is this due to the fact that the actual rate of inflation is perceived as being higher by those who saw themselves as most hurt

Table 9   Perceived Change in Financial Situation versus Perceived Effect of Inflation in 1969

Financial situation	Harm from inflation				
	None	A little	Much	Very much	N
Better	17.6%	62.6%	10.1%	9.7%	(455)
Same	14.4	61.5	12.1	12.0	(527)
Worse	6.0	47.1	19.4	27.5	(397)

The questions were, "We are interested in how people are getting along financially these days. Would you say that you and your family are *better off* or *worse off* financially than you were *a year ago*?" and "Would you say that you and your family were hurt by inflation very much, much, a little or not at all?"

Kendall's Tau $C = -0.204$ Significance $= 0.001$
Gamma $= -0.334$

Source: *Survey of Consumer Finances* (Ann Arbor: University of Michigan), Fall 1969.

financially. Controlling for the perceived rate of inflation made virtually no difference to the relationship.

It is possible to object to this last test on the grounds that even if large groups are not substantially affected by inflation and even if other variables have greater real effects on individuals, it might nonetheless be true that the financial situation of some individuals is worsened by inflation. It would therefore be desirable to find a group some of whom clearly benefitted both in the long and the short run from inflation and others of whom had lost, and to see whether this was reflected in their feelings about inflation.

Fortunately such a test is possible. Table 10, taken from a 1966 Michigan Survey of Consumer Finances survey, divides people according to their house and mortgage ownership status and their attitude to inflation. It is fairly obvious that with fixed-rate mortgages any unanticipated rise in inflation leads to a gain for the mortgagor and that this gain will be larger the more time is left on the mortgage. Further, house ownership is a traditional inflation hedge. Thus if actual short- or long-term effects were the primary explanation of people's attitudes, we would expect that holders of long-term mortgages would be substantially more favorably inclined toward inflation than their less fortunate peers. In fact, as we can see in table 10, we find nothing of the sort. There does not seem to be any significant tendency for holders of long-term mortgages to be even slightly more favorably inclined toward inflation, and house owners are, if anything, marginally more against inflation than renters.

Our results so far seem to show that people regard inflation as lowering their real income and tend to blame inflation for income losses caused by other factors such as recessions or reduced demand for their services.

Table 10   Attitude toward Inflation in 1966 by House Ownership and Mortgage Status

Price increase	No house	House-no mortgage	1–10 year mortgage	11–20 year mortgage	21–40 year mortgage
Bad	82.1%	85.4%	85.6%	84.2%	79.4%
No difference	10.1	7.8	5.6	9.6	11.8
Good	7.9	6.8	8.8	6.1	8.8

The questions were, "Do you own this home, or pay rent, or what? Do you have a mortgage on this property? How many years will it be before the mortgage is paid off? Do you think that these rising prices would be good, or bad, or what?" (asked only of those who had previously said prices would rise).

Raw chi-square = 4.570 Significance = 0.802
Kendall's Tau C = 0.009 Significance = 0.330

Source: *Survey of Consumer Finances* (Ann Arbor: University of Michigan), Summer 1966.

But it remains possible that much of the negative feeling about inflation could be due to its perceived non-income effects. These could be uncertainty costs, activity costs, or other less rational anxieties aroused by inflation, such as that it causes alienation, reduces American power or (yes, it has been claimed) causes a decline in moral standards and sexual ethics.

Available evidence tends to support the idea that people dislike inflation, at least in part, for reasons other than its effects on their incomes. Between July 1977 and July 1979, the Harris Poll asked people on five occasions whether they would prefer a loss of real income with inflation controlled or a rise in real income with inflation not controlled. The results, shown in figure 23, indicate heavy majorities willing to pay a real cost in terms of their own income to bring inflation under control. This in turn indicates that inflation's effects on their income are not the only reason that people dislike it. Even though the size of the majority is indubitably affected by the fact that the question was asked in the inflationary 1970s, rather than the less inflationary 1950s and 1960s, responses to similar questions asked

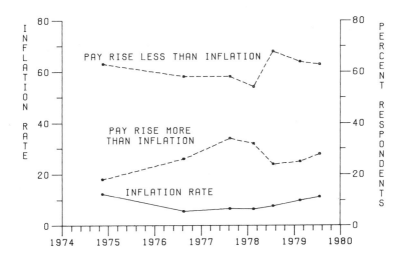

Figure 23   Willingness to sacrifice pay increase to get lower inflation. The question was, "Let's say you were up for a raise in pay. How would you feel about these two situations. One would be your getting a pay increase *lower* than the rise in the cost of living, but with some assurance the cost of living was being brought under control. The other situation would be your getting a pay increase higher than the cost of living, but with no assurance the cost of living was being brought under control. Which would you choose?" Source: Harris Poll data supplied to author.

both in the United States and elsewhere in the earlier period indicate that, even then, a substantial part of the population was willing to incur real income costs to curb inflation.

Even though this does provide solid evidence that the non-income effects of inflation are a worry, it does not indicate which non-income effects. There is however some additional evidence pointing to the uncertainty effects of inflation as explaining at least a part of the above results. In June 1978 the Harris Poll asked respondents, "Now here are two possible economic situations. If you had to choose between the two, which would you prefer? 1. An expanding economy that would give you a chance for higher income and a higher standard of living, but would be accompanied by rising inflation and periodic recessions. 2. An economy with little growth which would allow for only a slow but steady increase in your standard of living and your income, but would also mean little inflation and few recessions." Only 9 percent preferred having higher income in a more uncertain economy, while fully 81 percent preferred lower income growth in a more predictable economy.[7]

Media Evaluation

A last explanation for the highly negative evaluation of inflation is the elitist and Marxist one that people obtain their information about the economy from the media and that the information is manipulated to make inflation seem more serious and other economic problems less serious than they really are. We have already seem that there is some evidence that people get their information about inflation from the media rather than from direct experience. But is information from the media skewed in the way that the Marxist and elitist arguments posit?

Table 11, showing data on the direction of economic messages received from the media, tends to support the arguments. White and blue-collar workers were asked in each of 11 quarters, from the third quarter of 1968 to the first quarter of 1971, "During the last few months, have you heard of any favorable or unfavorable changes in business conditions? What did you hear?" Responses to this and similar questions on future business conditions were then categorized according to whether the news item was about employment or business conditions, prices or inflation, the international situation or domestic political policy. Six of the quarters were characterized by rising inflation and five by falling inflation. Unemployment fell in two of the quarters, was unchanged in four, and rose in five. Thus one might expect a preponderance of unfavorable items on unemployment and an even balance on inflation in a neutral press.[8] What we actually find however, is that while respondents reported an equal number of favorable and unfavorable items about unemployment and business conditions, they reported a heavy preponderance of unfavorable

Table 11   Respondents Citing Favorable and Unfavorable News Items on Different Topics

	White-collar	Blue-collar	All persons[a]
News of employment or business conditions			
average % favorable	33%	29%	31%
average % unfavorable	31	29	24
% of total unfavorable	48	50	44
News of prices and inflation			
average % favorable	8	5	5
average % unfavorable	18	14	14
% of total unfavorable	69	74	74
News of international situation			
average % favorable	6	5	7
average % unfavorable	4	4	4
% of total unfavorable	40	44	36
News of domestic political policy and events			
average % favorable	10	8	9
average % unfavorable	10	10	10
% of total unfavorable	50	56	53

Data represent averaged figures for ten quarterly surveys asked in the fall 1968 to spring 1971 period.

[a]The figures for all persons average data from fourteen surveys from Fall 1967 to Spring 1971 and hence are not comparable with the white and blue collar figures.

Source: Burkhard Strumpel et al., "The Function of Consumer Attitude Data: Beyond Econometric Forecasts," in Lewis Mandell et al., *Surveys of Consumers 1971–72* (Ann Arbor: University of Michigan, 1973) pp. 282–83.

items on inflation and price. This clearly lends support to the view that negative media evaluations are partly responsible for the public's negative view of inflation.[9]

Actual and Perceived Effects by Group

Thus far we have concentrated primarily on the perceived impact of inflation across the whole population. It remains to look at the factor income groups in the models and assess the degree of consistency between the effects on those groups as outlined in chapter 3 and their perceptions of the way inflation affects them.

It will be recalled that the actual long-term effects on the different groups seemed to be small, with some redistribution from the lowest 20 percent and top 5 percent toward the rest. When we looked at the short-term correlations between inflation and the different incomes we found a high negative correlation between inflation and wage and salary income, a somewhat smaller negative correlation between inflation and profits and small business income, little correlation with transfer income and a moderate positive correlation with farm income. Thus if people reacted on the basis of inflation's long-term effects we might expect shareholders, transfer income recipients, and possibly blue-collar workers to be mildly opposed to it, and other groups to be mildly in favor. If, on the other hand, people reacted to the short-term correlation between inflation and their income, we might expect wage and salary earners to be strongly opposed, profit receivers and small businessmen to be mildly opposed, transfer income recipients to be largely indifferent and farmers to mildly support it.

As we can see in tables 12 and 13, the actual distribution of perceived impact among the different groups does not appear to match either of these patterns. In terms of the short-term results, farmers for example are no more likely than self-employed businessmen to feel unharmed by inflation, and seem a little more likely to consider inflation an evil. Those receiving transfer incomes, far from feeling indifferent, are more likely to claim they are being harmed and more likely to feel inflation is bad than any other group. Lastly, salary earners seem less rather than more likely than wage earners to feel inflation harms them. In terms of the long-term results the two tables clearly do not fit a pattern of those in the middle, such as salary earners, perceiving themselves as gaining from those at the top and bottom.

Instead both the perceived impact and opinions as to the desirability of inflation seem to better approximate a model where those who have

Table 12   Perceived Harm from Inflation by Occupational Group in 1969

| Occupation | Perceived harm | | | | |
	None	A little	Much	Very much	N
Shareholders	25.4%	57.0%	11.4%	6.1%	(114)
Small business	15.2	63.6	10.6	10.6	(66)
Farmers	15.9	56.8	18.2	9.1	(44)
Salary earners	11.7	65.2	10.4	12.7	(385)
Wage earners	11.5	56.9	14.8	16.8	(506)
Welfare Pool	12.0	49.5	15.9	22.6	(283)

The question was, "Would you say that you and your family were hurt by inflation very much, much, a little, or not at all?"

Both chi-square and Kendall's Tau C were significant at the .002 level.

Source: *Survey of Consumer Finances* (Ann Arbor: University of Michigan), Fall 1969.

Table 13   Attitude toward Inflation of Those in Selected Occupations in 1962 and 1966

| | 1962 | | | 1966 | | |
	Bad	Good	N	Bad	Good	N
National	76.1%	16.2%	(585)	83.7%	7.1%	(967)
Occupation						
Fixed income	82.3	10.5	(124)	89.7	2.7	(233)
Wage earner	78.3	14.3	(203)	82.3	9.8	(338)
Salary earner	68.9	21.8	(193)	80.6	5.6	(284)
Self-employed	78.5	16.9	(65)	83.9	11.6	(112)
Farmers	94.4	5.6	(18)	84.5	12.1	(54)
Non-farm	72.3	21.2	(47)	83.3	11.1	(58)

Those who had said they expected prices to rise in the next year were asked, "Would you say that these rising prices would be good, or bad, or what?"

In 1962 chi-square was significant only at the .25 level but in 1966 it was significant at the .01 level.

Sources: *Survey of Consumer Finances* (Ann Arbor: University of Michigan), Fall 1962, Summer 1966.

the most are less opposed to inflation, and those those who have the least are most opposed, with a majority of all groups being strongly against it. This pattern, which clearly accords with the income transference explanation advanced above, is seen most clearly in table 12. When we look at those with more than $30,000 worth of shares we find 25 percent felt no harm from inflation and 6 percent felt they were harmed very much. At the other end of the scale only 12 percent of transfer income recipients felt that they were unharmed by inflation and 23 percent felt severely harmed. This picture seems also broadly consistent with the results shown in table 13, with the single exception that the self-employed seem more opposed to inflation than they "should" be.

If this income transference explanation were correct we might expect that if we could somehow get below the level of conscious thought to that of unconscious associations, we might find a much closer relation between the perceived impact of inflation on one's income and the actual short-term correlation. Table 14 shows two successively more ambitious attempts to reach this level of unconscious association. The first represents a very crude attempt to control for the conscious income-transference effect. Here I look only at those who claim their financial situation has worsened and see the degree to which those in different occupational groups give inflation as the primary cause. The second takes answers to separate questions on the degree to which money income and the financial situation of the respondents in different occupational groups has improved and assumes that those who give more positive answers with regard to

Table 14   Two Measures of Felt Harm from Inflation in Years with Different
                Inflation Rates

| | Percentage of those whose financial situation had worsened in the past year giving inflation as the primary cause | | | Percentage of respondents saying money income exceeded real income minus percentage saying opposite (*P* scores) | |
	1962	1966	1969	1962	1966
All respondents	15.6%	40.5%	45.0%	7.5%	18.6%
Occupation					
Self-employed	5.4	24.2	22.0	−5.8	9.6
Salary earners	20.9	45.8	46.7	11.1	18.6
Wage earners	17.6	44.2	48.1	9.6	24.0
Fixed income	12.6	38.5	46.1	5.8	10.7
Yearly inflation	(1.3%)	(3.5%)	(5.75%)	(1.3%)	(3.5%)

Source: *Survey of Consumer Finances* (Ann Arbor: University of Michigan), Fall 1962,
Summer 1966, Fall 1969.

their money income than with regard to their financial situation are un-
consciously indicating that inflation has eroded their real income. It is
encouraging, although given the roughness of the tests hardly conclusive,
that the results approximate the short-term correlations much more closely
than those in tables 12 and 13, and that the second test approximates
them better than the first.

Conclusion

In this chapter we have examined how the general public perceives and
evaluates inflation. We found that while most of the public is reasonably
sensitive to the rate of inflation, there is a minority that is not. In looking
at the evaluation of inflation, we found that it is regarded more negatively
than any other domestic problem and that this negative view is shared by
large majorities in all population groupings. In seeking to account for this
negative evaluation, we found evidence to support the view that inflation
was largely evaluated on criteria other than its actual effects on the real
incomes of respondents, in part because of income illusion and demand
transference.

At several points it became possible to test between views that would
seem more reasonable on pluralist assumptions and views that would
better fit Marxist or elitist models. With the exception of the results on
the degree to which inflation was perceived, the actual data seemed to

better accord with Marxist or elitist models. However, the importance of this should not be overstated. Not everyone will agree with my interpretation of what "their" model would predict and, in any case, the cumulative effect from testing all stages of the model is far more important than the results from any one part.

5 Inflation and Political Demands

In the last chapter we examined the way that people perceive and evaluate inflation. In this chapter we look at the degree to which the negative evaluations we found are translated into political demands by the public. We will look first at attitudes toward direct action to compensate for inflation. We shall then turn to what citizens think the political system should do about inflation, looking first at what is thought to cause inflation, then looking at the policies the public advocates to control it and then looking at who is thought to be responsible for inflation and who might do the best job of curing it. Lastly we will look at the degree to which people use their vote to try and affect the rate of inflation.

The major theoretical point at issue in this chapter is the degree to which people translate their negative feelings about inflation into demands for policies that would actually correct inflation. The pluralist model clearly implies that people do make demands upon the political system and that these demands are appropriate to the problem. Elitist theories would lead us to expect little translation of feelings into political demands and little reason to expect what demands there were to be appropriate. Traditional Marxism would lead us to expect demands to be made, but for the demands to bolster the ruling class rather than solve the problem. Structural Marxists would expect the working class to call for policies that would aid them, with capitalists being opposed to these policies.

Personal Adaptation to Inflation

This chapter is primarily concerned with people's political demands and political actions. Before we examine these however, it is worthwhile to look at the degree to which people feel capable of compensating for the effects of inflation on them and their family and whether the means they might employ would have the anticipated effect. While this section is not central to our models, we might expect pluralist man to adapt rapidly and appropriately to inflation and for the citizen envisaged by elitist and traditional Marxist models to adapt more slowly and less appropriately.

There are two major types of direct economic adaptation to inflation; to attempt to increase one's income, or to change one's spending and saving patterns. Some limited evidence on both adaptations can be found in a fall 1969 poll conducted by the Michigan Survey of Consumer Finances, at a time when the rate of inflation for the previous year was 5.7 percent. Respondents were asked whether they could protect their family and their savings against inflation and, if so, how. They were also asked whether they bought anything because it would cost more later and, if so, what.

Looking at the responses to the family question in table 15, the most striking result is that a solid majority think that there is nothing they can do to protect their families from inflation. Just as important are the responses to the question on what can be done. Here the striking point is that respondents do not consciously think of changes in income as a means of protecting their families from inflation. Only income from savings is seen as possibly protectable and this by only 3 percent of the population. Nor is this latter figure the tip of an iceberg. When asked specifically about savings, only 18 percent of respondents thought it possible to protect them. Surprisingly, protecting one's family by getting wage or salary hikes is not mentioned at all. This does not mean that people do not in fact do this. Other data indicates that, when asked why they need pay raises, the reason most frequently given by workers is that inflation has eroded their standard of living. Most probably it reflects the fact that most workers do not see pay raises as under their control, as well as the fact that inflation is seen more as an expenditure effect than a real-income effect.

In fact, the chief means of protection cited is an alteration in spending patterns. However, we find some surprises here too. Although economists generally consider anticipatory spending as the rational reaction to inflation, two opposing courses of action are in fact possible. One is to increase spending in order to take advantage of the current relatively low prices and have assets in inflation-proof goods rather than inflation-prone cash or savings accounts. The other is to reduce current spending, to provide savings as a hedge against expected lower real income in the future, or against increased perceived uncertainty. One might expect the first reaction when wage and salary income was thought likely to outpace inflation and the latter when income was thought likely to fall behind.

Table 15   Perception of Ability to Protect One's Family and Savings from Inflation

Can something be done to protect family?	All families	Income $10,000 or more	Can something be done to protect savings?	All families	Income $10,000 or more
Yes	27%	40%	Yes	15%	30%
Possibly	10	12	Possibly	3	4
No	56	45	No	71	61
Don't know	7	3	Don't know	11	5
Total	100%	100%	Total	100%	100%

What can be done?			What can be done?		
Buy less; postpone buying certain things	19%	25%	Put money in stocks	7%	14%
Buy cheaper goods; economize	6	8	Put money in real estate	4	8
Buy where prices are lower	2	3	Put money in other investments	3	6
Buy stocks, real estate	3	6			
Direct political action	2.5				

The questions asked were, "Would you say that someone like you can do something to protect his family against price increase? What can you do?"; "Think of your savings, do you see any way to protect them against inflation? What can be done?"

Source: Jay Schmiedeskamp, et al., *1969 Survey of Consumer Finances* (Ann Arbor: University of Michigan, 1970), p. 242.

We find, consistent with our findings in chapter 3, that inflation has negative short-term but negligible long-term effects on earnings, that the savings reaction seems much stronger than the spending reaction. To the question how respondents would protect their families against inflation the overwhelming response was a savings reaction. A full 19 percent said they would buy less, 6 percent said they would buy cheaper goods and another 2 percent said they would buy where prices were lower.

This impression that the saving reaction predominates is reinforced by another set of data. Figure 24 shows answers to a Harris poll question asked fourteen times between September 1973 and April 1975, a period when inflation varied between seven and twelve percent. After being asked a question on what future prices they expected, respondents were asked, "At this time, do you feel it is best to put away what money you can for a rainy day, to invest it in something that will grow as inflation

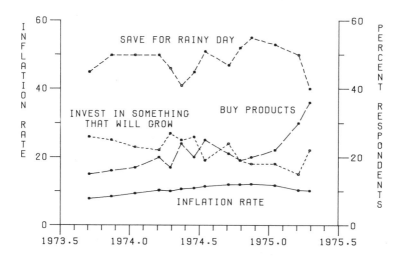

Figure 24   Propensity to save, invest and buy in the face of inflation. Sources: *The Harris Survey*, April 3, 1975, and May 15, 1975; U.S. Department of Commerce, *Handbook of Cylical Indicators* (Washington, D.C.: Government Printing Office, 1977).

increases, or buy things you want and need before prices go up further?'' Looking at the data, it is clear that the savings reaction predominates. If one regresses both the percentage opting to save and the percentage opting to buy now against inflation in the year preceding, one finds both reactions increase with inflation but the savings reaction increases more rapidly. The savings regression yields a value of 1.1 for the inflation b coeficient, with the equation accounting for 12 percent of the variance, while the buying regression yields a value of only 0.37 for the inflation coefficient, with the equation accounting for a bare 4 percent of the variance. These results should be taken cautiously as neither b was significant at the .05 level.

However, these findings are consistent with those of Juster, who found a positive relation between actual savings and both inflation and a direct measure of inflation expectations in the 1952-1973 period. Further, he found an even higher relation between savings and the variance of expected inflation, lending some support to the idea that the uncertainty associated with inflation is partly responsible for the savings reaction.[1]

A more detailed breakdown of spending changes in response to rapid inflation is available from a Gallup poll question asked in August 1974, when inflation had risen to 11 percent. Asked, ''Have you or your family already reduced spending on anything as a result of rising prices or inflation?" 68 percent of respondents claimed to have already reduced their spending and a further 7 percent planned to, with younger people, middle-income earners, blue-collar workers, whites and the college-educated more likely than others to claim to have reduced their spending. Asked which items they were spending less on, 55 percent mentioned food, 21 percent mentioned clothing, 21 percent mentioned automobile related matters, including gas, and between 8 and 12 percent mentioned vacations, entertainment, power and fuel, and luxuries.[2]

Although the savings reaction predominates, there is some evidence to show that a small, and possibly increasing, part of the population follows the logic of the spending reaction. In table 16, which shows responses to a fall 1969 Michigan Survey of Consumer Finances question on anticipatory buying, 12 percent of the respondents claimed to have bought something in the last few months in anticipation of a cost increase. It is interesting to note that whereas the savings reaction resulted in a change in spending primarily on non-durable goods, the spending reaction was

Table 16   Anticipatory Spending Increases as a Hedge against Inflation in 1969

	All families	Less than $3,000	$3,000 −4,999	$5,000 −7,499	$7,500 −9,999	$10,000 or more
			Family income			
Anticipatory Buying						
Yes	12%	11%	14%	11%	12%	12%
No	88	89	86	89	88	88
Item Bought						
Car	2%	1%	2%	3%	1%	2%
House; real estate	1	*	2	1	2	2
Appliances, furniture	3	2	4	3	2	3
Clothing, house furnishings	2	3	2	1	2	1
Food	1	2	3	*	2	*
Repairs of home	1	1	*	1	1	1
Other small items	2	1	1	2	2	3
Total	12%	10%	14%	11%	12%	12%

The questions asked were, "Did you or your family living here buy anything during the last few months because you thought it would cost more later? What did you buy?"

* Less than 0.5 percent.

Source: Jay Schmiedeskamp et al., *1969 Survey of Consumer Finances* (Ann Arbor: University of Michigan, 1970), p. 243.

concentrated on higher-value durable goods, with spending on cars, houses, appliances and furniture figuring prominently.

There appears to be some evidence that the minority favoring the spending reaction is increasing. A Michigan Survey of Consumer Finances poll taken in the summer of 1979, when inflation was 10.7 percent, found 25 percent of respondents favoring advance buying, up from 12 percent in 1969, and 24 percent thinking it was a bad idea to save in times of rapid inflation. Moreover, while there was little class difference in the tendency to favor advance buying, there was a large difference on the savings question, with 40 percent of college graduates thinking it was a bad idea to save in periods of rapid inflation, as opposed to only 10 percent of those who left school before high school graduation.[3]

Overall then, it seems that on the conscious level consumers see their direct response to inflation as being one of decreasing rather than increasing spending. More important, they do not volunteer increasing their income as a means of protection.

The fact that people generally feel that there is little they can do directly to soften the impact of inflation on their family, combined with our earlier observations on the high awareness of inflation, leads us to expect a strong political response to the problem. Table 15 shows that 2.5 percent of the population is prepared to volunteer a direct political response to inflation in answer to a question that does not point in that direction, and it seems reasonable that a much larger number might have a less direct political response. In order to see whether this is in fact the case, we will look at whether people think there are political solutions to inflation, what people think is the cause of inflation, what they think should be done about it, who is blamed for it and who they think should solve it.

Can Inflation Be Reduced?

People do not think that all problems can be solved through political means. Indeed, many problems are seen as insoluble. It behooves us to see whether inflation is this kind of problem, or whether it is seen as something amenable to solution through the political system. Figure 25 presents evidence from somewhat scattered Harris, Roper and Time polls asking people whether they think inflation can be avoided and whether it will be controlled. As can be seen, the evidence seems to indicate that, until the mid-1970s, most people thought that inflation could and would be controlled. However there was always a substantial minority, varying between 20 and 45 percent of the population, who thought that inflation could not be controlled, and a somewhat larger group, varying between 35 and 60 percent of the population, who thought that inflation would not in fact be controlled.

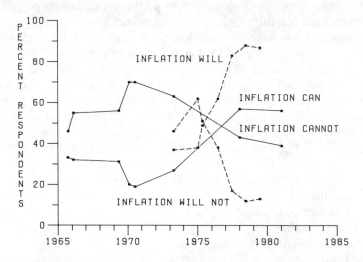

Figure 25   Propensity to believe inflation can and will be controlled in the 1965–
                 1979 period. The questions were variants on "Do you think that rises in
                 the cost of living are bound to happen or do you feel they can be
                 avoided?" and "Do you feel that inflation will be halted after a while, or
                 that it has become one of the facts of life and is here to stay?" Sources:
                 Data supplied by Harris polls; Louis Harris, *The Harris Survey Year-
                 book of Public Opinion 1970* (New York: Louis Harris, 1971), p. 158;
                 Louis Harris, *The Harris Survey Yearbook of Public Opinion 1973* (New
                 York: Louis Harris, 1975), p. 331; *Public Opinion,* May–June 1978, p.
                 34; December–January 1980, p. 41; *New York Times,* February 15, 1981,
                 section IV, p. 4.

During the 1970s there appears to have been continual erosion in the
belief that inflation was controllable, probably because people were faced
with continued high rates of inflation. After 1975 a steadily increasing
majority thought that inflation would not be controlled by government.
By the time that another year or two had passed, a majority thought that
control was not so much unlikely as impossible. It seems worth noting
that the change coincided with an increased tendency for national politicians to claim that inflation was very difficult to control, although the
cause-and-effect relationship is by no means clear. In addition, the highly
publicized Whip Inflation Now program of President Ford in the fall of
1974 may partly explain both the increase in short-term optimism and the
increase in long-term cynicism apparent in figure 25. We must be cautious
however not to read too much into the figures from the late 1970s. As
late as 1981, 25 percent thought it was possible for President Reagan to

keep prices from going up and an additional 14 percent thought it would be possible given a different president.[4]

Thus it appears that up to the mid-1970s and probably after that, inflation was seen as a problem that the political system could solve, although the confidence with which this view was held clearly declined over time. Let us now turn to the perceived causes of inflation.

The Causes of Inflation

The bias of the pluralist models is toward a rational and informed citizen, who not only can perceive problems accurately, but can diagnose their causes and press for solutions. Marxist and elitist models, on the other hand, with the possible exception of the structuralist model, would lead us to expect such knowledge, together with the ability to effectively press for solutions, to be primarily lodged in the ruling class or elite. It is therefore worthwhile to investigate the extent to which the public understands the causes of inflation and can press for appropriate solutions.

There are two methods of attempting to uncover the perceived causes of inflation. One is to ask an open-ended question seeking to elicit opinions and the other is to provide a closed-ended list of alternative causes for respondents to rank. Table 17 presents the results of an open-ended question asked in a September 1974 Gallup survey. Table 18 shows the results

Table 17   Perceived Causes of Inflation, September 1974: Open-ended Question

	All	Professional and business	Clerical and sales	Manual workers	Non-labor force
Price-Wage Spiral	26%	24%	22%	28%	28%
Poor government planning	12	9	14	11	17
Government overspending	11	14	10	9	9
Consumer overspending	8	7	14	5	10
Good of people	8	6	7	9	8
Labor-wage demands	6	10	6	3	8
Excess business profits	6	8	6	6	5
Fuel prices	5	9	6	4	4
Others	22	25	16	24	17
Don't know	18	13	16	17	17

The question asked was "What, in your opinion, is the chief cause of inflation?" Totals exceed 100 percent due to multiple answers.

Source: *Gallup Opinion Index*, October 1976.

of a closed-ended question asked by the Michigan Survey of Consumer Finances in fall 1969, and table 19 shows responses to closed-ended questions asked by the Harris survey at various dates between 1970 and 1978. The first impression is that although relatively few people felt unable to assign a cause to inflation—only 18 percent of those answering the Gallup poll for example felt that they did not know the cause of inflation— the combination of causes offered lacks coherence and seems quite different from the reasons discussed in chapter 2. Insofar as coherent views emerge, it seems that people are most inclined to blame inflation on the wage-price spiral and government spending. Thus the open-ended responses in table 17 show 26 percent of respondents giving some version of the wage-price spiral as the primary cause and another 11 percent citing government spending. This is supported by the answers to the closed-ended questions shown in table 19, which show large majorities of respondents agreeing that business price rises, union wage demands and federal spending are major causes of inflation.

This all seems to indicate a coherent, albeit simpleminded and tautological view of the causes of inflation. Other data however muddies the picture. Thus, as we can see from table 19. there is a marked tendency to attribute inflation to whatever relative price increase is currently in the news. In addition there is some data indicating that virtually any economic

Table 18   Perceived Causes of Inflation, Fall 1969

	All		Income over $10,000	
	Agree	Disagree	Agree	Disagree
The government spent too much on Vietnam	69%	20%	72%	22%
The government spent too much on other things	69	19	65	26
The government did not tax enough	9	85	15	81
Labor and trade unions demanded and obtained too large wage increases	65	24	75	19
Business firms raised prices too much	65	26	58	36
Consumers spent too much	58	31	56	37
Consumers borrowed too much	69	18	73	19

The questions asked were, "People have different ideas about why we have inflation. On this card is a list of reasons for inflation which some people have mentioned to us. First, do you agree or disagree that (first item) is a reason for our having inflation? Second . . . ?"

Source: Jay Schmiedeskamp et al., *1969 Survey of Consumer Finances* (Ann Arbor: University of Michigan, 1970), p. 244.

Table 19   Perceived Causes of Inflation, 1970–1978

	Feb. 1970	Jan. 1971	1972	April 1973	Nov. 1974	Oct. 1975	July 1977	Oct. 1978
Federal spending	67%	65%	72%	68%	76%	62%	76%	78%
Defense-Vietnam War spending	74		56	49	58	45		
Welfare and relief spending	39				43	54		
High interest rates	56	61				58		
Too much money	26							
Taxes	50							
Union wage demands	52	61	59	57	51		57	65
Business profits too high	52		60	56	65	65		
Business raising prices			66	64	74	70	60	72
Food prices		70		65		72	74	80
Health and medical costs							75	78
Energy costs							59	65
Oil-producing countries						64		83

The question from 1972 to 1975 was, "Do you feel that (read list) is a major cause of inflation, a minor cause, or hardly a cause at all?" On the other dates there were minor variations in this wording. Only the percentage saying the item was a major cause is reported above.

Sources: Louis Harris, *The Harris Survey Yearbook of Public Opinion,* 1970, 1971 and 1973 (New York: Louis Harris, 1971, 1975, 1976). The Harris Survey 11/7/74, 10/23/75, 9/29/77, 11/2/78.

phenomena, and many non-economic ones, are seen as causes of inflation. In October 1975, for example, 55 percent of respondents to a Harris poll thought lack of leadership in the country was a major cause of inflation, 73 percent blamed major oil companies and, at a time when defense spending was decreasing, 45 percent blamed defense spending.[5]

Just as interesting as the causes given for inflation are those which were de-emphasized. Most economists in the late 1960s and early 1970s felt that inflation in the post-1966 period was due either to President Johnson's failure to persuade Congress to impose a tax increase or to the rapid increase in the money supply. Tables 17–19 however show that neither was thought by the public to be a major cause of inflation. Neither reason was mentioned in the open-ended responses and both were heavily devalued in the closed-alternative responses. Thus in 1969, 85 percent disagreed that the reason for inflation was that the government did not tax enough and only 9 percent agreed. Looking at the 1970–1978 Harris results in table 19, we note that people appear to think high taxes cause, rather than prevent, inflation, although the question was not clear enough for us to be certain. The questions on the two polls do not enable such a direct test of the public's feelings about money and inflation. However the fact that only 29 percent of the respondents to the Harris survey thought that inflation was due to people having too much money to spend is at least indicative.

The final lesson to be drawn from the results in tables 17–19 is that people generally do not seem to have any firm perception of the causes of inflation. The categories used to aggregate the open-ended responses are vague, and responses to the closed-ended questions point to somewhat contradictory views on the mechanisms behind inflation. In fact the 1969 Michigan Survey of Consumer Finances used a closed-ended question format because it had been found during pre-testing that most people were unable to clearly express themselves on the causes of inflation.

It is notable that many of the results can be explained as arising from the strain between solving inflation and other problems—the strain being relieved, in accord with theories of cognitive dissonance, by a misperception of the relation between the competing goals. This can be seen in the 1969 survey in the refusal to allow that higher taxes could cause inflation and in the 1970 survey by a distinction between welfare spending and health spending as causes of inflation. Because an outcome of this nature is most likely to occur when there are shallow cognitive structures underlying opinions, the results afford a reasonable indication that respondents' perceptions of the causal relations between inflation and other variables are not deeply rooted.

Anti-Inflation Policy Preferences

Turning from the public's perception of the causes of inflation to preferred solutions, we find evidence of both simple-minded consistency and underlying uncertainty. Looking at table 20, it is clear that, left to propose its own solutions, around 32 percent of the public tends to emerge with one or another form of wage-price policy. This impression is strengthened by the fact, shown in table 21 and figure 26, that there is generally a majority in favor of using wage-price policy as a weapon against inflation. This seems consistent with our earlier data on the causes of inflation. Extrapolating from the two sets of data, it seems the public has a fairly simple notion that as inflation is caused in part by business increasing

Table 20   Attitudes toward Anti-inflation Policies, Fall 1969

	All families			Income over $10,000		
	Agree	Disagree	Don't know	Agree	Disagree	Don't know
Income taxes should be raised	9%	85%	6%	15%	83%	2%
Interest rates should be raised	12	81	7	15	83	2
The government should spend less	89	11	9	81	13	6
Consumers should spend less	67	24	9	67	28	5
Consumers should borrow less	80	11	9	82	15	5
The government should control prices	45	46	9	34	58	8
The government should control wages	33	56	11	25	65	6

The question asked was, "Here is a list of things which, some people say, should be done in order to slow down inflation. First, do you agree or disagree that (first item) . . . ? (second item) . . . ?"

Source: Jay Schmiedeskamp et al., *1969 Survey of Consumer Finances* (Ann Arbor: University of Michigan, 1970), p. 245.

prices and unions increasing wages, the best way to stop it is to forbid the price increases and control the wage increases.

It also seems possible to find evidence that would support the proposition that many in the public have a very simple version of demand inflation in the back of their minds. Thus as shown in table 21, 8 percent of the respondents volunteered that lowering government spending was the best way to reduce inflation and another 8 percent thought that less spending by the public would be the best anti-inflation policy. These figures are supported by the closed-ended responses in table 22, showing that for the dates for which we have data, over 85 percent of respondents giving a definite answer thought that it would help reduce inflation if government spending was lowered and consumers spent less. When combined with the data in tables 17, 18 and 19, which emphasizes government and consumer spending as causes of inflation, it implies that much of the public thinks that the more people are bidding for a good, the higher its price is likely to go, and that we should therefore try to cut down on spending by both government and the public to lower demand and the consequent tendency for prices to be bid up.

Table 21   Preferred Anti-inflation Policies in September 1974 by Occupation
                  Open-ended

	All	Professional and business	Clerical and sales	Manual workers	Non-labor force
Wage-price controls	12%	17%	9%	10%	10%
Price controls	13	10	14	16	11
Wage controls	3	4	1	3	2
Government control businesses	4	3	3	4	4
Cut government spending	8	12	8	7	6
Consumers spend less	8	8	9	7	8
Cut foreign aid-exports	5	6	4	6	4
Others	23	23	29	21	24
Don't know	36	30	33	37	40

The question was "How, in your opinion, should inflation be dealt with." Totals exceed 100 percent due to multiple responses.

Source: *Gallup Opinion Index*, October 1974.

The other fairly consistent tendency in the data is resistance on the part of the public to solutions to inflation that involve real sacrifice. It is not that the public consciously chooses inflation as a lesser evil than high taxes or interest rates. Rather, as we saw in tables 17, 18 and 19, it refuses to admit that such measures are effective ways to fight inflation, something consistent with the cognitive dissonance explanation. Despite the fact that there has always been much more agreement among economists on the efficacy of tax and interest rate increases than on wage-price policy as anti-inflation measures, and despite attempts by President Johnson and others in the late 1960s to persuade the public of the necessity of a tax surcharge, 87 percent opposed using higher interest rates and 90 percent opposed using higher tax rates to fight inflation in the fall of 1969. In addition, although I know of no direct evidence on the subject, much indirect evidence points to an unwillingness by the public to see inflation as being in a trade-off relationship to unemployment and recession, even in the short run. Thus table 22, taken from the fall 1969 Michigan survey, at a time when most economists and policy makers accepted the original Phillips curve, shows no tendency for those who expect inflation to be higher to also expect unemployment to be lower. This is not, in my view, the result of a prescient public anticipating monetarist arguments, but more probably derives from the belief that in economics one bad thing

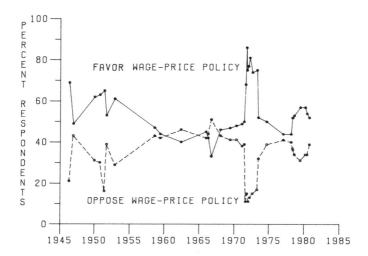

Figure 26   Attitude toward wage-price policy in the 1946–1979 period. The form of
the question has varied considerably. It was similar to the question, "It
has been suggested that both prices and wages be 'frozen'—that is, kept
from going any higher. This means that wages couldn't go up and prices
couldn't go up. Do you think this is a good idea or a poor idea?" During
wars the question usually added a qualifier such as ". . . as long as the
Vietnam war lasts." For a list of most of the questions asked see *Public
Opinion*, May–June 1978, p. 26. In the period November 1971 to April
1973 the question was "Do you think price-wage controls should be
made more strict, less strict or kept the same?" I have included both the
'more strict' and 'same' responses as positive and this may have a small
upward effect on the favorable category in this period. Source: George
Gallup, *The Gallup Poll* (New York: Random House, 1972); *The Gallup
Opinion Index*, various issues.

leads to another. And it is probably not accidental that successive Democratic platforms and many Republican politicians have asserted that it
is not necessary to use unemployment to deal with inflation.

However we should not overstate cognitive dissonance as an explanation. It does not really explain why such a large percentage favors
government spending as a cause. Nor is it very consistent with fall 1969
Michigan data showing that, despite the fact that fixed income receivers
pay few taxes and receive large payments from government, 90 percent
of those with an opinion favored reducing government spending to reduce
inflation, while only 10 percent favored raising taxes.[6]

A last conclusion that can be drawn from the data in tables 20 and 21
is that, as we might expect given the complexity of the issues and the
often confused way that leaders deal with them, people do not seem to

Table 22   Expected Unemployment, Expected Business Conditions and Expected Price Change in 1969

Expected price change	Expected unemployment[a]				Expected business conditions[b]			
	Less	Same	More	N	Bad	Pro-con	Good	N
Up 10% plus	13.3%	24.0%	62.7%	(75)	47.0%	7.6%	45.5%	(66)
Up 6–9%	5.9	17.6	76.5	(34)	45.2	19.4	35.5	(31)
Up 3–5%	9.3	37.2	53.5	(473)	36.8	9.1	54.1	(405)
Up 1–2%	12.5	37.3	50.2	(440)	35.4	5.3	59.4	(379)
No change	12.3	35.5	52.3	(220)	40.2	7.8	52.0	(179)
Down	9.2	28.9	61.8	(76)	31.4	7.1	61.4	(70)

The questions were: "Talking about prices in general—I mean the prices of the things you buy—do you think they will go up in the next year or so, or go down, or stay where they are now? How large a price increase do you expect? Of course nobody can know for sure, but would you say that *a year from now* prices will be about 1 or 2 percent higher, or 5 percent, or closer to 10 percent higher than now, or what?" "And how about a year from now, do you expect that in the country as a whole business conditions will be better or worse than they are at present, or just about the same?" "How about people out of work during the coming twelve months—do you think that there will be *more* unemployment than now, about the *same*, or less?" I also ran expected unemployment and business conditions against a question measuring expected *changes* in the rate of inflation. These were more significant, but in both cases in the "wrong" direction.

[a]Kendall's Tau C = 0.031 Significance = 0.092

[b]Kendall's Tau C = −0.039 Significance = 0.061

Source: *Survey of Consumer Finances* (Ann Arbor: University of Michigan), Fall 1969.

have firm, well-developed positions on how best to deal with inflation. We have already seen that such consistency as there is seems to be based on somewhat shallow reasoning and that the solutions advocated most strongly by economists tend to be rejected by the public. Further examination of table 21 indicates that a majority of the public does not even have the minimal understanding of anti-inflation policy that the above discussion indicates. Thus 22 percent of respondents named a wide scattering of unrelated issues and a full 36 percent could not think of any policy to deal with inflation.

We obviously must be cautious in generalizing from the above data into the pre-1966 and post-1978 periods. But it seems probable that despite attempts by government leaders and economists to persuade the general public of the efficacy of tax increases and decreases in the money supply as anti-inflation policies, the public has clung to the belief that wage-price policies and reductions in government spending are the most desirable anti-inflation policies. It should be noted that the preferred policies are simple to understand and involve little direct sacrifice by the citizenry, while those rejected are both more difficult to understand and require more sacrifice.

The Trade-offs

The question therefore arises as to what degree of sacrifice people might be willing to make to reduce inflation. If they could be persuaded that a painful policy such as a tax increase would reduce inflation, would they consider the gain worth the pain?

We saw in the last chapter, especially in figure 23, that people are prepared, at least verbally, to incur substantial costs in terms of their real income to reduce inflation. It makes sense then to think that they would be prepared to accept policies they dislike once they accept that such a trade-off exists.

Some limited evidence suggests that people might indeed behave in this way. In February 1967 the Harris survey asked respondents if they favored a 6 percent tax surcharge proposed by President Johnson. They found 24 percent in favor, 65 percent opposed and 11 percent not sure. They then followed this by asking "Would you be more in favor of this tax increase if you were convinced that it would help pay for the war in Vietnam and would help check inflation at home, or wouldn't this make any difference?" On these assumptions 51 percent favored the tax increase, 43 percent were still opposed and 6 percent were not sure.[7]

A more comprehensive question, and one without the Vietnam war complication, was asked by Harris in July 1970. Respondents were asked, "If you could be sure the cost of living would stop going up as a result, would you favor or oppose each of the following . . . ?" Results are shown in table 23. Omitting the 15 percent or so who were unsure we find a full 88 percent of respondents would be willing to cut government spending to reduce inflation and a solid plurality of 60 percent would support wage and price controls if they would stop inflation. But 74 percent said they would oppose higher taxes and 89 percent said they would oppose higher interest rates even if these would halt inflation. This is a very significant finding when we bear in mind our earlier findings about the relative importance of inflation as a problem. It is also a finding with considerable policy implications. Even if political leaders could delineate the links between tax hikes or money supply changes and inflation, there is little reason to think this would add significantly to support for such measures and some reason to think it might serve to reduce the emphasis placed on ending inflation.

Table 24, taken from the fall 1969 Michigan survey, is doubly interesting in view of our findings in table 21. There we saw that wage-price policy is one of the two most highly recommended anti-inflation policies. But the implementation of wage-price policy often means a short term slowing

Table 23   Anti-inflation Policies Favored by the Public, 1966–1970

| | Harris data | | | | | Michigan data Fall 1969 | |
	May 1966	Oct 1966	Oct 1967	June 1969	July 1970	All	$10,000 or more
Lower government spending	88%	89%	86%	93%	88%	88%	86%
Wage price controls		59	53	66	60		
Price controls	58					49	37
Wage controls	49					37	27
Raise income tax	20		16[a]	26[a]	26	10	15
Higher interest rates		15			11	13	15
Tight money			23	41[b]			
Consumers spend less						74	71
Consumers borrow less						88	86

The question asked by Harris from 1966 to 1969 was, "To keep inflation in check would you favor or oppose (read item)." The Harris question in 1970 was, "If you could be sure the cost of living would stop going up as a result, would you favor or oppose each of the following?" The Michigan Consumer Survey question was, "Here is a list of things which, some people say, should be done to slow down inflation. First, do you agree or disagree that income taxes should be raised, Second . . . " The percentages shown are the percentages of the "agree" and "disagree" answers after excluding "don't knows."

[a]People were asked in 1967 if they wanted to impose a 10% tax surcharge and in 1969 whether they wanted to retain the surcharge.

[b]The difference between this figure and those for interest rates may reflect confusion over what tight money is. A full 36% gave a "don't know" response to this question.

Sources: Jay Schmiedeskamp et al., *1969 Survey of Consumer Finances* (Ann Arbor: University of Michigan 1970), p. 245. Louis Harris, *The Harris Survey Yearbook of Public Opinion 1970* (New York: Harris, 1971), p. 160. Survey 5/16/66, 7/25/66, 10/26/66, 10/16/67, 6/23/69.

of income increases, particularly for wage earners. This is especially likely during wage-price freezes. Thus it is important to know people's willingness to have their wage increases limited to the rise in the cost of living. Table 24 shows that even people who were not expecting a pay increase were unwilling to have their future income change limited to the change in the cost of living. Those who were expecting substantial increases were even less willing. The two polls point to the sort of wage-price policy outcomes that we have actually observed, with the policy being imposed in a burst of public favor and then undermined by groups unwilling to accept the limits such policies put on their own incomes. However this material is not entirely consistent with that in figure 23 and it is possible

Table 24   Willingness to Limit Increases in Incomes to Increases in Prices in 1969

Income expectation for next year	Willing to limit income increase to price increase			
	No	Possibly	Yes	N
Better	60.8%	6.1%	33.1%	(477)
Same	52.4	6.1	41.5	(559)
Worse	47.9	5.3	46.8	(190)

The questions were, "We are interested in how people are getting along financially these days. Would you say that you and your family are *better off* or *worse off* financially than you were a year ago?" and "In order to slow down inflation, it has been suggested that increases in people's incomes should be limited to whatever amount the cost of living goes up. Would *you* personally be willing to have a limit like this placed on the amount of your next year's income?"

Kendall's Tau $C = -0.084$ Significance = 0.001

Source: *Survey of Consumer Finances* (Ann Arbor: University of Michigan), Fall 1969.

that willingness to pay a real price to control inflation may have increased in the 1970s.

Overall this material seems inconclusive as a test between the major theories. The consistency between people's perception of inflation's cause and its cure, the fact that it is possible to infer patterns of belief that seem reasonably consistent with people's direct experience of the economic world and people's refusal to believe leaders' statements that unpleasant policies are necessary to halt inflation, all seem evidence for pluralism and possibly the structuralist model, and against the traditional elitist and Marxist models. Yet the confusion among the public, the failure to propose policies that would actually be effective, and the pattern of strongly disapproving of income tax increases while strongly supporting government spending reductions, even when this is clearly against the individual's interest, seem to better fit Marxist or elitist explanations.

Who Is Responsible?

We have looked at what the public sees as the causes of inflation and we have seen what policies they propose to deal with it. We now turn to the question of who is thought to be responsible for inflation and who is in the best position to cure it. The different theories imply different predictions on these points. Pluralist theory would lead us to expect government to be stressed most, both as a causal agent and as a policy maker. The rational man variant of pluralism in particular tends to assume responsibility is primarily in the hands of the president and Congress. Marxist theory sees inflation as a way that business can reassert its share of the GNP in the face of collective bargaining. Thus if the system were characterized by class consciousness, as structuralists maintain, we would expect blue-collar workers in particular to blame business. If, as traditional Marxism maintains, the system were characterized by false consciousness, we would expect successful attempts to shift the blame to government or, even better, unions. Lastly elite theory would lead us to expect that people would either come to blame themselves or, while seeing government as responsible, see government as out of their control.

The only open-ended polls available on the question of who is to blame for inflation are two 1947 Gallup polls in which people were first asked if anyone was to blame for high prices, and then the 50 percent who said yes were asked who? Averaging the two polls, 16 percent blamed government, 15 percent blamed business and industry, 10 percent blamed labor and 7 percent blamed everyone, with a small percentage blaming business or Republicans.[8] In more recent times only closed-ended Gallup polls are available. I have data from four polls taken in the 1958–1962 period which asked people whether business or labor was most to blame; from seven polls from the 1959–1978 period asking whether business, labor or government was most to blame; and from a 1974 poll giving a choice between government, business, labor and the people themselves. Data from the two latter questions is presented in figure 27 and table 25.

Figure 27 shows a number of things. The first and most obvious, that there appears to have been a change from seeing labor as most responsible to seeing government as most responsible for inflation, should be taken cautiously. Whereas the increased tendency to blame government is probably real, the four Gallup polls taken between 1958 and 1962 that asked people whether business or labor was more to blame found 30 percent blaming business, 33 percent blaming labor and around 31 percent blaming both, implying that the 1959 labor figure is abnormally high.

The increased tendency to blame government is more interesting when we see it in the context of our earlier data dealing with the question of whether anything can be done about inflation. The two sets of data seem at first to be in conflict, for whereas in the above data we see an increasing tendency to place the responsibility for inflation with government, presumably more controllable than business or labor, the earlier data showed that people think inflation is becoming less rather than more controllable. The obvious resolution, which seems to best fit the structuralist variant of Marxism, is that people think their ability to influence government on such matters is decreasing and government is less controllable than it was.

The second thing we notice is that there appears to have been a long-term erosion in the tendency to blame business rather than labor, with the 1947 gap being reversed by the 1960s, and that in the most recent

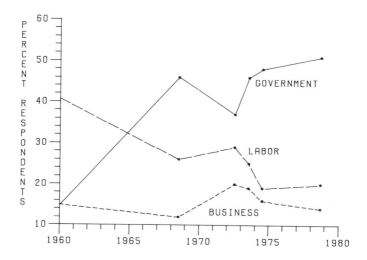

Figure 27   Perceptions of who is most responsible for inflation. The question was
                "In your opinion, which is most responsible for inflation—government,
                business, or labor?" Source: *Gallup Opinion Index*, September 1974, p.
                31; George Gallup, *The Gallup Poll 1978* (Wilmington, Delaware: Schol-
                arly Resources 1979), p. 250.

period fewer people have blamed business than blamed either labor or
government.

Finally, although I have chosen to leave it off the figure, uncertainty
has also declined, with the 30 percent who had no opinion on the question
in 1959 falling to between 10 and 17 percent in the 1968-1978 period.[9]

Table 25 also contains useful information. We can see that when the
category of "people themselves" is added as an alternative to government, business and labor, more people choose it than choose business or
labor, something consistent to some degree with the elitist model. It is
also interesting to see the occupational breakdowns. Although, as we
might expect, manual workers are less likely to blame labor than other
categories, they are no more likely than professionals and businessmen
to blame business and are somewhat more likely to blame the people
themselves.

As with the data on how to deal with inflation, that dealing with who
is to blame yields no conclusive results on the validity of our models but
does contain some lessons. The low percentage in 1959 who looked to
government can be seen as evidence against the pluralist models, as can
the large numbers blaming the people themselves and the fact that blue-
collar workers are no more likely than others to blame business. On the

Table 25   Perceived Groups Most to Blame for Inflation, July 1972 and August
                1974

	Government	Business	Labor	People	No opinion
July 1972					
All respondents	48%	16%	19%		17%
Occupation					
Professional/business-					
men	42	18	25		15
Clerks/sales workers	51	20	21		8
Manual workers	51	18	15		16
Non-labor force	46	9	20		25
August 1974					
All respondents	44%	15%	13%	23%	9%
Occupation					
Professional/business-					
men	45	18	16	18	7
Clerks/sales workers	47	11	17	25	6
Manual workers	47	18	9	25	7
Non-labor force	37	10	16	25	15

The questions were, "In your opinion which is most responsible for inflation—government, business or labor?" (July 1974) and "In your opinion, which is more to blame for inflation—government, business, labor, people themselves?" (August 1974). Totals may exceed 100 percent since some people gave multiple responses.

Sources: *Gallup Opinion Index,* September 1974, p. 31, and October 1974, p. 6.

other side, the increasing number blaming government could concievably evidence a move to a more pluralist process, and the tendency of blue-collar workers to blame labor less than other groups is consistent. The traditional Marxist view is consistent with the findings that business is usually least blamed and with the fact that blue-collar workers are no more likely than other groups to blame business. Both these facts work against the structuralist explanation. However the decline in the percentage blaming labor, and the fact that in the later period blue-collar workers are least likely to do so, could possibly be seen as indicating some increase in class consciousness. Finally the elite models seem consistent with the large number of respondents blaming the people themselves and/or labor and with the low percentage blaming business. However, the increase in the tendency to blame government is evidence against standard elitism although less so when coupled with the increase in the numbers thinking inflation is uncontrollable. It does not however seem opposed to a challenging elite theory, as the challengers would presumably seek to arouse anger against the incumbents.

Occupational Groups and Economic Policies

We have looked at the aggregate policy preferences of the population taken as a whole. We shall now turn to the differences in preference of the groups specified in our models.

In the fall 1969 Michigan Survey of Consumer Finances there are a number of questions aimed at eliciting public preferences. Of these I will look at five: whether raising taxes is a good policy for combating inflation; whether raising interest rates is a good method; whether government spending reductions would help; whether government price control is a good policy; and whether government wage control is a good policy. It should be recalled that these questions were asked after several years of attempts by the president to raise taxes and interest rates to combat inflation. Considerable publicity had been given to the necessity of doing so, while reductions in government spending had generally been de-emphasized by the Executive and wage-price policy was generally in disfavor with both the Executive and the public. Table 26 gives responses of the various occupational groups to questions regarding the five kinds of anti-inflation policy. Looking first at the proposal that income taxes should be raised in order to reduce inflation, we note that all occupational groups reject this policy by large margins—probably for reasons of cognitive dissonance. There is however some variation in the strength of opposition to the policy, almost certainly as the result of the different educational endowments of those in the different occupational groups. Only 5 percent of the less educated wage earner group versus almost 14 percent of the more-educated salary-earner group supported the proposal.

Raising interest rates, a proposal that takes the monetary rather than the fiscal route toward dampening demand, meets a reaction similar to the proposal to raise taxes. Again overwhelming majorities in all occupational groups oppose the proposal. As with the tax increase proposal the occupations containing those with the most education are more likely to support the proposal. Thus 15.8 percent of salary earners supported the proposal but only 8.4 percent of wage earners did so.

Thus if interest group leaders were to follow the wishes of their constituents, we would expect them all to oppose both increases in taxes and reductions in the rate of growth of the money supply, with the strongest opposition coming from unions.

Turning to the other possible leg of a restrictive fiscal policy—decreases in government spending—it is clear that the majorities in favor, in all occupational groups, are as large as the majorities against the other two policies. We can see that 80.7 percent of the population favors reducing government spending while only 10.8 percent oppose it. More interestingly, there is almost no variation between the various occupational group-

Table 26   Policies Advocated to Control Inflation by Occupational Category in
                1969

	Fixed income	Wage earner	Salary earner	Self-employed	All re-spondents
Raise income taxes[a]					
Disagree	78.5%	90.3%	84.2%	85.9%	85.3%
Can't say	12.6	4.8	2.2	2.2	5.5
Agree	8.9	5.0	13.6	11.9	9.2
N	(326)	(544)	(448)	(135)	(1453)
Raise interest rates[a]					
Disagree	72.4	85.9	81.1	85.2	81.3
Can't say	16.3	5.7	3.1	3.0	7.0
Agree	11.3	8.4	15.8	11.9	11.7
N	(326)	(524)	(450)	(135)	(1455)
Reduce government spending[b]					
Disagree	9.2	10.1	13.1	9.6	10.8
Can't say	9.5	10.1	6.0	8.1	8.5
Agree	81.3	79.7	80.9	82.2	80.7
N	(326)	(542)	(450)	(135)	(1453)
Government control prices[a]					
Disagree	39.6	38.6	60.2	47.0	46.3
Can't say	10.9	9.4	5.1	10.4	8.5
Agree	49.5	52.0	34.7	42.5	45.1
N	(321)	(540)	(447)	(134)	(1442)
Government control wages[a]					
Disagree	46.0	54.1	69.6	48.5	56.5
Can't say	15.1	11.3	4.5	11.9	10.1
Agree	38.9	34.7	26.0	39.6	33.4
N	(324)	(542)	(447)	(134)	(1447)

The question asked was, "Here is a list of things which, some people say, should be done
to slow down inflation. First do you agree or disagree (first item) . . . ? (second item) . . . ?"

[a]Chi-square significant at the 0.001 level.

[b]Raw chi-square = 8.926 Significance = 0.178

Source: *Survey of Consumer Finances* (Ann Arbor: University of Michigan), Fall 1969.

ings. Particularly noticeable is the fact that transfer income receivers are
no more likely than the other groupings to favor high government spending, despite the fact that increased transfer payments were primarily responsible for the increase in government spending as a percent of GNP
in the 1960s. Thus if interest groups were to represent their constituents'
desires, we would expect virtual unanimity on the desirability of reducing
overall government spending by the representatives of all occupational
groups.

Whereas there are heavy majorities on all three of the above policies, there are much more even splits on wage and price policy. We should note before analyzing these splits that wage-price control is not invariably perceived by the public as a single, unified policy. Although almost 88 percent of those advocating wage control also advocate price control, only 65.6 percent of those advocating price control also advocate wage control. This points to some support amid the public for price controls unaccompanied by wage controls.

Looking at table 26 we can see that government price control is supported by aproximately half of the population. Further, unlike the other responses, the breakdown by occupation makes a considerable difference. Both the self-employed and salary earners show majorities opposed to government price control, with almost twice as many salary earners opposing it as supporting it. Wage earners and transfer income receivers, on the other hand, strongly support price control, with 51.8 percent of the former and 49.5 percent of the latter supporting. The occupational distribution of support for price control seems consistent with pluralist self-interest—the groups most associated with management oppose it and groups most likely to see price increases from the viewpoint of the pure consumer support it.

Government control of wages was thought a good means of controlling inflation by only 33.4 percent of respondents and was opposed by 56.5 percent. No occupational group has a majority of respondents in favor of wage control, but the degree of support for the policy nonetheless varies considerably by occupation. Not surprisingly, the self-employed and transfer income recipients are more likely to favor government wage control than the other two categories. Around 39 percent in these two occupational groups are in favor of government wage control, and around 47 percent are opposed. Of the other two groups it is interesting that salary earners are much more resolutely opposed to the policy than wage earners, with 69.6 percent of salary earners and 54.1 percent of wage earners opposing the policy.

It is possible that these policies could be held very shakily by citizens and that the answers could represent more or less random responses to the questions—something that would be in accord with other studies of public opinion on particular policies. If this were so, it would obviously be less reasonable to expect leaders to follow the policy cues of their constituents. In order to test for coherence I decided to cross-tabulate responses to questions in the fall 1969 Michigan Survey of Consumer Finances that asked people what they thought caused inflation, with responses to the above questions asking them what policies were appropriate for controlling inflation. Table 27 shows the resultant gamma values.

Table 27   Gamma Values on Causes of Inflation and Policies for Solving It

Causes Policy	Taxes too low	Govt. Viet. spending	Other govt. spending	Firms over raised prices	Wage increases too large	Consumers overspent	Consumers over-borrowed	Inflation inevitable
Increase taxes	.79	−.03	−.08	−.13	.05	.13	−.03	.21
Increase interest rates	.40	.02	−.11	−.22	.03	.08	.07	.18
Decrease govt. spending	−.18	.43	.62	.14	.17	.18	.22	−.20
Govt. control prices	−.04	.06	.02	.25	−.22	−.02	−.14	.20
Govt. control wages	.09	.00	.02	.11	−.00	.01	−.07	.21
Consumers spend less	.16	.12	.13	.09	.14	.73	.53	−.05
Consumers borrow less	.08	.12	.16	.17	.14	.52	.78	−.18
Inflation inevitable	.11	−.09	−.17	−.11	−.18	−.13	−.16	−.76

Source: *Survey of Consumer Finances* (Ann Arbor: University of Michigan), Fall 1969.

It is clear that there is in fact a reasonable degree of coherence exibited, with the gammas in all cases being higher for the "proper" relation.

We must be careful however not to overinterpret this result. Although table 27 does show that people's remedies for inflation usually correlate with their perception of the causes of inflation, it also shows that this is not always the case. Moreover, as we noted earlier, it is likely that people's perceptions of the causes of inflation are influenced by a desire to reconcile their different goals, rather than by a carefully thought-through model of the inflation process. Thus the policy positions of the different groups shown in table 26 can probably be taken as real indicators of the preferences of people in those groups, but we should not overstate the depth of those preferences.

What can we conclude about the policy preferences of the different occupational groups? We have found very little group difference on most of the policy alternatives presented. Thus strong majorities in all groups favored reduced government spending and opposed increases in taxes and interest rates. However there were differences in attitudes toward wage and price policies in a direction generally consistent with pluralist ideas.

It seems likely that although the views were held fairly strongly, and were reasonably coherent, the public is most likely to think a policy will solve inflation if it already favors it on other grounds.

Political Parties and Inflation

To some degree the question of what the public thinks about curing inflation may be moot. Although American governments indubitably take some note of public opinion, the average citizen is hindered from directly implementing his view by the very structure of government. Group pressures, such as those we will examine in chapter 6, are one means by which the citizen's preferences could get translated into action. One alternative means is through people with different opinions collecting around different political parties and trying to influence their party's policy. Another is through the use of the vote to influence the policies of the current administration and replace it if necessary. We will look in this section at the degree to which party membership is differentiated by views on inflation, before turning in the next to the question of the degree to which the vote is used to reward and punish administrations.

It is not entirely clear which party might most reasonably be expected by the voter to lower inflation. The vast majority of economists and political scientists would indubitably see the Republican party as most likely to keep inflation low. Both in its ideological statements and in its economic policies, the Republican party has given much more emphasis than the Democratic party to the goal of reducing inflation and less to the competing goals of full employment and economic growth. Furthermore, the policy that the public most unambiguously favors as a way of reducing inflation—that of reducing government spending—is a distinctly Republican policy. However, the rate of inflation has been little different under presidents of the two parties. Although this is possibly due to the lagged effects of Democratic presidents, and the efforts of successive Democratic Congresses, this would not necessarily have been perceived by the average voter.

What evidence there is seems to indicate that it has been perceived but only to a very limited degree. Figure 28 shows answers to Gallup questions asked in the postwar period on which party can best handle the problem of inflation. Although sixteen data points do not allow certainty, the most reasonable interpretation of the data would seem to be that the Democrats are normally seen as the party best able to solve inflation but that the Republicans were seen as best able to handle the problem in the wake of the inflationary periods during and after the Korean and Vietnam wars. For some of the periods in which the question was asked it was possible to compare the inflation answers with answers to similar questions on the

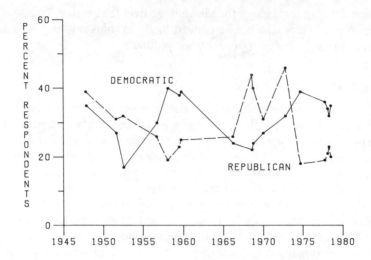

Figure 28   Perceptions of which is the better party to handle inflation. The actual
                   words used in asking voters their opinion vary from survey to survey.
                   The two most common were, ''Which party—the Republican or the
                   Democratic—do you think can do the better job of dealing with infla-
                   tion?'' and ''Which party—the Republican or the Democratic—do you
                   think will do the best job of keeping prices down during the next four
                   years?'' Sources: George Gallup, *The Gallup Poll* (New York: Random
                   House, 1972); *The Gallup Opinion Index,* various issues.

relative ability of the two parties to handle foreign policy and to ensure
prosperity. At these points it was generally the case that inflation was in
an intermediate position, with more seeing the Democrats as able to ensure
prosperity and more seeing the Republicans as able to handle foreign
policy well.

   Despite this evidence that people do not always see their party as best
able to handle any important problem, there is evidence that people iden-
tifying with either of the two parties are disproportionately likely to see
their own party as best able to handle the problem. Table 28 shows this,
as well as showing that independents in September 1974 were much more
likely to see the Democrats as the party best able to solve inflation. This
is not however a typical period. Extrapolating from table 28 to the sixteen
time points shown in figure 28, and bearing in mind that there are almost
twice as many Democrats as Republicans, it seems likely that we would
find independents fairly evenly split over the period as a whole. The best
overall conclusion would seem to be that it is the Democrats, not the
Republicans, who are usually seen as the party best able to handle inflation, but that this may be due in part to Democrats who support the party

Table 28   Political Party Perceived as Best Able to Deal with Inflation by Selected
Groups, September 1974

	Republican	Democratic	No difference	No opinion
National	18%	39%	30%	13%
Education				
College	23	35	31	11
High school	17	40	30	13
Grade school	14	40	30	16
Politics				
Republican	46	8	34	12
Democrat	4	61	23	12
Independent	14	32	38	16
Occupation				
Professional/businessmen	23	32	34	11
Clerks/sales workers	22	35	26	17
Manual workers	13	45	29	13
Non-labor force	21	37	29	13
Union Status				
Labor union	14	48	28	10
Non-labor union	10	35	32	14

The question was, "Which political party, the Republican or the Democratic, do you think
can do a better job of dealing with the problem of inflation?"

Source: *Gallup Opinion Index*, October 1974.

for other reasons automatically assuming it will handle most policies better.

The above discussion was predicated on the possibility that people
might change to the party more against inflation as concern over the issue
rose. There remains the possibility however that parties' policies might
prove to be in part the result of attempts to please those who already
identify with the party. For this notion there is some limited support. Table
29 shows mean figures for three questions asked of people by the Harris
poll over the 1974 to 1979 period, broken down by party. It is clear that
Republicans are more likely than Democrats to prefer lower inflation to
higher income, that they are more likely to see inflation rather than unemployment as a problem for themselves and are also more likely to see
it as a greater problem for the country. Hibbs also finds Republicans
placing more weight on inflation and Democrats placing more weight on
unemployment.[10] We cannot properly infer from these results that people
have joined the Republicans because of their stand on inflation as the
differences are almost certainly a side-effect of differences in the socio-
economic makeup of the two parties. It does however seem reasonable
to infer that Republican leaders should be under more pressure than their

Table 29   Party Differentation on Importance of Controlling Inflation, 1974–1979

| | Mean figures from eight surveys | | |
	Republicans	Democrats	Difference of means
Most important problem for respondent[a]			
Inflation	86.8%	80.5%	6.3%
Unemployment	9.1	11.5	−2.6
N	(22,294)	(48,523)	
Most important problem for country[b]			
Inflation	51.8	41.4	10.4
Unemployment	32.5	38.3	−5.8
N	(22,602)	(48,954)	
Preference for higher income or less inflation[c]			
Lower inflation	64.0	59.9	4.1
Higher income	23.6	27.4	−3.8
N	(16,309)	(33,814)	

The questions were: (a) "As far as you personally are concerned, which is a more serious problem for you and your family today—rising prices or high unemployment?" (b) "If you had to choose, which do you think is a more serious problem for the country today—rising prices or high unemployment?" (c) "Let's say you were up for a raise in pay. How would you feel about these two situations. One would be your getting a pay increase lower than the rise in the cost of living, but with some assurance that the cost of living was being brought under control. The other situation would be your getting a pay increase higher than the cost of living but with no assurance the cost of living was being brought under control. Which would you choose?"

The first two questions were asked in January 1975, March 1975, July 1975, August 1976, August 1977, February 1978, July 1978 and February 1979. The last question was asked in November 1974, August 1976, August 1977, February 1978, July 1978, February 1979 and July 1979. The figures shown are the means from all of these points.

In all cases chi-square is significant at the 0.001 level for the pooled samples.

Source: Harris Poll data supplied to author.

Democratic counterparts from their party faithful to take strong stands against inflation. But even this should not be overstated. It is important to notice that the difference between party supporters on the relative importance of inflation does not appear to be large and that in all cases majorities of Democrats as well as Republicans appear to consider the control of inflation as most important.

Inflation and Voting Models

We have looked at what the public thinks about inflation, what it thinks should be done about it and who it blames for it. But how relevant are these opinions to the shaping of macroeconomic policy? Marxist and elitist theories maintain, by and large, that they are not very important because in a capitalist state the mass of the people lacks the means to shift the levers of power. Thus they would predict that voting would have little effect on economic policy making and that people would be misled into voting against their real economic interests. Given our previous discussion, this implies that the vote would not be primarily determined by economic variables and that what influence there was would be as likely to come from inflation as from changes in unemployment and real income. Pluralists, on the other hand, maintain that people have the ability to shape policy and that they use that ability.[11] Thus they would generally expect people to have considerable influence on policy and to vote to maximize their true economic welfare. Logically this should lead us to expect a heavy influence from economic variables, with the major impact coming from personal income change rather than inflation.

One of the means by which people could affect policy, the formation or use of interest groups, will be examined in chapter 6. We will also defer to chapter 6 the examination of policy actions of elected politicians. Here we examine the relation between change in economic variables and support for elected officials.

Primarily because of the availability of hard data, this question has absorbed the energies of most contemporary political scientists interested in the relation between economic policy and politics. Virtually all of this literature has followed the assumptions of the rational actor variant of pluralism, and the majority has been concerned with proving or disproving the first part of the theory of the political business cycle. This holds that people vote their economic interest, but that because people have a short memory, governments only give them what they want—economic stimulation—near election time.

Leaving aside for the moment the problem of the degree of short-term control over the economy possessed by elected officials, let us look at the logic of the notion that people vote their economic interest. At first thought nothing would seem more plausible, and this initial plausibility is responsible for much of the model's popularity. Further thought reveals many obstacles. In the average national election half the eligible citizens do not vote.[12] When they do, their vote is often determined by long-term factors, such as ethnic and racial loyalty, intergenerational transmission of party affiliation, region of origin or habit.[13] Even where they are influenced by more recent events, non-policy considerations, such as charisma, perceived trustworthiness, or incumbency are often determinative.[14] Finally, even if one were prepared to ignore all this, or argue, with Fiorina, that they are lagged functions of economic change, there still remains the overwhelming problem that while there are many important policy issues, there is only one vote.[15]

There are further problems. It is not obvious whether one should change one's vote for the president, one's senator, one's representative, or all three. It is not clear whether, as the literature almost universally assumes, one should vote against the incumbent,[16] or whether one should vote for the party or individual thought best able to solve the problem, whether currently in or out of office.[17] Lastly, even if economic issues did influence voting, given the short-term trade-off between inflation on the one hand and income and employment growth on the other, it is not obvious that voters would reward stimulation, and it seems possible that the variables might have a cancelling effect on one another.

Given all this, what does the available evidence indicate? As one might expect, since most of the literature originates with authors embedded in the rational actor paradigm, there is primary emphasis on the "real" variables of income growth and unemployment, but many authors have also looked at inflation "because it was there." The bulk of the literature has been cast in the form of a prolonged debate between those who find a significant relation between political popularity and changes in income and employment, and those who do not, with the implicit model resembling those developed by Frey and Schneider.[18] As is often the case in this kind of exercise, the significance of the relation depends to a great extent on technical questions: the choice of the dependent variable, the particular series used, whether the data are monthly, quarterly or yearly, the assumptions underlying the form of the equations and the choice of methodology.

It is particularly important to note that those, like Monroe, using monthly data tend to find much less correlation between economic change and political support than those, like Hibbs, who use quarterly data, or those, like Tufte, who use yearly data. This is partly because the dependent survey variable in monthly data contains more white noise from sampling error. Probably more important however is the fact that the multitude of very short term events that have a temporary effect on presidential popularity, such as the timing of the Iranian hostage release just before the 1980 election, tend to get washed out in the longer-term figures, increasing the percentage of the variance explained by events, such as economic changes, taking place over longer time spans.

Congress

The literature dealing with the relation between change in economic variables and congressional voting falls into three major divisions. The early literature deriving from Kramer, and relying on aggregate data, dealt with the relation between general economic conditions and the share of the congressional vote going to the party of the incumbent president. The next approach used election year surveys to link individuals' economic fortunes and opinions with their self-reported vote. The most recent approach looks at changes in economic conditions in individual constituencies and sees how these affect the vote for the congressmen representing those constituencies.[19]

Although there is now a large literature dealing with the question, it is unfortunately still not possible to say conclusively whether or not economic conditions affect the vote for congressmen. The bulk of the literature takes the first of our three approaches. Most of it finds some relation between economic conditions and incumbent party vote, but some of it does not. Further, even the authors who agree that there is a relation disagree on which economic variables are significant, whether the effect is symmetric or asymmetric and whether it is turnout or the party share of the vote that is primarily affected.

Thus Kramer in his original 1971 article found that in the 1896-1964 period, excluding war years, changes in nominal income, real income and inflation had significant effects on the vote, while unemployment had insignificant results in the wrong direction.[20] Stigler, reanalyzing the Kramer data, with slight changes in the years examined, found that the results were very sensitive to inclusion or exclusion of particular years and that only inflation had any effect on voting, and not a large one.[21] In a later reanalysis of his own data, Kramer found that income had no significant effect after all, leaving only inflation significant.[22]

A new attack on Kramer, this time by Arcelus and Meltzer, found a relation between economic changes and turnout, but none between economic change and share of the party vote.[23] Goodman and Kramer objected to the statistical methods of their critics, and wrote a reply that found significant effects.[24] Bloom and Price, also taking off from the original Kramer article, found that voters punish the incumbent party when the economy is worsening in the year preceding the election, but are less inclined to reward success.[25] Li, using an auto-regressive moving average technique to reanalyze the Kramer data, found that there was a small effect from unemployment but none from inflation or income change.[26] Finally, Tufte, confining himself to the 1946-1976 period, finds a strong relation between change in real disposable income and the party vote, but does not consider, or control for, the effects of unemployment or inflation and lays himself open to the objection that the number of elections his regressions are based on—eight—is too small for any certainty.[27] Overall, this literature based on aggregate data must be adjudged inconclusive with regard to whether there is an effect, what the effect might be on, and which economic variables, if any, have an effect.

A second, smaller group of writers have used survey data to see if there is a linkage between the effect of economic conditions on individuals and the congressional vote. This literature shows more agreement than that based on national-level aggregate data. Most articles find a small or non-existent effect of personal economic fortunes on voting. Wides found a small positive effect of change in personal income during the 1964, 1968 and 1972 elections.[28] Klorman also claimed to find a similar effect on elections between 1956 and 1974, but most of his results are not significant at the .05 level, and nine of the thirty-one coeficients are in the wrong direction.[29] Fiorina finds a weak effect on on-year elections but none on off-year ones.[30] Kinder and Kiewiet, using the most comprehensive data base of any of these works, find the effect of unemployment and income dissatisfaction to be very small in the eleven elections between 1956 and 1976, leading them to claim that "congressional voting is seldom motivated by perceptions of declining personal financial well being or by unemployment experiences."[31] But they found that there was a generally significant relation between voters' views as to how good business conditions were and their vote, giving rise to the view that it was people's general view of the economy rather than their own economic fortunes that influenced their voting behavior.[32] This finding was partly confirmed by Wides and Kuechler, who found, looking at the 1976 election, that personal fortunes did not explain the vote for Congress but that the perceived economic competency of the President did.[33] It is also consistent with Levenson and her associates' analysis of a 1956, 1958, and 1960 panel survey which showed no correlation between objective or subjective personal income change and congressional voting.[34] Finally it is largely consistent with the findings of Kuklinski and West, who found that if one chose a year (1978) when conditions were optimal for inducing personal economic voting, one could find a small effect on voting for Senators but still none for members of the House.[35] Kinder and Kiewiet see the tendency to vote according to general perceptions of the economy rather than effects on the individual voter as essentially other-regarding behavior. But a more plausible view is put forward by Feldman who attributes it to a tendency by that majority of Americans who believe in individual responsibility and the virtues of the free enterprise system to blame their economic misfortunes on themselves.[36] Taken overall this literature seems to show a weak to non-existent relation between personal income change and congressional voting and some evidence that people's general view of the economy affects their vote.

The most recent approach compares economic conditions in individual constituencies with the vote for the congressman representing that constituency. Pierson, looking at the 1974 election, finds no relation between economic conditions in the district and district voting, but is prepared to entertain a relation between national trends and local voting.[37] A more recent and complete analysis by Owens and Olson for the 1972, 1974 and 1976 elections finds "no linear relationship between changes in the vote for individual candidates and changes in real income and inflation,'' either for actual incumbents or for members of the president's party.[38] But their tables do allow the conclusion that local inflation may have an effect on the vote for congressmen of the president's party, with that effect concentrated in safe districts. This latter possibility is upheld by Hibbing and Alford who find that there is an effect of personal financial situation on the Congressional vote, but only in the safe seats where it doesn't matter.[39]

Summarizing, the overall thrust of this congressional literature is that, at least in the last thirty-five years, there appears to have been some relation between changes in economic variables and the national share of the congressional vote going to the party of the incumbent president, although both the size of the effect and the economic variables that have the effect are open to question. The relation however does not seem to be due to people voting against congressmen when their own personal economic situation worsens. Rather they vote on the basis of what they think is happening to the national economy, and even this effect seems weaker in marginal seats, where incumbents campaign harder.[40]

The President

Prima facie it seems more reasonable to expect voting for the president to be affected by economic conditions, than voting for Congress. Economic policy is, after all, primarily formulated in the executive branch and the president's role is far more visible. In addition, we have seen that the literature on congressional voting does not claim that the party forming the majority in Congress is punished when economic conditions are bad, but rather that voters punish candidates of the president's party.[41]

The work seeking to determine the effect of economic conditions on presidential elections falls into three groups. The earliest approach, as with the congressional literature, examined the relation between national-level aggregate economic data and the vote for president. The next approach looked at the same national-level economic data and correlated it with presidential popularity, using a monthly Gallup series. Most recently, while work in the earlier traditions continues, there has been some use of survey data to see whether changes in the economic fortunes of individuals affected their presidential vote.

In principle the first of these approaches is probably the best, as it avoids the twin problems that people's expressed opinions do not always reflect their real feelings or their actions, and that people receive and absorb more political information near election time, thereby widening the basis upon which they judge incumbent presidents. However, these advantages tend to be outweighed by the fact that there have not been a lot of elections for which reliable economic data has been available—even fewer if one restricts oneself to the postwar era—making the statistical reliability of tests based on this data highly dubious. In addition it seems reasonable that presidents might pay more attention to their current popularity than the (yet unknown) vote they will get in the next election when judging the effect of their policies on their electoral fortunes.

As was true for the congressional literature, each of the approaches yields somewhat different results. As was also true there, the combination of these results does not yield a fully coherent or consistent answer to the central question, namely whether changes in economic variables affect the fortunes of presidential candidates in a consistent manner.

The three major pieces that correlate the presidential vote with changes in aggregate economic variables are those by Kramer, Fair and Tufte. In the first of these, Kramer, while finding that personal income had a large effect on the congressional vote, found that economic variables had only a small effect at best upon presidential elections in the 1896-1962 period, a result later confirmed by Stigler.[42] This conclusion was challenged by Fair, who argued that by constraining his presidential equation in the same way as his congressional one, Kramer had missed a significant effect. After using a variety of different lags, he found that growth in real per capita GNP in the year preceding the election had an effect in the right direction, but one that was not strong enough to be significant at the .05 level.[43] Tufte, looking only at the eight elections in the 1948-1976 period, finds that change in disposable personal income has a significant effect on the vote for president, but unfortunately fails to look at inflation and unemployment, the former of which I found significant on rerunning various versions of his basic equation.[44] In general it seems to me that the weight of the evidence from these works points toward there being some sort of relation between personal income and the presidential vote, but the result is dependent on which years are included or excluded, a hardly satisfactory situation. Further, none of the works above deals with more than sixteen data points, making their results, as Fair points out, highly contingent.[45]

This last caveat is the primary explanation for the fact that most of the work on the effects of economic variables upon presidential fortunes has used presidential popularity rather than the presidential vote as the dependent variable. Though there is considerable variability in this work, the overall trend has been to find personal income is an insignificant predictor, and unemployment only a little better. Inflation, on the other hand, which seemed an unimportant predictor in the works based on the presidential vote, emerges as by far the most significant predictor of postwar presidential popularity.

The earliest of these works, that by Mueller, found that unemployment did not have an effect per se, but that if unemployment worsened after a president took office, his popularity fell.[46] A recalculation of these results by Hibbs however, adjusting the data to remove the serial correlation in the residuals in Mueller's original study, found no evidence that unemployment affected presidential popularity at all.[47] A more systematic reanalysis of the Mueller data by Kenski, which looked for effects from both inflation and unemployment, also found unemployment an insignificant predictor, but found inflation to be significant.[48] However, these results too showed evidence of serial correlation, and when Kenski used the rate of change in inflation to take out the serial correlation, the relation vanished.[49]

The two most methodologically advanced works in this tradition are those by Kernell and Monroe. Kernell used six-month moving averages of inflation and change in unemployment, controlling for the effect of wars and some other variables.[50] Looking separately at each president, and using a variety of tests, he found change in unemployment to be an insignificant predictor, for all presidents except possibly Johnson. He finds inflation to have stronger effects overall, but only in the Johnson and Nixon years is the inflation coefficient significant at the .05 level. Overall his results seem to indicate that inflation is the only economic variable with significant effects on presidential popularity and that the effect is more important when inflation is high. Monroe's two articles use the Almon distributed-lag technique to allow for the fact that economic change may have a cumulative effect on presidential popularity and uses the Cochrane-Orcutt technique to adjust for auto-correlation in the residuals.[51] She tries a variety of models in the two articles, but comes to the conclusion in both "that inflation and military expenditures are important influences on popularity and that unemployment and income are not."[52]

Recent work by Levi and Monroe and by Michaels has tried to assess whether there might be a greater negative effect on the incumbent's popularity from unexpected than from expected economic change. Levi and Monroe found that whereas unexpected economic growth increased presidential popularity, unexpected inflation had no effect.[53] Michaels, looking at inflation, found both expected and unexpected inflation had weak and unstable results, with anticipated inflation having more negative impact than unanticipated inflation.[54] However, the measures of expectations in these works—a panel of businessmen and economists in the first, and an auto-regressive twenty-four-month moving average of inflation in the second—though commonly used in the economic literature, have obvious weaknesses which should induce caution in accepting the results at face value.

Somewhat in opposition to these more recent works, Frey and Schneider find unemployment highly significant and inflation and real consumption not significant in the most convincing of their six equations.[55] But their extensive use of dummies, particularly their popularity depreciation dummies, seems to this writer a less satisfactory procedure than that employed by Kernell in his similar work as a way of dealing with the different popularity functions of each president, and reduces my faith in their results.

Recent work by Hibbs, generally accepted as the most methodologically sophisticated of the writers in this area, aggregates the Gallup monthly presidential popularity series into a quarterly series enabling a finding that inflation, unemployment and income change all significantly affect presidential popularity. In three sucessive attempts inflation has gradually replaced unemployment as the major explanatory variable. In a first attempt, using quarterly data from 1961 to 1976, he attempted to estimate the relative effect of unemployment and inflation on presidential popularity and found, contrary to most other writers, that unemployment was more important throughout the period, though much more so during the 1960s than the 1970s.[56] Two later more careful pieces, using quarterly data from the 1960 to 1979 period, compare the relative effects of inflation, unemployment and change in real disposable income. In the first he finds that in the 1960s the rate of unemployment had the greatest effect on presidential popularity, with inflation almost as important and change in personal income somewhat less so, while in the 1970s inflation has almost twice as large an effect as either of the other two variables.[57] His most recent piece shows inflation as the most important single economic variable for the 1960-1979 period taken as a whole and further finds it most important for each of three occupational groups and for Republicans, Democrats and Independents, even though his equation controls for the effects of inflation on real income.[58] Finally, it is worth noting that noneconomic events Hibbs includes in his equations, such as the Vietnam war, Watergate, presidential personality and a foreign affairs "rally" variable adopted from Mueller, generally seem to have larger effects on popularity than economic variables.

The third approach, that of using cross-sectional studies of voter perceptions near election time, has been less used for presidential than for congressional voting. Wides performed a preliminary exploration of the effect of change in an individual's financial situation on the 1964, 1968 and 1972 presidential vote with generally inconclusive results. Despite his claim that he shows that "self-perceived economic change . . . is related to relative support of the incumbent presidential administration," the reported gammas and r's seem low and unstable and possibly, at least in 1964, not significant.[59]

Much more satisfactory is Fiorina's analysis of the 1976 presidential election, in which he attempts to show the influence of economic variables on both the short-term expectations and the long-term party identification of respondents.[60] Though the cross-sectional approach is not ideal for the second of these aims, the results are nonetheless interesting. Using quite different assumptions and employing different more subjective variables, he comes to similar conclusions to the bulk of the popularity literature. He shows that expectations of parties' ability to handle inflation are more important than expectations of their ability to handle unemployment and that "Judgements about past economic performance seem to matter, though the direct effect may be limited to evaluations surrounding inflation performance."[61]

What one makes of the presidential literature obviously depends on which method of approach seems most plausible. The voting approach leads to the conclusion that personal income has an effect and that the effect of inflation is smaller or non-existent. The popularity approach points to inflation as a significant variable, with most of the work showing unemployment and change in personal income to have weak or non-existent effects. For the reasons of statistical reliability cited earlier, my own preference is for the second approach, but a case for the first approach can clearly be made.

Class Differences

A few writers in the political business cycle tradition have pushed on from consideration of aggregate patterns to consideration of whether different groups in the population, with different economic interests, might have different political support patterns. Wides breaks down his sample by self-reported class and income and attempts to ascertain whether class makes a difference to the relation between change in financial position and presidential support in 1964, 1968 and 1972.[62] He finds minor class differences in what is in any case a weak relation, but they seem to vary from election to election, making generalization difficult.

In a somewhat more sophisticated development of the Wides logic, Weatherford, looking at data from a panel study taken in the 1956-1960 period, when economic conditions were unusually bad but inflation was not, found some evidence that changes in the financial situation of the working class affected their vote, but that changes in the financial situation of middle-class respondents had little effect.[63] He explains this by saying that the working class is worst hit in recessions, but it is not evident to this reader why the nature of his dependent variable does not already control for this; so the finding remains essentially unexplained.

Though interesting in their own right, these works have only limited interest for us because of their concentration on change in financial situation as the single dependent variable and because of their weak theoretical base. Much more interesting in both regards is the work of Hibbs. In most of his work Hibbs pursues a notion most consistent with pluralist democracy and structural Marxism. Following the logic of the business cycle theorists discussed in chapter 3, he reasons that those in the working class are most subject to unemployment and lose most in recessions, and hence that we should find working-class respondents much more likely than others to worry about unemployment. Thus given a choice between unemployment and inflation, we should find more working-class people seeing unemployment as the major problem and more middle-class people viewing inflation as the major problem. From this it follows, he argues, that we should find working-class people more inclined to support presidents who lower unemployment and middle-class people more prepared to support presidents who lower inflation.

This notion, reasonably common among British economists in the early seventies and reminiscent of Hirschman's and Meier's work on inflation as the product of class conflict, was first proposed by Hibbs in the mid-seventies in an article in which he attempted to demonstrate that it explained the different Phillips curve trade-offs of different developed Western nations.[64] In two recent articles he looks at effects of inflation, unemployment, real income growth and various non-economic variables on presidential popularity among blue-collar workers, white-collar workers, and those not in the labor force, as well as among Republicans, Democrats and Independents.[65] He expected to find people "voting" their objective interest, with blue-collar workers most worried about unemployment and real income growth and white-collar workers most worried by inflation. He finds that all groups are most worried by inflation but that there appear to be small differences in the expected direction between white- and blue-collar workers[66] and rather larger ones between both sets of workers and those not in the labor force. He also finds somewhat larger differences, again in the expected direction, between those in different parties. While Hibbs takes these results as confirming the idea that people vote their interest, and they clearly can be interpreted that way, the fact that blue-collar workers are more worried by inflation than unemployment, the fact that the differences between the party identifiers, who have heterogeneous economic interests, are larger than those between the occupational groups, with more homogenous economic interests, and the fact that it was not possible to control occupation by party, should make us cautious in accepting this interpretation. Further it is important to remember that Hibbs, like others who use the Gallup series, cannot control for turnout.[67] This is important because there is evidence that both unemployment and lowered income decrease turnout.[68] This naturally raises the possibility that decreased turnout could offset negative voting in the affected groups.

Summary

What overall conclusions can be drawn from the voting literature? First it seems likely that normal economic fluctuations, ceteris paribus, do have a small-to-moderate effect on political popularity and that major depressions have quite large effects. However it seems equally true that other problems, especially foreign affairs problems, often swamp economic ones, that other factors such as party identification or presidential personality are generally more important, and that what effect there is is more important for the president than for congressmen. Second it appears likely that voters' perceptions of the general economic climate, rather than their direct personal experience, explains what effect there is, a point obviously not favorable to my pluralist models. Third it is not clear whether inflation on the one hand, or unemployment and decreases in personal income on the other, are more likely to lead to vote loss. With the bulk of the presidential literature favoring the former and the bulk of the congressional literature favoring the latter explanation, it even seems possible that a president and members of his party in Congress might have opposite interests in whether the economy is inflated or deflated.

Given that economic variables do have some effect on political support, does this support the pluralist case as Tufte among others claims? The answer seems to be that on balance it does not appear to. The congressional literature clearly does not support pluralist notions of representation whether one believes those who claim there is an effect on the vote or those who claim there is not. If there is not, then the obvious question for pluralist theory is why not. If there is, it does not seem to be the sort of effect that, as the theory requires, would give congressmen a consistent incentive to change policy to achieve the desired results. The articles showing an effect, it will be recalled, show that voters punish not the majority party in Congress for bad economic conditions but the party of the incumbent president. Thus when Congress and the presidency are controlled by different parties, as they have been for half of the postwar period, the congressional majority would actually have an incentive to make economic conditions worse. When we look at the remaining half of the period there still does not seem to be a strong positive incentive. Even those like Tufte who have claimed a strong effect on the vote have been careful to point out that the number of incumbent congressmen who lose their seats for all reasons is small and has declined over the postwar period. And those congressmen with the greatest influence over policy, the members of the key economic committees, are buffered even against this, as they are chosen in part on the grounds of how safe their seats are.

The presidential literature can more easily be reconciled with pluralist assumptions, but here too there are problems. The overall thrust of the evidence seems to support the proposition that in most presidential elections the state of the economy is one reasonably important determinant of the vote, and this is in line with pluralist assumptions. However it also seems to be true that on most specifications of the underlying equation, inflation rather than unemployment or real-income growth seems the most important predictor. This seems incompatible with the normal assumption that inflation is only important insofar as it affects real income. Further, to the extent that policy makers change their policies in order to lower inflation by deflating, they are acting against what most pluralists see as the short-term interests of the population. Even if one ignores the bulk of the literature, and looks only at the work of those like Hibbs and Frey and Schneider that find unemployment and changes in income also have a significant influence, one is left with the somewhat unsatisfying conclusion that the president is being signalled to both inflate and deflate.

The class literature, or at least the results of Hibbs, offers in my view the strongest support for the pluralist postition. Working-class people are most affected by unemployment and, although the middle classes seem to marginally benefit from inflation in the long run, one can make a case that salaries are worse hit than wages by inflation in the short term. Thus it is reasonably consistent to find, as Hibbs does, that blue-collar workers are more likely to support presidents that reduce unemployment than their white-collar counterparts and that the reverse holds for presidents that reduce inflation. However, one must bear in mind the dependence of Hibb's latest results on a questionable lag coefficient, the fact that all the groups seemed to place more weight on inflation than on the "real" variables of unemployment and income, even though the effect of inflation on real income was controlled for, and Hibb's inability to control his occupational results for party or turnout.

Conclusion

In this chapter we have looked at the way in which people convert their evaluations of inflation into political demands. The major findings of the first part of the chapter are that most people feel unable to cope with inflation and that the policies they seem to want would not generally achieve the anti-inflationary result they appear to desire. In the second part we found that although there may be some conversion of economic desires into votes, especially for the president, the economy appears to be only a minor determinant of voting and much of the voting is counterproductive. In the next chapter we will look at how the representatives of the people actually make policy.

6 Making Inflation Policy

So far we have looked at the first two stages of our three-stage model, focussing on the effect that inflation has on different groups within the nation, and the reaction of the people in those groups to the phenomenon. It now remains to take up the third stage of our model and look at the attitudes and actions of the group leaders—those people whom pluralist-democratic theory identifies as the real policy makers. We will look at who these leaders are, the extent to which they are involved in macroeconomic policy making, the patterns of influence between them and the degree to which their actions and statements reflect the views and experiences of the groups they represent.

In order to understand why leaders think and act as they do, it is necessary to view them in the context of the policy making process. We will look first at who is involved in this process, second at the more detailed operation of economic policy making and lastly at who is not involved and the criterion for exclusion.

The Policy Makers

Inflation can be seen as resulting from actions taken outside the political process as we normally visualize it. Here the thousands of collective bargaining processes and the even larger number of price decisions by firms could be seen as the cause of inflation and essentially beyond the control of any more centralized group. This view obviously has some merit. There is abundant evidence that more than one wage-price policy has failed owing to the failure of these many smaller decision makers to exercise voluntary restraint.

However, as we saw in chapter 2, economists generally believe that if policy makers are willing to bear high costs in terms of other goals it is possible to lower the rate of inflation. Usually these goals are seen as low employment, price stability, GNP growth, a reasonable balance of payments and the maintenance of free enterprise institutions.[1]

The Executive

Who are the people primarily involved in this difficult task? Within the formal governmental structure the task is handled primarily by a number of specialized federal agencies and by a number of somewhat less specialized congressional committees. The chief agencies involved in macroeconomic policy making are the Federal Reserve, the Treasury, the Office of Management and Budget, the Council of Economic Advisers and the White House staff. The Federal Reserve, formally independent of presidential control, handles the day-to-day management of the money supply and sets targets for monetary growth—usually with some regard to prevailing interest rates. The Treasury is the government agency primarily responsible for debt management, the balance of payments and the estimation of government revenues. The Office of Management and Budget is responsible for preparing the annual budget and coordinates government expenditures. The Council of Economic Advisers estimates GNP growth and has formal responsibility for advising the president on macroeconomic policy. The White House Staff provides general coordination and often arbitrates disputes. These agencies and quasi-agencies work together reasonably well, partly because their heads tend to have similar economic philosophies at any given time, partly because each commands resources that are necessary to the creation of any unified program and partly because if the agencies work against one another the resulting economic policy mixture is likely to be one none of them would have wanted.

There are however occasional differences of opinion between the agencies, some arising from fairly permanent biases within the different bodies, deriving from their roles in the management of the economy and some arising from the particular personalities leading the bodies at a given time. Generally the Treasury, responsible for refinancing debt and most open to balance of payments pressures, is relatively conservative.[2] The Federal Reserve also tends toward conservatism, partly because of the banking background of most governors and the pressure they receive from the banking community and partly because its natural tendency to emphasize the role of the money supply in economic management is more consistent with conservative economic theories.[3] The Council of Economic Advisers is normally the most liberal of the bodies, reflecting its base in the generally liberal academic community and its lack of responsibilities.[4] The Office of Management and Budget is normally most concerned to maintain the integrity of the president's programs and will shift its position as this aim dictates. These normal biases can however shift with changes in leadership. Differences are often compromised first between members of an informal troika of the Office of Management and Budget, the Treasury and the CEA and then between the troika and the Federal Reserve. The balance is held in the White House, with White House staff often arbitrating disagreements and the final say being in the hands of the president, who usually works with his chief economic adviser. Influence with the president is the key to the balance of power between the different bodies, with marked shifts in power sometimes taking place when a presidential intimate is appointed to head one of the bodies.[5]

Congress

On the congressional side the picture is much more confusing. Several committees in the House and Senate, a joint committee and the congressional leaders, all share varying degrees of power, and the congressional membership as a whole has some ability to set limits to changes in economic policy.

In the House, the generally conservative Ways and Means and Appropriations committees have traditionally been the two most important committees for economic policy making, with the former bearing primary responsibility for revenue bills and social security and the latter for government expenditures.[6] Partly because of a demonstrated inability of these committees to work together, a Budget Committee was established in 1974 with the task of reconciling revenues and expenditures in congressional budgets.

This generally moderate body has had some impact on the timing of budget approval, positive at first and negative later, but, except in 1981, little on the substance of the budget. Though House co-ordination of taxes and expenditures has been somewhat improved the difference is not major.[7]

Of lesser importance are the more liberal Banking, Finance and Urban Affairs Committee and the highly liberal Education and Labor Committee. The former committee is responsible for price control legislation and has some nuisance power in the area of monetary policy. The latter committee has jurisdiction over manpower policy, and wage control legislation and has some effect on appropriations through its responsibility for anti-poverty programs.

Most other House committees are not very important for major economic policies, although the Agriculture, the Armed Service and the Public Works and Transportation committees have some minor influence through the sheer size of the economic sectors for which they are responsible. Also the Foreign Affairs Committee has some importance in foreign trade matters and the Energy and Commerce Committee has minor relevance through its regulatory and foreign trade responsibilities. Outside the substantive committees the Rules Committee has occasionally bottled up major economic legislation.[8]

Within the committees the chairmen and, to a lesser extent, the ranking minority members have much more power than anyone else. Some chairmen, such as Wilbur Mills, have in the past been able to completely dominate their committees.[9] More recently there has been a steady increase in both the number and the power of subcommittees. Most committees have between six and thirteen subcommittees and the power of the subcommittee chairmen has increased at the expense of the power of the full committee chairmen.[10]

The leadership of the House is also important in deciding the fate of major presidential legislation to regulate the economy.[11] The Speaker and House Majority Leader are important in blocking the proposals of presidents from the opposing party and in working out compromise replacements. More importantly, they are often necessary to get their president's proposals through Congress. The House Minority Leader can also be important. His role is particularly relevant in the sustaining of his own president's vetoes.

In the Senate the structure of power for macroeconomic policy making is very similar to that in the House. Again, two committees—the Finance Committee which handles revenue and the Appropriations Committee which handles expenditures—have been the dominant committees for most of our period. The Senate too formed a Budget Committee in 1974. Though it has been more influential than its House counterpart, the Finance and Appropriations Committees remain more important.[12] As in the House, the Banking, Housing and Urban Affairs Committee, which is responsible for price controls but has some say in monetary policy, and the Labor and Human Resources Committee, which is responsible for wage controls and manpower policy, are next in importance. In addition, the Foreign Relations, Commerce, Agriculture and Forestry, Armed Services, Science and Transportation and the Environment and Public Works committees play roles similar to their House counterparts, although individual jurisdictions vary somewhat. Although power was never as centralized in the Senate as in the House, here too there has been a steady devolution of power to the chairmen of the steadily increasing number of subcommittees. The Senate majority and minority leaders are also highly influential, albeit somewhat less so than the House leadership.[13]

The major differences in this area between the House and the Senate are the greater relative importance of committee chairmen and party leaders in the House vis-à-vis other committee members and the membership as a whole, the fact that senators are generally less knowledgeable on the subjects dealt with by their committee, and, prior to 1981, the more liberal complexion of the Senate.[14]

Finally the joint committees such as the Joint Economic Committee and the Joint Tax Committee perform a primarily educational function. However, the staff of the Joint Tax Council and the jointly shared staff of the Congressional Budget Office do have some influence, especially on legislation where technical issues are important.[15]

Interest Groups

Although a large number of interest groups maintain some degree of peripheral interest in macroeconomic policy making, active participation comes basically from the representatives of labor and big business, with small business, farm, banking and insurance groups taking a smaller but still significant role.

Labor input into the macroeconomic policy process is largely centralized in the hands of the AFL-CIO, although some of the larger craft unions, particularly those from the highly cyclical construction sector, will sometimes give independent testimony. The major exception to this rule of centralization is the role played by the United Automobile Workers Union, which has a more liberal position, a more economically sophisticated research staff and a more cyclical production cycle than the bulk of American unions.[16]

The input from business is more diverse. The major peak interest groups—the National Association of Manufacturers and the Chamber of Commerce of the United States—respectively represent large manufacturers and common views of large, medium and small businesses. Two other groups—the Committee for Economic Development and the Business Roundtable—represent large corporations. In addition to these peak associations[17] there is occasional action by individual corporations such as the Ford Motor Company and by various groups of businesses in specialized areas such as retail trade and transport.

Small business also has some input into the policy process. The U.S. Chamber of Commerce represents the views of small as well as big business, and the National Federation of Independent Businessmen gives more specific expression to small business interests.[18] In addition, there is diffuse influence through pressure on congressmen at the local level. There is also occasionally some influence from professional groups such as the American Medical Association, though economic policy is not their main interest.

The financial sector is also influential, particularly for monetary policy.[19] Here the American Banking Association is the primary influence, but there is also influence exerted through the Life Insurance Association of

America, the National Association of Mutual Savings Banks, the Independent Bankers Association and some of the larger individual banks such as the Bank of America, Chase Manhattan and the First National City Corporation.[20]

Farm groups too have some importance for economic policy making, although outside the agricultural sector they are more evident in public activities such as testimony, than in private lobbying. Most activity here is funnelled through three major farm groups—the conservative American Farm Bureau Federation and National Grange, and the liberal National Farmers Union. The Farm Bureau, easily the largest and most conservative of the three, primarily represents the affluent farmers of the Midwest and the poor farmers of the South and has strong ties to the Agriculture Department. The smaller and somewhat less conservative National Grange primarily represents Northeastern farmers. The Farmers Union, much smaller and much more liberal than the other two peak groups, primarily represents the farmers of the Midwest and Northwest. Almost all farm influence in major economic policy comes from these organizations.[21]

Another strong influence on economic policy making is the intellectuals—primarily academic economists. Their major influence is to push policy in the direction of innovation and growth. In terms of traditional ideologies they are found more often on the liberal side than the conservative side and are found chiefly in a handful of Washington research foundations and the country's top university economics departments. The liberal intellectual effort is spearheaded by the Brookings Institution and some smaller Washington groups like the Conference on Economic Progress and the Urban Institute and is supported by the Ivy League schools of Harvard, MIT, Yale, Princeton, Columbia and a variety of other schools. The less influential conservative response finds its Washington home in foundations such as the American Enterprise Institute and the Heritage Foundation, and its regional base is in western and midwestern universities, such as Chicago, Michigan, Stanford and UCLA. The intellectual community influences policy in the long run through the education of bureaucrats and politicians and through its media efforts. Short-term influence is through its institutional extensions in the Council of Economic Advisers and the Joint Economic Committee and more directly through individual testimony and influence with lawmakers.[22]

Parties

Finally, although party organizations per se have little influence on economic policy, parties, seen as shared ideologies, shared interaction patterns, shared electoral fortunes and bodies that have an effect on policy makers' career prospects, do have an effect both in the Administration and in Congress. Both congressmen and potential members of administrations interact within party-based networks that reinforce the Democratic stress on growth and employment and the Republican stress on moderating inflation. Presidents of both parties pick their economic advisers from pools of businessmen, academics and economist entrepreneurs who generally agree on such things as the virtues of a mixed economy that stresses the private sector, the allowable policies with which to manipulate it and the general mix of economic goals. However, Republican presidents normally choose their advisers from Republican activists linked by policy research bodies such as the American Enterprise Institute. Similarily Democratic presidents choose their advisers from Democratic activists within the pool or from a similar Democratic network clustered around research groups such as the Brookings Institution. Party is also important in Congress. Both roll call analysis and more informal studies show greater party cohesion for voting on economic policy issues than on almost any other policy issues. Although cohesion on economic as on other issues is greatest among Republicans the difference between Northern and Southern Democrats is far less on economic than on social or agricultural issues.[23]

Although we have now briefly examined the institutions most important for macroeconomic policy making, a listing of influential institutions gives only the skeleton of the policy making process. It remains to flesh out the picture. In order to do so, we will examine the way in which policy makers view the inflation process, the broad coalitions between insititutions, the shifts over time in those coalitions and the process of exclusion from the policy arena. We will then look briefly at the institutional groupings which surround particular economic policies, before turning in the next chapter to examine the relations between leaders and members of some important groups.

Ideologies in the Policy Process

We saw in chapter 5 that the ordinary person does not have a very clear conception of the relation between economic variables and is particularly averse to the proposition that there are trade-offs in which progress on one front comes at the expense of retreat on another. The economic assumptions of the policy making elite are quite different. We will look first at the assumptions that are more or less shared by all the participants in the policy making process and then briefly at the ideological differences within that shared framework.

The first thing to note is that, although it is not always apparent from their public utterances, virtually all active participants in the process believe that there are trade-offs between the major economic goals and particularly between the goals of reducing unemployment and reducing inflation, though the extent of these trade-offs is disputed. Another characteristic of the process is the level at which debate takes place. A large part of the effective debate is conducted not by the leaders of the institutions mentioned earlier, but by their house economists. This has the effect of raising the ante for participation in policy making, helping consensus by ensuring that disagreement is filtered through a group with very similar training and making the policy choices opaque to the public. Another major difference between elite opinion and that of the public is the time frame in which it works. While the public, as we saw, concentrates on the very short-term effects of inflation, policy makers tend to think in terms of years rather than months and, with the possible exception of the pre-election period, are more concerned with long-term trends and business cycles than with short-term fluctuations. Overall then, we are in a different world, one where policy makers talk to each other in the language of economics and where the conceptualization of the economic process is considerably more sophisticated—if not always more accurate—than that of the public at large.

One should not get the idea however that economic policy is made in a spirit of harmony and consensus. Disagreement among policy makers is extensive. The basic pattern is a liberal ideology facing a conservative one, with the specific content of the opinions held under these labels undergoing steady change during the postwar period. Throughout the period it was true that liberals placed the greatest stress on lowering unemployment and conservatives were much more concerned with restraining inflation. As one might expect, liberals are much more inclined to stress the degree to which the economy can be positively manipulated by government policies and conservatives are much more inclined to downgrade the extent to which the economy can be improved by government policy and to point to "natural" limits to economic intervention. In practice, as we saw in chapter 2, this has often led to policies that resulted in business cycles when the conservative ideology was dominant, and either steady or runaway growth when the liberal ideology dominated.

Over time, both the liberal and the conservative ideologies have changed under the influence of changing economic theory and a changing economic environment. The liberals originally followed Keynesians, such as Hansen, and were primarily preoccupied with preventing a recurrence of the prewar depression with its attendant unemployment and with the general stimulation of demand, relying largely on fiscal policy. In the late 1950s and early 1960s the concern with unemployment was supplemented by a desire for steady growth, with inflation controlled by "fine tuning" of the economy and by wage-price controls. By the late 1960s when the choices were seen to be more inflation, or more growth and unemployment, the liberals were clearly in favor of trading off higher inflation for lower unemployment, generally holding that this choice was possible in the long run. In the mid-1970s many liberals, faced with stagflation, lost their faith that such a trade-off was possible, but nonetheless maintained their stress on moderating unemployment.

The conservative ideology has also evolved over the period. During the late 1940s and through the 1950s, conservatives stressed keeping inflation low by balancing the budget, following the "natural" business cycle and relying mainly on monetary policy to control the economy, with interest rates being the indicator to be watched. During the 1960s the need for a balanced budget was de-emphasized, the money supply replaced interest rates as the primary indicator, the new wage-price policies fell into disfavor and the acceptance of the doctrine that unemployment could be traded off for inflation led to an emphasis on trading somewhat higher unemployment for lower inflation. In the late 1960s and early 1970s most conservatives came to accept the monetarist doctrine that there was no long-term trade-off between inflation and unemployment and came to advocate steady growth at the "natural" rate of unemployment, a doctrine inaccurately labelled "the old time religion."[24] Toward the end of the 1970s some conservatives flirted with the version of supply side economics embodied in the Laffer curve, but this never became the dominant view among conservatives even after its official adoption by the Reagan administration.

The Coalitions[25]

We have looked at the participants in the policy process and at the ideological frameworks dominating the policy arena. It remains to combine these by showing the broad coalitions dominating macroeconomic policy making and the changes that have taken place in these coalitions.

The coalition process is found at three levels. At the first level, there is a general consensus on the rules of policy making, who should participate in the process and the limits that should inhibit policy making. The most important of these limits is agreement on the maintenance of what is generally called the "free enterprise system," by which is generally meant maintenance of private property and a somewhat oligopolistic industrial base. This first-level consensus is essentially a coalition of the "ins" against the "outs," whereby the participants logroll to protect each other's power bases. This process has been important in maintaining such things as the archaic congressional committee system, the distance of labor leadership from its constituency, the domination of monetary policy by the executive branch and bankers, free collective bargaining and a number of other practices. Substantively, it has resulted in a tacit agreement to ignore or downplay popular wishes when these wishes are "irrational" or overly "selfish," to increasingly rely on professional

economists to guide economic policy, to de-emphasize integrated economic planning, and to prefer "voluntary" methods of controlling the
economy to coercive ones, even if these former should be less efficient.

The Liberal Coalition

At the next level, we have broad conservative and liberal coalitions
holding the ideologies discussed above. Though the coalitions are fairly
loose, they are extraordinarily stable. Membership has not changed much
since 1947, although a few new groups have entered the coalitions and
there have been shifts in the relative importance of others.

At the heart of the liberal coalition are the politicians belonging to the
Democratic Party, and the leaders of the labor unions. Allied with these
are liberal citizens groups such as the Americans for Democratic Action,
Common Cause and Ralph Nader. Also allied with the liberal coalition is
the eastern intellectual establishment, spearheaded by academics from
the Brookings Institution, Harvard and Yale, and supported by the liberal
press—particularly the *New York Times*, the *Washington Post* and the
television news networks. In addition, the National Farmers Union, black
groups and welfare groups can usually be counted on to support liberal
economic legislation.

Among the federal agencies the most liberal departments—HEW and
HUD—are not very important in our area. The Department of Labor,
another generally liberal agency, is important primarily for manpower and
wage-price policy. The really important executive agencies and groups—
the Office of Management and Budget, the Council of Economic Advisers,
the Treasury and the White House staff—are among the more conservative of federal agencies but generally are in the liberal camp during
Democratic presidencies. Under both kinds of administrations there is a
tendency for the CEA to be the most liberal and the Treasury the most
conservative of these bodies.[26]

Congress has moved from being part of the conservative coalition in
the late 1940s and 1950s, to being part of the liberal coalition in the late
1960s and early 1970s and then to a more conservative stance in the late
1970s and early 1980s. Change in the committees has tended to lag behind
this, largely because of the seniority system. Further, the fact that seniority is most easily achieved by representatives of conservative one-party
areas has meant that for the bulk of the period committee leaders, particularly those on the Finance, Ways and Means and Appropriations committees, have been less liberal than senators and representatives as a
whole.

The Conservative Coalition

At the heart of the conservative coalition are business interests, particularly the old line interests represented by the National Association of Manufacturers, the U.S. Chamber of Commerce and the Republican Party politicians. Backing these up were the two major farm groups, particularly the American Farm Bureau Federation, and a group of old-line southern Democrats.

Intellectual support came from groups such as the American Enterprise Institute, the Heritage Foundation, right wing economists (particularly those at Chicago, UCLA and Michigan), the bulk of the nation's newspapers and from influential business publications such as *Business Week*, the *Wall Street Journal* and *Fortune*.

The presidency is part of the coalition during Republican administrations, during which time all major economic groupings within the executive branch are also part of the coalition. In addition, the Commerce Department and, to a lesser extent, the Treasury are often found in the conservative coalition even during Democratic administrations. The Federal Reserve can also generally be found in the conservative camp. This is invariably true during Republican administrations.

Congress, as we saw, has been a part of the conservative coalition at the beginning and, to a lesser extent, at the end of the period we are concerned with. However the key economic committees have been a conservative force for most of the period. Only the two labor committees have been outside the conservative coalition for a majority of the period.

Balance of Power

There has been considerable change in the strength of the two coalitions over the period. The long-term trend has been a decline in conservative strength and a rise in liberal strength. The move from farming into urban occupations has reduced the strength of the big farming organizations as well as the number of conservative congressmen in both the north and the south. There seems also to have been a slight long-term decrease in business influence and a shift in the balance of power within the business community. Thus the corporate-managerial philosophy represented by the Committee for Economic Development has gained at the expense of the old-line, anti-government, free-enterprise beliefs represented by the National Association of Manufacturers. Additionally, the rising educational level of the American people has been associated with a rise in the influence of the generally liberal academic community and a softening of the conservative attitudes of the nation's media—a change particularly noticeable in the relatively new medium of television. These changes have led not so much to a change in the numbers calling themselves liberal or conservative but to a change in what those terms mean. Although it is currently fashionable to point to liberal congressmen adopting conservative camouflage, the change in conservative attitudes has been greater in the long run.

Within this long-term trend there have been a number of medium-term influences. Predominant among these have been the effects of elections.

For most of the period power in Congress has been uneasily shared by the Democrats and a loose coalition of Republican and Southern Democratic congressmen generally referred to as the Conservative Coalition.[27] Elections have strengthened or weakened these two elements. Particularly important were the Republican victories in 1946, 1952 and 1980 and the influx of liberal Democrats in 1964 and 1966. Much more important however have been changes in administration, with Republican and Democratic presidents swinging many of the key policy making bodies into the conservative or liberal camp respectively.

The balance of power has also been affected by the creation of new institutions and by the occasional, but usually temporary, defection of old ones. An example of the latter phenomenon was the defection of the Teamsters Union during the Nixon administration. Examples of the former were the growing influence of television, the growth of the generally liberal consumer movement behind Ralph Nader and Common Cause, the growth of ideological, conservative Political Action committees, and the establishment of the budget committees. Lastly, particular policies have often split the coalition, with examples being labor's opposition to wage-price policy during the Nixon administration and Eisenhower's support for free trade during the 1950s.

The Major Policy Arenas

So far we have looked at macroeconomic policy making as a whole, at the participants, their ideologies and the broad coalitions. This however gives a somewhat misleading picture of the policy process. While it is true that those taking part in macroeconomic policy making are in some respects different from those in other policy areas and while it is true that there is some approximation to unified policy over the whole area, what makes American economic policy making distinctive is the degree to which macroeconomic policy emerges as the result of competition, compromise and contradiction between a number of semi-autonomous policy arenas—each dealing with a different aspect of economic policy, each with its own structure of power and each jealous of the others. These arenas are defined by the policies around which they form, with distinctive clusters around manpower policy, wage-price policy, monetary policy, expenditure policy and revenue policy.

Fiscal Policies

The single most powerful tool available for the management of the economy is fiscal policy.[28] In most countries fiscal policy is integrated so that revenues and expenditures are coordinated to achieve the desired effect on the economy and specific actions taken are balanced against one another to achieve a predetermined amount of stimulus or restraint. This happy situation is at best roughly approximated in the United States. Instead of a unified system the United States has separate systems for determining expenditures and revenues, with the co-ordination lying in the hands of a few rather weak groups. The major exception to this statement is the system of automatic stabilizers that has been built up since the 1930s. Mildly progressive tax rates act as a brake on the economy when inflation increases, while unemployment and other welfare payments pump money into the economy as it slows down. But these automatic stabilizers only compensate for 30 percent of the total economic change, leaving plenty of room for discretionary economic manipulation.

Expenditure Policy

The determination of government expenditures is an extraordinarily diffuse process. It is important in terms of overall stimulus to the economy both what total government spending is and how that spending is distributed by region and class. In the United States a large part of both decisions takes place at the state and local levels, with state and local spending rising from 36.8 percent of all government spending in 1950 to 43.5 percent in 1979.[29] One should note however that the federal government has some control over state and local spending through federal subsidies to various categories of spending. However, even if we concentrate on the federal level, input into decision making is very diffuse.

Figure 29 indicates roughly the major channels of influence in the expenditure policy process at the present time.[30] The reader should note that although the process has not varied greatly over the postwar period, the power of the expenditure subcommittees has increased over the period and there were no budget committees before 1974. Further, the diagram severely understates the complexity of the process. Bargaining goes on between all the participants at all stages of the process and a complex system of alliances further complicates the picture. Furthermore the diagrams completely leave out the equally complex alliances between those governmental subgroups, private interest groups and corporations in the various spending areas.

The complexity and instability of these relationships make it virtually impossible to regulate the distribution of government spending so as to allow easy movement in the stimulation of different parts of the economy, in accord with an overall plan. At best, bills can be proposed to stimulate

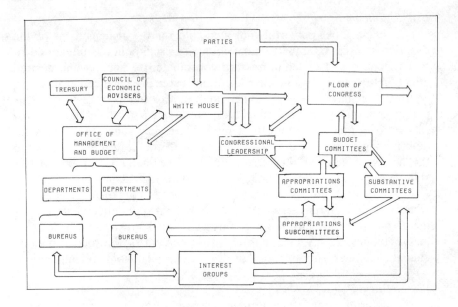

Figure 29   Major channels of influence for expenditure policy. The size of the box
                is meant to designate the relative importance of the institution and the
                width of the arrows the relative influence. Variation in both across time
                mean this is only a very rough guide. These qualifications apply also to
                figures 30 and 31.

a particular lagging economic sector, such as construction or public employment, but secondary effects on the economy are often ignored.

    Usually the best that can be done in this area is to specify an overall
dollar total for expenditures and try to keep spending within this. The
pattern is for the executive branch to recommend a total and for Congress
to alter it. Within the executive branch the decision is made through a
process of consultation between members of the troika and the White
House. The president is usually more active here than in other areas of
macroeconomic policy making. The use of the budget for stabilization
purposes is restricted by the long lead times prior to impact on the economy, by the fact that a majority of the items in the budget are mandated
spending, by the difficulty of getting major changes through Congress and
by the informal norm among government economists that one should
"avoid changes in government expenditures, because it is almost impossible to change them without sacrificing efficiency in resource allocation."[31] Nonetheless some attempt is usually made by presidents to use
the expenditure level as a stabilization tool, with Democratic administra-

tions often trying to expand the level and Republican administrations typically trying to reduce the level of government expenditure.

Once this request has been determined and allocated among the agencies, it goes to Congress, where it has usually been increased during Republican administrations and reduced during Democratic ones.

Within Congress the appropriations process was fragmented until the establishment of the Budget committees in 1974, with authority to set an overall spending total. Decisions on individual items were made by twelve specialized subcommittees of the House Appropriations Committee and reviewed and usually increased by the thirteen subcommittees of the Senate Appropriations Committee. Fragmentation was further increased by a long-term trend whereby the substantive committees removed increasing portions of the budget from the immediate control of the Appropriations committees, primarily through the creation of entitlement programs. Extensive pressure to increase particular items came from private interests, the agencies and programs, and members of congressional committees dealing with the subject area. What typically emerged from this process was an expenditure total uncoordinated with the revenue total and not ideal for regulating the economy.

Although it is too early to say for certain, the institution of the Budget committees seems to have altered this process a little,[32] making the political process in the appropriations arena somewhat more like Lowi's redistributive process and less like his distributive process.[33] The effect is to encourage coalitions, with the liberal coalition and the conservative coalition gaining power at the expense of their constituent parts.

Overall then the key institutions in the appropriations arena are the Office of Management and Budget, the White House, the two Appropriations committees and the two Budget committees, with continuing pressure from private interests for more spending in their area and strong ideological influence deriving from the party of the current administration. No group however can be said to have firm control of the process—a fact which has de-emphasized changes in appropriations as a regulatory method.

Revenue Policy

A much more common way of attempting to regulate the economy is through changes in revenue raising practices. Again, the control in the United States is less complete than in other countries. Sales and property taxes are essentially reserved for the state and local levels and tariffs have little importance in a country where imports are only 9 percent of GNP. Furthermore, of the three major taxes raised at the federal level—social security taxes, income taxes and corporate taxes—only the latter two are used extensively to regulate the economy. Social security taxes are treated

as insurance payments and are usually raised when social security payments are increased.

Changes in corporate and income taxes are of three types. One is the
steady increase in income tax receipts brought about as inflation moves
people into higher tax brackets. Although we have seen that this does not
result in steady revenue increases it does change the political balance in
the revenue raising area. By making increasing income taxes the status
quo, it obviates the need for the rate increases that would otherwise be
necessary and makes it possible for those powerful in the area to periodically reduce taxes without reducing long-term revenues. Second, there
are fairly regular but minor changes in such things as rates of depreciation
and income tax deductions, aimed at stimulating lagging sectors or providing mild overall stimulus or restraint to the economy. There are also
periodic major changes in the income tax rates, aimed at providing major
stimulus to avoid or correct recession or as a major restraint to an over-
heated economy. Though participants in making these two latter kinds
of tax change are roughly the same, their relative importance varies with
the impact of the proposed change.

Figure 30 shows the major actors and channels of influence in the
revenue policy process for major tax changes.[34] It is also the normal
process for the medium impact tax changes that take place on a yearly
basis. Although it does not provide an accurate description of the tax

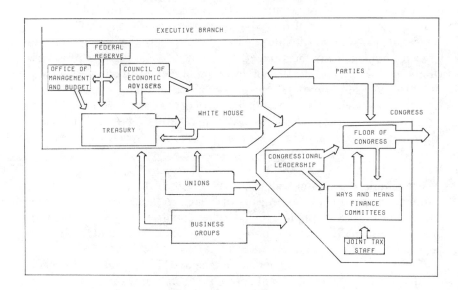

Figure 30   Major channels of influence for important tax changes

loophole changes that are the basis of most debate in this arena, it does provide a rough description of the process for those tax changes with the most impact on the economy. It is somewhat misleading however in de-emphasizing interest group influence in the process and in understating its complexity.

In the executive branch the troika is again the primary group for decision making. But instead of the Office of Management and Budget dominating, the Treasury is the most important agency. The Council of Economic Advisers is more important for revenue policy than expenditure policy but is still somewhat less important than the Treasury and the White House.

In Congress the Budget committees, despite their name, are not very important for tax policy. The primary power is held by the House Ways and Means Committee and the Senate Finance Committee, with the lead-ership of the two houses becoming important for major tax changes. Subcommittees are much less important in this area than in the appro-priations process although their importance has increased. The Ways and Means Committee has tended to be more important than the Senate Fi-nance Committee in the revenue process, though the replacement of Wil-bur Mills by Al Ullman, in 1975, reduced the difference considerably.

Private interests are also important in the revenue arena. Part of the process consists of a steady stream of particular tax changes, aimed at benefitting particular companies or industrial sectors and achieved through pressure from the businesses involved on members of the two congres-sional committees. The resulting special provisions are subject to periodic attacks by the liberal coalition, which sometimes manages to abolish some of them. Private interests also have a considerable voice on larger changes in tax laws, with the general rule being continual pressure from the unions and liberal academics to increase the deficit and from business and farm groups for restraint, although these latter would prefer that restraint to come about through lower government expenditures.[35] Private interests are important too for the occasional major tax changes. It is extraordi-narily difficult to enact a major change opposed by either labor or busi-ness.[36]

Our account so far may have overstated the flexibility in the revenue policy arena. Overall, the most obvious fact about the political system in this area is its resistance to change. Once a tax provision favoring some interest is incorporated into the tax code it is very difficult to remove it, even if the conditions that led to the passing of the provision have changed.[37] More importantly, major tax changes, such as the 1964 income tax re-duction or the 1968 tax surcharge, are difficult to pass and usually require a consensus building process that may take several years. The process works best for changes that affect the whole economy but not to a large degree, possibly because these changes are typically tax reductions.

Monetary Policy

The distinctive feature of monetary policy making in the United States is the degree to which control is vested in a single non-elected body and a single narrow interest. The body is the Federal Reserve Board of Governors—the apex of a system of twelve regional Federal Reserve Banks—charged by Congress in 1933 and 1935 with the regulation of the nation's money supply and the controlling of its banking system. The narrow interest is the banking and insurance industry, whose generally conservative pressure on the Federal Reserve and independent actions on such things as interest rate levels, has considerable effect on monetary policy.

Figure 31 shows the rough outlines of the policy process in this area. Formal power to control the nation's money supply is shared by a seven-member Board of Governors of the Federal Reserve and a twelve-member Federal Open Market Committee which comprises the seven governors plus the New York Bank president and four other regional bank presidents. The chairman of the Board of Governors is more powerful than the other members of these two bodies. The two bodies also pay considerable attention to the views of the twelve regional boards, especially the powerful New York Board which is traditionally somewhat more expansionary than the others. The banking industry is very important in setting the

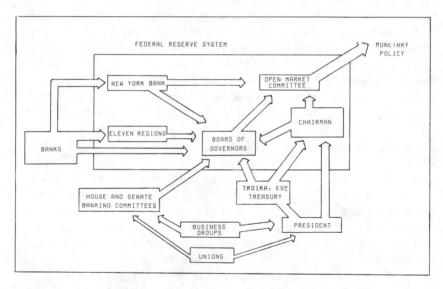

Figure 31   Major channels of influence for monetary policy making

general guidelines for monetary policy both because of its heavy representation on the federal and regional boards[38] and because monetary policy
requires the cooperation of the banking community if it is to work smoothly.

The Federal Reserve is unique among the important economic agencies
in being formally free from presidential control. Formally the Federal
Reserve is an independent body under the control of Congress, with board
members appointed by the president, subject to congressional confirmation, for fourteen-year terms. In practice however the president has somewhat more control than Congress. The banking committees in the two
houses of Congress can and do apply pressure but, despite occasional
threats, leave their formal control in abeyance.[39] The president on the
other hand can exercise some control through appointment authority,
because turnover makes the average term of a governor nine rather than
fourteen years, and through his partial ability to counteract the effects of
monetary policies he dislikes through fiscal measures.[40] Exactly how much
power the president has over the Federal Reserve is controversial, but
the bulk of the literature asserts his influence is substantial.

Despite its great measure of formal independence, the Federal Reserve
in fact determines monetary policy in consultation with the members of
the troika. Of these by far the most important is the Treasury, which,
through its power to finance the national debt by issuing securities, is the
second most important institution in the monetary policy arena. It can
and has negated Federal Reserve attempts to restrict the money supply,
notably during the Truman administration.[41] Cooperation between the
Federal Reserve and the troika comes about, not just because of the power
of the Treasury to offset Federal Reserve actions, but because both fiscal
and monetary policies become much more effective when co-ordinated.
This is not to say that this is always the case, and there have been times,
particularly under the Truman and Nixon administrations, when the Federal Reserve has followed an independent economic course, with the aim
of forcing the administration to adjust its policies in the direction of more
restraint. The more normal relation however, is one of week-to-week
consultation between the troika and the Federal Reserve to coordinate
policies, with the troika being typically somewhat more important than
the Federal Reserve in determining the broad policy outlines to be followed.[42]

As was mentioned earlier, the Senate and House Banking and Currency
committees are fairly ineffectual in the monetary policy area, with heavy
pressure coming from the committees only at times, like 1956 and 1966,
when the troika and the Federal Reserve disagree.[43] Even then the pressure is rarely effective. More important is the role of private interests.
Preeminent here are the views of the financial community, primarily bankers, which plays both a direct role, through its members in positions of

authority in the Federal Reserve System and the Treasury, and an indirect role through the pressure it can apply. The big union, business and farm groups have very little influence on monetary policy. This is a position quite different from that in the other economic arenas, and is one of the reasons monetary policy is so important in the United States.[44] Those groups do however give some indirect support or opposition to Federal Reserve policies, that may play some minor limiting role. The most important group, other than the financial community, is the academic community. The intellectuals effect changes in prevailing economic theories about the relation of the money supply to the economy, apply pressure in the media and journals and work directly, through the administrative role that academics such as Arthur Burns play, in monetary policy formulation. Although economists specializing in monetary theory are generally more conservative than other economists, they are somewhat less so than the bankers, who form the other major internal influence on the Federal Reserve.

Overall then, the major feature of the monetary policy arena is its domination by the Federal Reserve. The Treasury and the other troika members have considerable influence and the financial and academic communities have some influence too. It should be noted that the removal of monetary policy from the delaying influence of federal agencies, Congress and the major pressure groups, has long ensured it a much more dominant role in the total economic process than is normal in other countries.

Wage-Price Policy

Wage-price policy—using controls or persuasion to directly limit increases in wages or prices—is one that has been used less often and more hesitantly in the United States than in other developed countries. It was used in the 1942-1946 and 1950-1953 periods and in the 1971-1974 period. In addition, voluntary wage-price guidelines were adopted by the Kennedy and Johnson administrations in the 1962-1966 period. In comparison with programs in other countries, United States efforts were marked by the degree of voluntarism, concentration on prices rather than wages, and the selective nature of the controls in terms of the sectors of the economy and the size of firms concerned.

Wage-price policy is different from the areas we have so far examined, both in the relation between the president and Congress and in the direct role of the major interest groups in administering the policy. The relation between the president and Congress is interesting because it is one of very few legislative areas where initiative is as likely to come from Congress as from the president. Two of the four times the policy has been adopted, Congress passed standby authority enabling the president to impose controls when he saw fit, without the president asking for this authority.[45] In addition, on all four occasions Congress has played a reasonably active part in the development of the policy. This is due largely to three things. The first is that there is no permanent executive agency with a stake in promoting wage-price policy. As a result the policy is invariably administered by special temporary boards.[46] Second, wage-price policy is the province of the relatively liberal banking and labor committees—both more likely to recommend action than inaction. Last, as we saw in figure 26, the policies, at the times they are recommended, are generally politically popular.

A much more important feature of the wage-price arena is the direct role of business and labor. The nature of this role varies with the degree of voluntarism of the program. When a program is in its voluntary stage there is often direct pressure brought by the president on key sectors and sometimes even key firms or unions on those sectors.[47] When a policy is broader and includes guidelines for wage or price increases, there is usually considerable consultation and communication between the wage-price board that is typically established and the major interest groups, as well as with the individual firms or unions involved in particular cases. When a policy becomes mandatory and involves tight control of industry or labor, there is usually some attempt to devolve some authority for enforcement and lower level policy decisions onto a committee of representatives from business and labor.[48]

More important than these positive contributions of business and labor are their negative contributions. Neither business nor labor likes wage-price policy. It interferes with the ability of business to choose prices that will maximize profits, as well as labor's ability to secure wage increases in line with inflation. In addition, wage-price policy is inconsistent with the free enterprise and collective bargaining practices that bolster the current institutional arrangements within the business and labor sectors. This steady opposition, and the generally negative reviews from economists reared in the competitive pricing tradition, account in large part for the fact that wage-price policy has not been used for most of the postwar period, for the reluctance to use mandatory controls when it is implemented and for its increasing ineffectiveness if used over long periods.[49]

The pattern of forces described above typically results in a pattern of cyclical activity in this arena. Most of the time labor and business combine forces to prevent wage-price policy. When the rate of inflation begins to increase, however, wage-price policy becomes more popular with the public and it is instituted by the president, sometimes after considerable congressional prompting, usually according to one of two patterns. The first is a very strict policy, with an enforcement board that is accepted by labor and business for a short while. It then meets increasing resistance and is gradually scaled down, until finally abandoned amidst cries of failure.[50] The other pattern is for the policy to begin in a mild form, possibly even voluntarily, and gradually tighten up as business and labor find ways to slip through the mild restrictions.[51] It then follows the pattern described above.

Manpower Policy

Although manpower policy is the least important of the policies used to affect the inflation/unemployment trade-off, this is not an intrinsic characteristic. As we saw in chapter 2, it is the only policy tool that all economic schools can support and it has been successfully integrated into macroeconomic policy in other countries—most notably Sweden. Its unimportance in the United States as an economic tool is largely due to the fact that it has generally been considered a "distributive"[52] welfare policy[53] and that it has become enmeshed in the contradictions of United States federalism. In addition, the forces that control the arena have a vested interest in preventing innovation within their bureaucracies, preventing the establishment of rival programs and not allowing the consolidation necessary for successful economic manipulation.[54]

The chief loci of power in the area are the recesses of the federal bureaucracy, congressional labor committees, relevant appropriations subcommittees, big urban spokesmen and spokesmen for certain disadvantaged groups, mainly from the federal poverty programs. In addition business and the unions play a somewhat indirect though largely negative role. When discussing manpower policy it is important to bear in mind that since the 1960s there has been little disagreement that some form of manpower program is necessary. There has however been constant disagreement on how much should be spent, what kind of manpower program is preferable, and who should administer manpower programs.[55]

Within the federal bureaucracy the key department is the Labor Department. Since the early 1960s a struggle for control of the manpower programs has been going on between the secretary, who has an interest in expanding and controlling the newer manpower programs, and the old line Employment Service (ES), which supervises the State Employment Security system and has jurisdiction over the unemployment insurance and employment services programs. The secretary's allies include the agency staff and the new bureaus, such as OMAT (Office of Manpower Automation and Training) and OFMS (Office of Financial and Management Services), within the agency. In this struggle the secretary has generally had mild support from the White House. The ES has been supported by congressional committees, by the business-dominated state employment agencies and their lobbying arm—the Interstate Conference of Employment Security Agencies—and by the old-line Bureau of Apprenticeship and Training with its craft and building-trade union base.[56]

As well as fighting internally, the Labor Department was also battling OEO and HEW, particularly the old-line Office of Education, Vocational Division, and its lobbying arm—the American Vocational Association. In their struggles in and out of Congress, the Labor Department generally had union and some business support, HEW the support of local education forces and OEO support from minority and poverty groups. The interagency struggles for jurisdiction, carried on at all levels, led initially to the formation of a hierarchy of local, state and regional inter-agency committees called the Cooperative Area Manpower Planning System and later to the passage of the Comprehensive Employment and Training Act with its system of local prime sponsors responsible for deciding the local mix of programs. Although this, together with the virtual abolition of OEO under Nixon, did something to reduce overlap, it did little to resolve disputes.[57]

Also important are the House Committee on Education and Labor, particularly its Manpower, Compensation and Health and Safety subcommittees; the House Appropriations subcommittees on Labor, Health, Education and Welfare; the Senate Committee on Labor and Public Welfare, especially its Employment-Poverty and Migratory Labor subcommittee; and the Senate Appropriations subcommittee on Labor, Health, Education and Welfare. These various committees and subcommittees have been dominated by old-line liberal AFL-CIO supporters and could generally be relied on to push for appropriations for manpower legislation, whether or not the current administration wanted them. They also tend to support the old-line bureaus against their newer rivals. However, the ascension of Orin Hatch to the chairmanship of the Senate Labor and Human Resources Committee in 1981 considerably reduced the congressional support base for manpower programs.

Other major actors are big city mayors and minority groups, who generally unite to demand more extensive programs with local control, but divide over the issue of community or city control. Both tend to see manpower programs as another welfare program, while the mayors also view it as a form of revenue sharing.

This enumeration leaves out the actors who restrain the manpower program from growing faster than it has. Although most labor economists and manpower specialists are "positive" toward manpower programs, their generally negative evaluation of the success of current programs[58] has been picked up by business publications and newspapers and repeated in congressional testimony. This tends both to restrict the overall growth of manpower policy and to encourage the proliferation of new and underfunded programs, rather than the expansion of old ones. In addition, manpower policy must compete for funds before the Office of Management and Budget and the Appropriations committees, and although these are not hostile per se, they must balance manpower program needs against the needs of other programs. On a more negative note there are conservative congressmen in the Rules and Appropriations committees who feel that the rather limited success of current programs is the result of interfering with more efficient free enterprise mechanisms. These conservative congressmen have on occasion held up or defeated manpower program bills. Lastly, we should remember that the manpower program is essentially a Democratic policy whose primary beneficiaries are naturally Democrats. Republican administrations have ranged from the hostility of the Eisenhower administration to the general indifference of the Nixon administration.

Given the conglomeration of forces working on all levels and in all sections of the federal system, it is hardly surprising that manpower policy has emerged as a welter of contradictory programs, under the supervision of different bodies, delivering benefits to different clienteles. Largely because of this it is impossible to include manpower in a coordinated macroeconomic program even if top policy makers wished to do so. Thus the actual thrust of the program has made it more of a disguised welfare program and a counter-cyclical revenue-sharing program than a method of easing base-level unemployment.

Excluded Groups

We have looked in some detail at the institutions and groups that are influential in making economic policy, at their attitudes, at the coalitions between them and at the specialized economic policy areas where they wield the most influence. But in order to fully understand the bases of power in economic policy making it is also important to look at the groups that are excluded. Only by so doing can we perceive the larger processes serving to distribute economic power in the society, and thereby test the models presented in chapter 1.

Many groups and institutions have little power in macroeconomic policy making. Obviously we are not interested in all of them since there are many which have no reason to help make economic policy. But some seem to have good reasons for intervening in the process, yet fail to do so. Here we will briefly examine groups that ought to be important if various of the models in chapter 1 are correct. We will then look briefly at some reasons why these groups do not play a significant role in the policy making process.

What I have termed the group model would lead us to expect the emergence of specialized groups around particularly salient problems.

Yet, despite the fact that inflation has existed and has been perceived as a major problem for over thirty years, no specialized group—let alone one with any power—has emerged to fight it. The groups that might seem at first to be nearest to what pure pluralist theory would demand are consumer groups. These have indeed grown more important in recent years with the emergence of Common Cause and Ralph Nader and the National Taxpayers Union. It is possible that rapid inflation has contributed somewhat to this growth. But it is notable that neither these new groups nor the older ones, such as the Consumer Federation of America or the Consumers Union, have played any real part in the macroeconomic policy making which determines the rate of inflation. Indeed there is some evidence both that they do not want to take part in the process and that even if they did, they would be more inclined to emphasize lower unemployment than lower inflation.[59]

The pluralist-democratic model, which it is our primary concern to test, would also lead us to expect certain excluded groups to take a larger part in economic policy making. These are groups representing the poor, the self-employed, white-collar occupations and debtors. Of these, debtors are virtually unorganized, the self-employed and white-collar occupations have very little representation and the poor virtually none. All of these it should be noted, lack a peak group to speak for their overall interests.

In some ways debtors are the most interesting of these underrepresented groups. As we have seen, bankers—the prime creditors group—are heavily represented in the macroeconomic policy process. But debtors, who have more than anyone else to gain from unanticipated inflation, have almost no representation. Even obvious subgroups such as home owners have remained essentially unorganized.

The self-employed, on the other hand, are not unorganized. The three major farm groups, the National Federation of Independent Businessmen and groups like the American Medical Association, representing the self-employed, all take positions on macroeconomic policy and testify before congressional committees. Their influence is however minimal in this area, despite the considerable influence they can exert on policies more directly affecting the farm sector or small business.

White-collar workers have even less influence than the self-employed. The professional workers groups, such as the American Bar Association and the National Education Association, play no part in economic policy making. Managers groups, such as the American Management Association and the National Management Association, also play little direct part in the macroeconomic policy process—although, as Monsen and Cannon point out,[60] the Committee for Economic Development represents the managerial ideology to some extent. Finally the lower level white-collar occupations are underorganized in comparison with blue-collar occupations. Only government workers, retail clerks and musicians have significant representation and this mainly through a handful of white-collar unions such as AFSCME, AFGE, AFM, APWU, RCIA and the AFT.[61] These unions—all AFL-CIO affiliated—are not very united among themselves and their interests tend to be subordinated within the AFL-CIO to the numerically dominant blue-collar unions. As a result, they play little discernible part in macroeconomic policy making.

The most obvious absence from the arena of macroeconomic policy making is that of groups representing the poor. As with the other interests reviewed in this section there is no peak group representing the poor or all welfare recipients. Instead we find separate groups representing women, blacks, Spanish Americans, the aged and public welfare recipients. Only the black groups, such as the NAACP, the National Urban League, the SCLC, Operation Push, the Minority Coalition and the Black Caucus, have been at all successful in organizing their constituency. It is these groups that play the largest part in macroeconomic policy making. But this role, though expanding, is not yet significant outside the manpower policy area. Groups such as the National Council of Senior Citizens and the American Society of Retired Persons, the National Welfare Rights Organization (NWRO) and various church groups, which represent those on welfare; and the League of Women Voters and the National Organization for Women, either do not attempt to take part in macroeconomic policy or, like the NWRO, are not successful in their attempts. In view of our earlier findings that inflation has heavy negative short-term effects on welfare recipients and that fixed-income recipients see themselves as worse hit than any other group by inflation, this is a somewhat anomalous finding for the pluralist-democratic model.

What then explains the lack of influence of the various groups enumerated above? Though no answer can be complete, four factors probably provide most of the explanation. One factor that is particularly important in explaining the absence of debtors and consumer groups is information costs. As Downs points out, if one has the choice of organizing around one's consumer or producer interests, it is rational to organize around the latter.[62] This is because the costs involved in finding out what consumer interests are and in organizing people in a like situation to defend them are much higher than for organizing around producer interests. Also, because producer interests have a more concentrated impact on the individual, the logic of collective action indicates that the balance of costs and benefits attendant upon group action is more likely to be favorable when a group organizes around producer interests.[63]

A second major factor, especially for the poor, is that many excluded groups are characterized by limited resources with multiple demands on those resources. Thus welfare groups, whose clientele have numerous problems, have not managed to organize a large proportion of their potential membership. In any case their members are poorer, less likely to vote[64] and lack prestige in society. And although white-collar workers suffer from none of these defects, their representative groups have succeeded in enrolling only a very small percentage of the potential membership.[65] Furthermore, most of the subcategories among the poor are led by a number of small groups with non-overlapping memberships rather than by one or two peak associations, thus ensuring a further weakening of the resource base. This is particularly important when we remember that the level of debate on macroeconomic policy demands considerable expenditure for economists and other specialized and costly staff.

Another reason why many of these groups lack influence is that the logic of specialization acts against them. Their primary reason for organizing, in many cases, bears little relation to macroeconomic policy. This means both that their resources are not suitable for influencing macroeconomic policy and that success in this arena is less likely to expand membership or increase support from existing members.

A corollary is that few of these organizations occupy positions of economic power. Whereas cooperation from banks or labor unions is often essential to the success of economic policy, it matters less what welfare recipients or debtors do.

Finally it seems reasonable that, with low resources and specialized access channels, it may be far more rational for a group to seek compensation for inflation rather than attempt to alter the policy itself. This strategy is of particular use to the aged, the poor, white collar workers and the non-farm self-employed. But it could be one of the primary reasons why a strong consumer interest opposed to inflation has failed to emerge.

The reader should note that although these four explanations have sometimes been used in other contexts by self-professed pluralists, their logic is elitist. They all provide rational reasons why only a small part of the population will be able to influence policy making in an area of central importance to all citizens.

Conclusion

In the first sections of this chapter we looked at the pattern of macroeconomic policy making. We saw a large number of groups were important, some of them part of the formal governmental system and some of them part of the various "private" interests. Certain groups we saw as more important for some kinds of economic policy than for others, with power often being dependent on the necessity for that group's cooperation if there was to be effective policy making. Some groups we saw were potent over the whole range of economic policies, with broad liberal and conservative coalitions linking both these and other more specialized groups in a reasonably effective aggregation of elite group interests. Finally we saw that many interests with a considerable stake in economic policy outcomes had little or no influence in the policy making process.

7   Interest, Opinion
       and Representation

The relation between the objective interest of citizens, those citizens' opinions concerning which policies should be pursued and the actions and opinions of citizens' representatives lies at the heart of political theory. A number of variations are possible. The most straightforward is what is generally referred to as "representation," where the leader acts as his constituency would want him to. Another is what is generally referred to as "leadership," where the representative, possibly because of superior information, makes a decision contrary to the one his constituents would desire, but which conforms to the long-term real interests of his constituents. In political theories that predicate substantial democracy it is generally assumed that the "leadership" representative needs to, indeed will, persuade his constituents of the correctness of his view. A third variant is "statesmanship," where the representative sacrifices the real interests of his constituency in favor of a larger and more important group—generally one of which the members of his constituency are a part. A final variant is "organizational maintenance," in which real policy interests of the constituents are sacrificed to the imperatives of maintaining the organizational status quo or of keeping a particular leader in power.[1] It should be noted that when any of the last three variants describes the constituency/representative relationship, the representative has two choices in explaining his actions. He can explain the reasons for his actions in a way that would educate his constituents and persuade them that such actions were necessary. Or he can attempt to make constituents believe inaccurately that his actions conform

175

to their desires. This is often done, as Edelman points out, by stressing a symbolic victory while de-emphasizing a real defeat.[2]

In this chapter we will attempt to link our earlier analysis of the real effects of inflation on five occupational groups, and the opinions of those in those groups, with the actions and opinions of interest groups which represent those population groupings. We will look first at the profit sector and the self-employed, and then at salary earners, wage earners and welfare recipients.

The Profit Sector

Interest groups which represent profit receivers are of two types. One, which includes the National Association of Manufacturers, the United States Chambers of Commerce and the American Bankers Association, are groups that perceive themselves primarily as representatives, using the classical business ideology held by most businessmen as their base, and trying to move policy in that direction. These organizations are generally more concerned with acting as their constituents would desire than with ensuring that the policies which they support actually benefit the business community, although they generally believe both approaches to be synonymous. The other, in which the Business Roundtable, the Business Council[3] and the Committee for Economic Development are the most prominent organized interest groups, perceive themselves more as leaders, with occasional essays into statesmenship. Monsen and Cannon see this latter category as representing a managerial ideology and the first category as representing the business ideology.[4] But it would probably be more accurate to think of this second category as representing major corporations interested in maximizing actual profits over the long term and the first as primarily representing businesses outside the 100 major corporations and more intent on preserving its constituents' ideas of a free enterprise system.

As might be expected, the two groupings hold rather different attitudes toward macroeconomic policy. Business groups take the general position that less government is better government and, as such, are proponents of a balanced budget and reduced government income and expenditures, particularly expenditures. When it comes to the relative emphasis to be placed on growth, reducing unemployment and reducing inflation, they seem prepared to make great sacrifices on the unemployment front and some sacrifices on the growth front to keep inflation in check.[5] In addition when balance of payments problems loom, they are prepared to make some sacrifice in terms of other goals to keep the payments account in balance.[6]

Less worried about a government role in the economy and more inclined to believe in planning, the corporate groups have accepted Keynesian countercyclical policy and the resulting deficits, although in recent years they have edged toward a more monetarist stance. They do not however like deficits to get too large, or government spending to increase too rapidly.[7] When weighing the goals of reducing inflation, reducing unemployment and increasing growth, the corporate groupings place somewhat less emphasis than business groups on reducing inflation, a great deal more on increasing growth and somewhat more on reducing unemployment.[8] These modifications seem at least partially spurred by their feeling that profits increase most when growth is fastest and that high levels of unemployment breed discontent with the system.[9]

Having looked at the policy positions of the two groupings it remains to see what the relation of these positions is to the views and experiences of their constituents. Unfortunately it is not possible to get a proper sample of the views of large profit receivers with available data. We can however approximate by using data from the 1969 Michigan Consumer Survey broken down by categories of shareholding. Table 30 shows the degree to which the various categories of shareholders thought themselves adversely affected by inflation. As we can see, the more shares held by respondents the less likely they are to see themselves as hurt by inflation, with those owning over $25,000 in shares only half as likely as those with no shares to see themselves as seriously hurt by inflation. This is despite the fact that shareholders are likely to be older than the rest of the population. It should be noted that this finding—which is not very consistent with our finding in tables 1 and 2 that inflation has a moderately negative

Table 30   Perceived Harm from Inflation by Those Owning Different Share Values in 1969

Value of shares	Perceived harm from inflation				
	None	A little	Much	Very much	N
$25,000 plus	31.7%	51.7%	11.7%	5.0%	(60)
$10,000–24,999	19.0	59.5	14.3	7.1	(42)
$2,000–9,999	16.4	64.8	9.8	9.0	(122)
$1–1,999	10.6	63.5	9.4	16.5	(85)
No shares	11.6	56.8	14.5	17.1	(1084)

The question was, "Would you say that you and your family were hurt by inflation very much, a little, or not at all?"

Kendall's Tau $C = -0.072$ Significance $= 0.001$

Source: *Survey of Consumer Finances* (Ann Arbor: University of Michigan), Fall 1969.

short-term influence on profits or with Feldstein's position that inflation depresses stock prices[10]—points to some degree of money illusion possibly arising from failure to conrol for the effect of inflation on inventories and depreciation.

It is also interesting to look at the opinions on policy held by shareholders. Table 31 shows gamma values obtained from the contingency tables running shareholdings against various policy preferences. As we can see, this yields a picture which, while not radically so, is different from that of the general public for certain policies. These differences appear to conform with Monson and Cannon's classical business ideology[11] or Sutton and his associates' business creed.[12] Shareholders are more likely than non-shareholders to favor tax increases, presumably to help in balancing the budget, and are somewhat more enthusiastic about reducing government spending. In line with the business creed's enthusiasm for monetary policy, they are more likely to support increases in interest rates to control inflation. Furthermore, while they are more likely than non-shareholders to advocate voluntary changes in spending and borrowing to control inflation, they are much less likely to support wage or price controls both of which involve direct government control of the economy. Similar opinions seem to be held by business executives. A 1977 poll shows 75 percent of business executives think a balanced federal budget essential even if it results in lower government benefits or increased taxes, compared with only 47 percent of the general public. Likewise whereas only 46 percent of the general public agreed that keeping inflation under

Table 31   Degree of Share Ownership and Support for Selected Anti-inflation Policies in 1969

Policy	Gamma
Raise income taxes	.2760
Raise interest rates	.1919
Reduce government spending	.0545
Consumers spend less	.1957
Consumers borrow less	.1734
Government control prices	− .2920
Government control wages	− .1643
Inflation inevitable	− .2852

The cutoff points for shareholding were the same as in table 69. The question was, "Here is a list of things which, some people say, should be done to slow down inflation. First, do you agree or disagree that (first item) . . . ? (second item) . . . ?"

Source: *Survey of Consumer Finances* (Ann Arbor: University of Michigan), Fall 1969.

control is necessary even if it results in higher unemployment, 81 percent of business executives agreed.[13]

Turning from opinions to the actual effects of inflation on profits, it is clear that what we consider those effects to be depends on whether we think businessmen look at the long- or short-term effects. In the short term the relative effect of inflation appears moderately negative. This, combined with the moderately positive effects of unemployment, appears to outweigh the positive effects of GNP growth, giving profit receivers reason to support deflationary policies. In the longer term the effect of inflation appeared not to be negative at all, giving less reason for such a policy emphasis, unless businessmen were less concerned with the absolute level of profits than their relative size over the long run.

This brief summary of attitudes and of the relation of profits to other economic variables seems to show that business groups generally represent the interests as well as the opinions of their constituents. It is clear that the anti-government, pro-balanced budget and pro-monetary policy views of business groups are aimed at producing policies that will both satisfy those groups' constituents and increase profits. The somewhat greater emphasis on growth by the corporate groups is consistent with the known tendency of corporate executives to emphasise long-term growth and profits over short-term profits.

It should be clear that the linkages between the different stages in the profit sector do provide a reasonable fit to the pluralist-democratic model. The postulated ability to convert interests into demands and demands into representation does appear to exist in this sector.

The linkage pattern also however fits the Marxist and elitist models. It will be recalled that Marxist models postulate that only the capitalist class is able to secure effective representation, while elitist models see corporate leaders as the major component of the elite, and hence as properly situated to represent their own interests. However, the fact that inflation has been increasing in the face of business opposition to it does not seem easy to reconcile with the elitist model and can be reconciled with the traditional Marxist model only if we assume that capitalists are more interested in maintaining their relative position than maximizing their short-term profits. It seems somewhat more consistent with structuralism. On this view unemployment is a positive goal, serving to weaken the power of labor; inflation is a last ditch method of removing labor's gains, and growth is something that must sometimes be sacrificed to maintain control of the economy. In this context the different emphases of the corporate and business groupings can be viewed as a division of labor in which the larger, more complex business groups carry out the basic tasks of representing the interests of business, and the smaller, more flexible corporate groups adapt their postures to the realities of the political environment.

The Self-employment Sector

There is no single group claiming to speak for all self-employed persons. Instead there are separate groups representing the three major categories of self-employed persons—farmers, professionals and small businessmen. Two of these categories, self-employed businessmen and farmers, have declined drastically as a percentage of the work force in the postwar period. Thus between 1958 and 1972, self-employed small businessmen shrank from 5.62 percent to 2.08 percent of the labor force and farmers shrank from 4.89 percent to 2.10 percent of the labor force. This reduction in the constituencies of small business and farm groups seems to have decreased their influence in macroeconomic policy making, which was never in any case a major area of activity for these groups.

On most matters the three major farm groups, the American Farm Bureau Federation (AFBF), the National Grange (NG), and the American Farmers Union (AFU) are strung out in an ideological chain with the AFBF on the right, the AFU on the left and the NG in the center.[14] But on macroeconomic policy the AFBF and the NG have a virtually identical approach, one very similar to the classical business ideology of balanced budget,[15] low government spending,[16] low inflation,[17] and a "natural" rate of unemployment. The AFU, on the other hand, emphasizes high growth rates and high levels of employment, and while not in favor of inflation, tends to de-emphasize it. It is also much more open to Keynesian economic policy and is prepared to countenance unbalanced budgets.[18]

Small businessmen do not have strong independent representation, in part because on most matters the Chambers of Commerce and the National Association of Manufacturers represent their views fairly well. Easily the largest of several small groups is the National Federation of Independent Business, a group that has taken a somewhat spasmodic role in macroeconomic policy making, more in public than in private. Although it has differences with the major business groups on such matters as antitrust policy, it takes a very similar position on macroeconomic policy, with views that are perhaps just a little more conservative than those of business generally.[19]

The self-employed professionals are essentially without representation in the area of macroeconomic policy making. Although they have strong groups such as the American Bar Association, the American Medical Association, and the American Institute of Certified Public Accountants representing them, these groups have no impact on macroeconomic policy and on the whole have no position on the major policy choices.

Overall then, groups representing the self-employed tend to hold positions not very different from the classical business ideology, with the

NFU, the smallest of the major farm organizations, and some smaller black business groups being virtually the only exceptions. The control of inflation is heavily emphasized, while expanding growth and decreasing unemployment are not given high priority.

This ideology does not have a close fit to the opinions of the self-employed as to the appropriate policies to be followed, but neither is it completely inconsistent with them. As we saw in table 14, the self-employed are a little more likely than the other groups to favor controlling government spending and are more likely than wage earners or the welfare pool to favor raising taxes and interest rates to fight inflation, although a large majority opposes both measures. They also oppose price controls though less strongly than salary earners. As can be seen, this complex of views is not inconsistent with the classical business ideology.

What is inconsistent with it however is the degree to which they see themselves as adversely affected by inflation. As we can see in table 32, both self-employed businessmen and farmers are less likely than most other groups to see themselves as being harmed by inflation. Only 10.6 percent of self-employed businessmen and 9.1 percent of farmers saw

Table 32   Perceived Harm from Inflation in 1969

Occupational category	Perceived harm from inflation				
	None	A little	Much	Very much	N
Shareholders	25.4%	57.0%	11.4%	6.1%	(114)
Self-employed businessmen	15.2	63.6	10.6	10.6	(66)
Farmers	15.9	56.8	18.2	9.1	(44)
Professionals/technicians	12.4	67.5	10.1	10.1	(169)
Managers/officials	12.0	61.3	9.3	17.3	(75)
Clerks/sales workers	10.6	64.5	11.3	13.5	(141)
Craftsmen/foremen	10.4	53.8	16.5	19.2	(182)
Operatives	11.0	66.0	13.6	9.4	(191)
Laborers/service workers	13.5	48.1	14.3	24.1	(133)
Fixed-income under 65	10.4	49.6	18.4	21.6	(125)
Fixed-income over 65	13.3	49.4	13.9	23.4	(158)

The question was, "Would you say that you and your family were hurt by inflation very much, a little, or not at all?"

Raw chi-square = 71.787 Significance = 0.001

Source: *Survey of Consumer Finances* (Ann Arbor: University of Michigan), Fall 1969.

themselves as being very much hurt by inflation as compared to 15.6 percent of the population as a whole, although given the small number in each group we should not regard these results as firm proof.

The fact that the self-employed are both less inclined than other groups to see inflation as a major threat, and more inclined toward deflationary policies, would seem less contradictory if deflation held fewer perils for them than for others. At first sight this seems plausible. One of the aims juxtaposed against inflation by policy making elites, that of full employment, clearly is much less relevant to the self-employed than to employees. But offsetting this is the accelerated rate of business failure during recessions, and the fact that the income of the self-employed like that of other groups falls during recessions.[20] Farmers too normally lose in recessionary periods and gain during growth periods, but world price levels for agricultural products are a more important determinant of income.

If the opinions of the self-employed as to the extent they are being harmed by inflation do not seem to fit in with the opinions of their representatives, the actual effects of inflation provide only a marginally better fit. While table 1 did show a moderately negative short-term effect of inflation on the income of self-employed businessmen, table 2 showed a decline in this effect in the more recent period when inflation was higher. Further, farmers' incomes are positively rather than negatively correlated with inflation both in the period as a whole and in the more recent period. This relative freedom from harm, combined with the negative growth effects and the opinion data on effects of inflation on respondents' families, points to a set of real, perceived interests quite different from the policy views of the self-employed and their representatives.

What do these results mean in terms of our models? The first conclusion is that one crucial precondition of a pluralist-democratic system is met here. The groups do, by and large, represent the policies that their members favor.[21] A second crucial precondition, that the self-employed be aware of the actual effects of inflation on them, seems also to be roughly met. But a third crucial precondition, that the self-employed's solutions to the problem embrace their interests, seems to be violated. In fact the ideology put forward by the self-employed and their representatives seems to bear very little relation to their real economic interests. As in the profit sector, a Marxist or elitist explanation seems a more economical way of explaining the facts. According to these theories an ideology propagated by big business to protect its long-term interests is picked up and held by the petite bourgeoisie owing to their similar relation to the factors of production. This happens even though big business is remorselessly driving them into the ranks of the wage and salary earners. Thus, the actions of the interest groups representing the self-employed bear only marginal relevance to the real needs of their constituents.

The Wage Sector

As we saw earlier, labor's representation in the bargaining over macro-economic policy is much more monolithic than that of other sectors. Although many individual unions have their own lobbyists in Washington and their own ways of persuading particular congressmen to vote their way, most of the effort on major economic issues is coordinated by the legislative division of the AFL-CIO,[22] with the research division of the AFL-CIO researching and presenting testimony.[23] This does not stop other unions from taking part in economic policy formation, with the UAW, the United Steelworkers and the Ladies Garment Workers playing a particularly prominent part.[24] But their testimony and pressure is almost invariably coordinated with that of the AFL-CIO and even the defection of the UAW in 1968 did not halt cooperation in this area.[25]

The distinctive feature of labor's attitude toward macroeconomic policy is its emphasis on employment. Although growth is regarded as highly desirable, it is seen more as something ancillary to high employment, than as a distinct alternative goal.[26] The labor policy toward inflation is one of opposition through neglect. Although in their public statements labor leaders are careful not to say that they favor policies leading to inflation,[27] the more sophisticated seem to realize this is a consequence of the policies they advocate, and do not seem to be unduly perturbed by it.

In terms of the policy subareas looked at earlier in this chapter, the AFL-CIO places chief reliance on an activist expansionary fiscal policy. It prefers this expansion to come about through higher government expenditures benefitting the less well off members of society,[28] but will generally support expansion on the taxation side so long as the benefits do not go to corporations or the rich.[29] Labor would prefer less emphasis on monetary policy, and particularly dislikes its use to raise interest rates and restrain demand.[30] It strongly backs expenditures in the manpower sector, tending to emphasize job creation over retraining.[31] Labor departs from its normally liberal position on wage-price policy. It strongly opposes wage control, preferring reliance on traditional collective bargaining procedures. And, while it does not oppose price controls, it is not very enthusiastic about them either, largely because it sees them as the thin end of a wedge resulting in wage controls.[32]

In order to determine the extent to which this stance accords with the wishes of blue-collar workers, I will briefly reexamine three sets of findings—those showing blue-collar opinions on inflation, those comparing blue-collar workers' attitudes to inflation with blue-collar workers' attitudes toward unemployment and those detailing their policy preferences.

It will be recalled from table 32 that blue-collar workers are considerably more likely than salaried workers, the self-employed, or profit receivers to feel that they are being harmed by inflation. Furthermore we can see that when we break down the blue-collar category into its three components (craftsmen-foremen, operatives, and laborers-service workers) craftsmen-foremen, the group most influential in union affairs, are much more likely to consider themselves seriously harmed by inflation than operatives. Thus 36 percent of craftsmen and foremen fall into one of the two strongest categories as compared with 17.5 percent of shareholders, 23.6 percent of the self-employed and 23.1 percent of salary earners. These figures would lead us to expect truly representative unions to support policies that would reduce inflation.

But, as we saw earlier, labor unions do not see inflation as an isolated problem but as something to be seen in the context of the more important problem of unemployment. This makes it important to look at how blue-collar workers would deal with the problem of inflation defined in terms of a trade-off, though we should note that in doing so we are already moving a step away from true representativeness.[33]

It will be recalled that there are two methods of uncovering the priorities of workers. One is to ask them an open-ended question on what was the worst problem facing them or the country, while the other is to force them to choose between inflation and unemployment in a closed-ended format. As we can see in table 33, the first method tended to show workers thinking inflation is the more important problem, except when inflation was abnormally low and/or unemployment was abnormally high. The closed-ended method yields similar results. Figure 32 shows that workers almost

Table 33   Relative Importance of Inflation, 1974 and 1976

| | October 1974 | | | January 1976 | | |
	Infla-tion	Un-employ-ment	Other	Infla-tion	Un-employ-ment	Other
All respondents	79%	3%	32%	47%	23%	49%
Occupation						
Professional/businessmen	85	2	27	54	20	49
Clerical/sales workers	79	1	32	55	23	46
Manual workers	81	3	30	45	25	47
Non-labor force	73	2	38	41	23	53

The question was, "What is the most important problem facing the country today?" Totals add to more than 100 percent because of multiple responses. In October 1974 the unemployment rate was 6.1 percent and the annual inflation rate 12 percent.In January 1976 the unemployment rate was 7.9 percent and the inflation rate was 6.8 percent. The means for the 1948 to 1979 period were 51 percent for unemployment and 3.8 percent for inflation.

Source: *Gallup Opinion Index*, November 1974 and February 1976.

invariably think that inflation is a worse problem for them and their families but that they are normally a little more likely than the rest of the population to see unemployment as a problem for them and their family. Figure 33 shows that this awareness is not converted isomorphically into a feeling that what is worse for one's family is worse for the country, a point consistent with Kinder and Kiewiet's findings.[34] People in all groups are more likely to stress unemployment as a problem for the country than for themselves, although inflation is seen as worse by a majority except in periods of abnormally high unemployment. More interestingly, workers seem less rather than more inclined than the rest of the population to stress unemployment as a problem for the country, something that argues against a solidary class-conscious working class.[35]

Overall then the evidence seems to indicate that workers normally consider inflation a worse problem than unemployment both for themselves and their family and for the country as a whole. If therefore unions represented their members' views on what the trade-off should be we would expect them to lay some stress on keeping inflation low in normal periods.

Moving from blue-collar workers' views on which problems are most important, to their preferred policies, we find evidence of subjective policy preferences somewhat different from those displayed by unions, though still on balance expansionary. Table 26 shows wage earners as opposing tax or interest rate increases more than any other grouping, while strongly

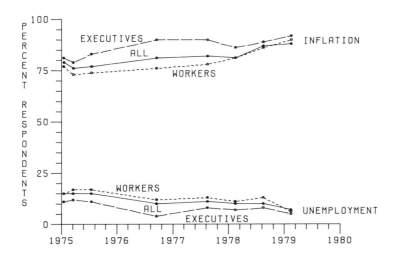

Figure 32   Unemployment versus inflation seen as a worse problem for individuals.
Source: Data supplied by Harris Polls.

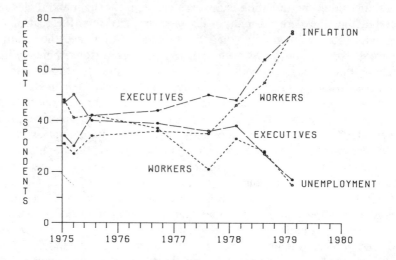

Figure 33   Unemployment versus inflation seen as a worse problem for the country.
                 Source: Data supplied by Harris Polls.

opposing increases in government spending. Although opposed to wage controls, their opposition is much less strong than that of salary earners, and they are in favor of price controls. This complex of preferences is much more like the policies advocated by business groups, it should be noted, than those advocated by unions.

If the opinions of blue-collar workers are a poor indicator of union performance, what of the actual effects of inflation and unemployment? Can unions be seen as leadership groups rather than representative groups?

We saw in chapter 5 that when we look at inflation as an isolated phenomenon the blue-collar worker loses from inflation in the short term, although not as heavily as his white-collar counterpart. Thus the anti-inflation stance of wage earners was, we noted, a reasonable expression of their interests.

But, as unions look at inflation in the context of growth and unemployment, it is necessary to consider the balance of costs and benefits for the wage earner arising from all three of these economic phenomena. Looking at the short-term regression of change in real wages against inflation, change in unemployment and change in real GNP, shown in table 1, it is clear that the effects of inflation remain important when we weigh those effects against the effects of the other two variables. However, in the longer term, GNP growth is a far more important determinant of wages than inflation and it seems reasonable to expect union leaders to perceive this.

But this is not all. The equation referred to above looked at wages adjusted for the number of workers. But workers who become unemployed suffer additional losses in income, and there are also psychic costs attendant upon unemployment. Figures 34 and 35 show the unemployment rates for the different categories of the work force and the percentage of the total work force likely to have suffered some unemployment in a given year.[36] As can be seen, the rate of unemployment in any given year is higher for wage earners than for salaried workers and there is also much greater fluctuation in their rate over the business cycle. Thus in the 1958–1977 period white-collar unemployment averaged 3.0 percent with a standard deviation of 0.8 while blue-collar unemployment averaged 6.95 percent with a standard deviation of 2.1. It should however be noted that craftsmen and kindred workers, who we have noted command disproportionate influence within the AFL-CIO, have somewhat lower unemployment rates than other blue-collar workers, and that union activists are almost invariably more senior than other workers and hence considerably less likely to become unemployed.

Looking at both the figures showing the income effects of changes in demand and the unemployment figures, it seems clear that wage earners have a heavy stake in policies that increase demand and reduce unemployment. Although wage earners as a whole do suffer from inflation in the short term, it seems clear that the long-term costs of inflation are

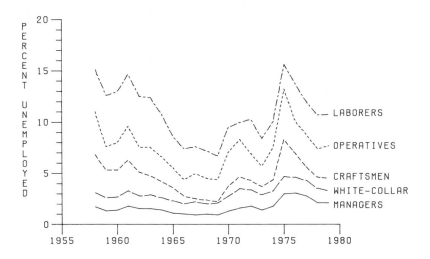

Figure 34   Unemployment rates by occupation. Source: U.S. Department of Labor, *Handbook of Labor Statistics* (Washington, D.C.: Government Printing Office, 1980), p. 73.

Figure 35   Two measures of the percentage of the workforce unemployed. The unemployment rate is obtained by averaging the monthly figures for unemployed adults who actively sought work in the past thirty days. The
figures for the percentage unemployed sometime during the year overstate unemployment somewhat as they include some double counting of
people unemployed more than once during the year. Source: U.S. Department of Labor, *Handbook of Labor Statistics* (Washington, D.C.:
Government Printing Office, 1980), pp. 61 and 98–99.

minor compared with those of high unemployment and slow growth and
we would therefore expect leadership directed unions to stress these latter.
This is less true if we see unions as organizations that respond primarily
to the interests of those workers most active in union affairs. If however
unions seek to lead all blue-collar workers,[37] including the less unionized
and less active, then support for activist, demand-oriented economic policies should be the major thrust of union policy.

It should be noted however that there is an alternative explanation of
union leaders' behavior that follows an organizational maintenance rather
than a leadership model, and hence is more elitist. We know that unions
typically gain members and bargaining strength in periods of strong demand for labor and lose both in deflationary periods. Hence union leaders
have an organizational as well as a representative reason to stress stimulative policy.

How well do the patterns described fit the pluralist-democratic model?
The answer would seem to be not very well. In an interesting reversal of
the situation we found with the major business groups, unions seem to
represent the real interests of their constituents well, but essentially to

ignore the policy preferences of those constituents. This "leadership" pattern is essentially inconsistent with pluralist-democracy, which assumes that people know their interests and that they can make their leaders represent their views.

Here a Marxist explanation provides a more economical pattern. In the Marxist schema the workers are subject to false consciousness, and the activist wing of the workers in the form of the union movement is meant to act as a vanguard correctly perceiving the "real" rather than the "subjective" interests of the working classes and acting upon that perception.

It should finally be noted that, despite Michaels emphasis on oligarchy in labor unions, the relations described do not fit the elitist model well. If this model obtained we would expect the observed discrepancy between the real situation of workers and their policy preferences, but we would expect the unions to pursue labor's subjective, rather than their objective, interests, or to be co-opted by management.

The Salaried Sector

While the representation of blue-collar workers is best described as monolithic, the representation of white-collar workers is the opposite. There is no organization which universally represents white-collar workers, or even any substantial division within union ranks. What organizations there are tend to cooperate with, or abstain in favor of, groups which primarily represent interests of other occupational sectors. Furthermore the various groups representing white-collar workers lean in rather different directions—often advocating contrary economic policies.

In order to understand this confusing process of representation it is helpful to divide white-collar workers by their relation to the means of production. Different organizations with different orientations represent the three major divisions—managers and officials, professional and technical workers, and clerical and sales workers. A fourth, cross-cutting division of government workers also provides an organizational focus. Even within these divisions however we cannot find groups representing the whole division. The salaried sector vies with the welfare sector for the title of least organized. A large percentage of the salaried do not belong to any occupational organizations and the groups that do exist are not aggregated into effective peak groups. Nonetheless, within the three organizational subdivisions, attitudes of the interest groups toward macroeconomic policy are reasonably consistent.

Although groups such as the American Management Association, the National Management Association, the Administrative Society, the Society for the Advancement of Management and the American Society for Public Administration represent managers and officials and tend to support

policies very similar to those advocated by business groups, they do lean
a little more toward the positions of the more moderate corporate groups
than those of the more conservative business groups.[38] As in the other
divisions, government employed public administrators tend to hold somewhat more liberal positions than privately employed managers. The most
noticeable fact concerning these organizations however is their virtual
absence from the macroeconomic policy process rather than their policy
positions. With memberships accounting for only a small proportion of
the potential universe, these organizations concentrate on professional
activities and managerial education while leaving their policy positions to
be represented by the business groups.

At the other end of the policy spectrum, sales and clerical workers find
their representation in the white-collar unions. As table 34 shows, only
about 10 percent of white-collar workers are unionized. Their membership
is concentrated among government clerical workers and the highly mobile
sales workers are the least organized. The major clerical unions are the
Communications Workers of America, the Office and Professional Employees International Union, the Brotherhood of Railway (etc.) Clerks,
the American Federation of Governmental Employees, the American Federation of State, County and Municipal Workers, and the California and
New York Civil Service Associations. Both the Teamsters and the UAW
also have a substantial number of clerical members. Although sales work-

Table 34   Occupations in Labor Unions by Race and Sex, 1970

Occupation of longest job held in 1970	Total	Race		Sex	
		White	Black	Male	Female
All occupations	20.4%	20.2%	21.8%	27.8%	10.3%
White-collar workers	9.8	9.3	16.6	12.5	7.4
Professional/technical	9.0	8.8	12.1	9.7	8.1
Managers/officials	7.5	7.3	14.2	8.3	4.1
Clerical and kindred	13.1	12.3	21.1	29.2	8.2
Salesworkers	4.9	4.8	7.3	5.5	4.2
Blue-collar workers	39.3	39.8	35.5	42.1	27.8
Craftsmen/foremen	42.7	42.9	39.8	43.8	20.1
Operatives and kindred	40.4	40.8	38.2	46.4	29.0
Nonfarm laborers	28.9	29.2	27.2	29.6	19.2
Service workers	10.9	10.9	10.8	20.1	5.7

Source: Bureau of Labor Statistics, *Selected Earnings and Demographic Characteristics
of Union Members, 1970* (Washington, D.C.: Government Printing Office, 1972), p. 6. I
have used this data because it is more reliable than that supplied by unions, and though
there have been some changes in the 1970 to 1980 period the proportions remain roughly
the same. The sample size was 50,000.

ers are concentrated in the 587,000-member Retail Clerks International Association, both the Retail, Wholesale and Department Store Union and the Communications Workers of America have over 35,000 members. Except for the two civil service unions, all of these are members of the AFL-CIO. In general, they let the AFL-CIO represent their interests even though they have little individual or collective influence within that organization. The one partial exception to this absorption of white-collar into blue-collar interests is the American Federation of State, County and Municipal Employees (AFSCME). But, although its leader, Jerry Wurf, has several disagreements with the craft union dominated AFL-CIO leadership, their views on macroeconomic policy are very similar. The only deviation is in the somewhat heavier stress placed on growth and public employment by AFSCME.[39]

Professional and technical workers make up the occupational sector that most resembles Mannhein's "free-floating intellectuals,"[40] or Marx's "intelligentsia."[41] The distinguishing features of this sector's relation to economic policy making are the large influence wielded by individual members, the assumption by most participants that this influence is disinterested and the rather limited influence wielded by any organization representing this sector's members.[42] Assessment of the degree to which professional and technical workers are represented in macroeconomic policy making is dependent on how one regards the unity of their interests and the disinterestedness of their specialist advice. Viewed as a class in which all members have a similar stake in macroeconomic policy and with advice dictated by class interests, professional and technical workers seem to be one of the most strongly represented groups, with economists and lawyers being their specialized class representatives for macroeconomic policy making. If however we view them as an occupational group which is represented in policy making through their interest groups and in which individual members may give disinterested advice, we must come to the conclusion that they have little influence on making macroeconomic policy and little desire to have such an influence.

Professionals are in fact rather well organized—more so than technical workers—and are represented by three distinct types of groups. Entertainers and federal government workers tend to be represented by unions; lawyers, doctors, academics, architects, engineers and accountants by professional associations; and teachers, nurses and state government workers by employee associations. Generally speaking, professional unions, like the clerical and sales unions, consider the AFL-CIO as representing their interests on macroeconomic policy. It should be noted however that peak organizations exist, such as the Council of AFL-CIO Unions for Professional Employees and the National Federation of Independent Unions, that could represent them. Rather than abstaining in favor of other organizations, professional associations and employee associations tend to abstain altogether. Even the American Bar Association and the American Economic Association, which represent the people most intimately involved in policy making, have very little say in making economic policy. The latter group however does add weight to those policies on which economists are most likely to agree.

If one took the views of economists as representing the interests of professional workers, then one would have to say that for most of the postwar period they favored mildly interventionist Keynesian policies that emphasized the use of fiscal policy to restrain demand, with monetary policy in an ancillary but cooperative role. Further one would have to say that they generally supported manpower policies, opposed wage-price policy and tended to stress growth and employment even at the expense of controlling inflation. If, on the other hand, one looked to the views of the individual representative organizations, one would have to say that the more unionized professions supported the strongly expansionary interventionist policies of the AFL-CIO, while the professional groups, organized in other ways, took a very weak position somewhere between the liberal and conservative coalitions by considering both inflation and unemployment as important problems.

Thus overall we have a tripartite system of representation in the white-collar sector—clerical, sales and lower paid professional workers align themselves with the blue-collar workers; managers and officials abdicate to corporate and business interests; and the bulk of professionals opt for indirect representation by technocratic professional economists, who take positions somewhere between the two major economic coalitions.

Given this rather wide range of representation within the white-collar ranks it does not make sense to look only at aggregate opinions. Therefore I will break down the opinion data by the three types of white-collar workers discussed above. Looking at both the impact they think inflation has had on them and at the policies they advocate, we will try to see if the differences found at the leadership level can also be found at the membership level.

Looking first at the figures on the perceived impact of inflation on respondents' families, shown in table 32, we find a situation somewhat different from the one we might expect. Given the interest group attitudes just examined, we might expect to find managers and officials seeing themselves as being most hurt by inflation, clerical and sales workers seeing themselves as least hurt and professional and technical workers in between. We do in fact find the managers and officials are most likely to report being harmed, with 26.6 percent claiming to be hurt more than a little by inflation. But clerical and sales workers, far from being the least hurt, are almost as likely to report harm as the managers and officials, with 24.8 percent of them reporting being hurt more than a little by infla-tion. Last, the professional and technical workers do not occupy an in-termediate position, but feel less hurt by inflation than either of the other groups, with only 20.2 percent claiming to be hurt more than a little.

When we look at shareholders we find that, although their represen-tatives' views on inflation do not "fit" with the degree to which they think they are harmed by inflation, they do "fit" shareholders' opinions on the issues. As we can see in table 35, which shows the percentage of different occupational categories in favor of various anti-inflation policies, this does not seem to be true for white-collar workers. Looking at the views of their representatives, we would expect that, in a pluralist-dem-ocratic system, managers and officials would be least likely to favor raising income taxes and having government price controls; most likely to favor raising interest rates, reducing government spending and lowering con-sumer spending and borrowing; and in the middle on government wage controls. We would also expect the clerical and salesworkers to be at the

Table 35   Occupational Categories' Agreement with Alternative Anti-inflation Poli-cies in 1969

	Shareholders	Self-employed	Farmers, Farm managers	Professional, Technical, etc.	Manager, Official	Clerical, Sales	Craftsmen, Foremen	Operatives, etc.	Laborer, Service	Fixed Income (under 65)	Fixed Income (over 65)
Raise income taxes	15.5	11.8	10.9	17.0	15.8	8.3	6.3	4.6	3.4	8.4	7.1
Raise interest rates	17.8	10.3	10.9	17.1	14.5	13.9	9.4	8.2	7.5	10.7	10.7
Reduce govt. spending	83.8	80.9	87.0	82.9	75.3	79.2	78.5	82.1	78.6	77.9	82.8
Consumers spend less	77.6	70.6	73.9	69.6	61.0	70.1	63.7	66.8	60.3	62.6	69.8
Consumers borrow less	87.9	82.4	80.4	82.5	79.2	84.0	78.0	81.6	78.1	71.5	76.5
Govt. control prices	29.3	55.9	28.9	32.1	36.4	41.0	47.1	56.1	54.2	50.4	50.0
Govt. control wages	27.4	52.9	26.7	26.0	36.4	21.7	27.4	39.5	38.6	31.3	44.3

The question was, "Here is a list of things which some people say, should be done to slow down inflation. First do you agree or disagree that (first item) . . . ? (second item) . . . ?"

Source: *Survey of Consumer Finances* (Ann Arbor: University of Michigan), Fall 1969.

other end of the spectrum on the first six issues but to be most opposed
to wage controls. In fact we find nothing of the sort. Managers and officials
are least likely to favor reducing government spending, and lowering
consumer spending and borrowing; most likely to favor government wage
controls; and in the middle on raising income taxes, raising interest rates
and government price controls. The opinions of the other two groups are
almost equally inconsistent with the policies promoted by their representatives.

If the positions of the representatives are not consistent with white-
collar opinion, are they consistent with the objective situation of the
different categories of white-collar worker?

As far as can be determined, using admittedly inadequate salary data,
the answer would seem to be that the objective situation is more consistent
with the opinion data than with the positions of the representative groups.
It will be recalled that in table 2, based on salary data for professional,
technical, clerical and sales workers, we saw that inflation is a more
important determinant of salary changes than either changes in GNP or
unemployment. Thus a percentage increase in inflation is associated with
a 0.43 percent decrease in salaries and the beta weight was substantially
higher than those for changes in GNP and unemployment.

These figures are drawn from an equation using salary data from two
of our categories. If there was a marked difference between salary change
in the clerical/sales division and the other divisions, this might account
for the observed differences in representation. But in fact, as we can see
in table 36, the salary changes for the clerical and sales workers are almost
identical to those for the professional and technical workers. This makes

Table 36   Annual Increases in Monetary and Real White-collar Rates, 1961–1973

Occupational group	Monetary			Real		
	1961–1966	1966–1972	1972–1977	1961–1966	1966–1972	1972–1977
All salaries	3.28%	6.49%	7.96%	1.45%	1.30%	−0.70%
Professional, administrative and technical	3.64	6.62	7.73	1.79	1.40	−0.86
Clerical and clerical-supervisory	2.85	6.62	8.12	1.06	1.41	−0.60

Sources: Bureau of Labor Statistics, *National Survey of Professional, Administrative, Technical and Clerical Pay* (Washington, D.C.: Government Printing Office, 1977), p. 2; Council
of Economic Advisers, *Economic Report of the President 1981* (Washington, D.C.: Government Printing Office, 1981), p. 289.

difference in salary changes an unlikely explanation for the differences in the attitudes of the representative groups.

It is also difficult to account for the attitudes of the groups by looking at the unemployment data shown in figure 34. It is true that the variation between the groups is consistent with the positions taken by their representatives. As might be expected, managerial groups, with a mean unemployment rate of 1.35 percent, suffer from less unemployment than the professionals, who have a mean rate of 2.0 percent. And these in turn suffer from considerably less unemployment than sales and clerical workers whose mean unemployment rates are 4.0 percent and 4.2 percent respectively. It should be noted however that all these unemployment rates are all well below the mean blue-collar rate of 6.95 percent. Thus, since inflation is so important in the determination of white-collar income and unemployment so unimportant, one might expect all interest groups representing white-collar workers to place a heavy emphasis on controlling inflation, but to be relatively unworried about unemployment. As we have seen, only the managers and officials seem to have representatives who have this emphasis.

One final point needs to be examined. We saw that overall the representatives of salaried workers took a rather passive role in macroeconomic policy making. This seems to have some justification in the economic conditions facing their constituency. Unemployment, as we saw, is far less of a problem for white-collar than for blue-collar workers. And whereas the average wage earner reaches an earnings plateau early in his working career, making any erosion of wage rates very painful, the salary earner is generally on a career ladder. Hence, for any given salary earner, erosion of salary due to inflation may be compensated for by increases in salary resulting from ascent of the career ladder. However, the short-term negative effects of inflation on salary rates seems higher than on wage rates. Further, while the slow long-term growth and the recent dip in salaries shown in table 36 are primarily due to changes in the supply of women and a more highly educated work force, the psychology of inflation, explored in chapter 4, would lead us to expect that substantial numbers of salary earners would blame both of these on increasing inflation.[43] Thus though there are some factors which should reduce the salience of macroeconomic policy to the representatives of this sector, the amount of inactivity actually observed seems extraordinary.

Overall patterns in the salaried sector do not seem to fit the pluralist-democratic model any better than patterns in other sectors. Although opinion and reality fit fairly well, only in the managerial and official division do we find patterns of representation that are in accord with the interests of relevant sets of workers. Even here the representation is more through abstention than direct representation. It is possible to "save" the pluralist model in this sector by claiming that white-collar workers are represented but by political parties rather than by interest groups. Seen in this light both the low levels and eccentric patterns of representation on economic policy would be due to the fact that parties not interest groups were the primary channel of representation and that this representation was effective enough to remove the need for the interest group channel. We will look at political parties as representation mechanisms later in this chapter. Meanwhile however it seems worth pointing out that white-collar workers do not seem notably satisfied with the parties or their policies, that they are more likely than those in other groups to be independents and that the party they generally vote for, the Democratic Party, does not generally represent either their economic views or their putative interests.[44]

A Marxist or an elitist model again seems to provide a better fit to the data. As we have seen, white-collar workers, whose economic interests appear from the data to be very similar, break down for purposes of representation into separate groupings defined largely in terms of their rank in the process of production. Marxists would see this as false consciousness and argue that this "new middle class"[45] has yet to develop full consciousness of its objective class position. But, as the rapid increase in unionization of this sector indicates, they are moving from a position where the managers, officials, professionals and clerks identify with the capitalist class, to one where they increasingly see themselves in a similar relation to the means of production as the blue-collar worker.

An elitist interpretation seems to fit even better. In this model managers and professionals would be viewed as an alternate functional elite challenging the old capitalist elite for power, but with interests very different from the working class and lower ranks of white-collar workers. For them, the economists' emphasis on rational planning of the economy, an emphasis echoed by the corporate interests, is the key point, since this inevitably expands their real power. Seen in this light their seeming abstention from power is due to the fact that individual informal action has already ensured the kind of policies they want, without them having to expose themselves by overtly "political" action. The fact that the clerical and sales workers fit increasingly with the blue-collar workers is a reflection of their exclusion from both the old capitalist elite and the new managerial/professional elite.

The Welfare Sector

The representatives of welfare pool members are as weak and disorganized as those of white-collar workers. But whereas white-collar workers seem to voluntarily abstain from the process of macroeconomic policy making, representatives of welfare pool members lack the organization and power to take part in the process, despite their desire to do so.[46] Instead they tend to pursue an explicitly compensatory strategy, seeking reimbursement, generally from the federal government, for economic policy outcomes that affect them adversely. This is particularly true for inflation, where the general tendency has been to seek cost-of-living increases in the various welfare payments.[47] In this more limited aim, these groups have enjoyed some success—usually as a part of a larger coalition in which labor has an important role,[48] and aided by the fact that most of the population views the poor, the old and those on fixed-incomes as suffering most from inflation. However, the success of the different groups in indexing their payments against inflation and protecting themselves against inflation has varied tremendously. Generally social security recipients, especially since 1972, have been almost fully protected against both inflation and recession while payments to AFDC recipients have been much less well protected.

Representation of welfare pool members is based on divisions of interest. The most important of these are race,[49] charities,[50] churches,[51] foundations,[52] and old people's groups[53]—all of which represent their own particularistic interests to a greater or lesser extent. All these interest groups are opposed to inflation and think their constituencies are particularly hard hit by it.[54] But, although none of the groups has a sufficiently developed economic theory to enable them to have clear positions on the marginal policy choices of most interest to the central policy makers, there are considerable differences in the degree of emphasis placed on inflation on one hand and unemployment and growth on the other. Old people's groups are most inclined to stress inflation[55]—almost to the exclusion of unemployment and growth[56]—and place almost equal stress on keeping down prices of such items as food and medical costs, which are of particular importance to the aged, and on indexing social security and medical benefit payments to lessen the impact inflation has on old people's incomes.[57] Welfare groups, charities, foundations and churches, which are united chiefly by their desire to ensure that losses to their constituency arising from unemployment, growth or inflation are compensated for by the federal government—an approach it should be noted that tends to expand government spending and hence place inflationary pressure on the economy—seem to have no very consistent emphasis.[58] Last, civil rights and urban groups, with large constituencies of working poor as well as fixed income recipients, place their primary emphasis on employment rather than inflation. Although they are as likely as the other groups to demand that the federal government compensate their constituents for losses due to inflation, their primary stress is on increasing growth through decreasing unemployment, primarily through the creation of new jobs programs for minorities.[59] When these three types of group coalesce and attempt to push a single set of recommendations, the better organized black and urban groups tend to predominate. The resulting proposed policies tend to be inflationary, by combining compensation for the victims of inflation with expansionary job and housing programs which would be only very partially offset by suggested cuts in defense spending.[60]

To what extent does this general overall policy set square with the opinions of those with fixed incomes? To what extent are the differences between the groups merely a reflection of differences in opinion among their constituents? Let us look at these questions in turn.

If we look at welfare pool members' opinions on how they are being harmed by inflation, the poverty coalition's expansionary policies seem inappropriate. As we saw in table 32, welfare pool members are considerably more likely than any other group, except laborers and service workers, to consider themselves much or very much hurt by inflation, making a deflationary policy more appropriate, prima facie, than an expansionary one. But this group, containing many marginal workers, is also very vulnerable to slow growth and unemployment. Thus it is important which set of problems is seen as more pressing. It is difficult to be certain, as I was unable to obtain relevant data broken down by welfare pool status. But what data there is suggests that black and non-black members of the welfare pool may think differently. Data from eight Harris polls over the 1975 to 1979 period shows a strong and consistent tendency for blacks to rate unemployment a more important problem than whites do, both for themselves and the country, something consistent with the fact that black unemployment rates are normally double those of whites. At the same time, groups such as those with an eighth grade education, those earning less than $5,000 a year and those over sixty-five showed a weak tendency to consider inflation the more important problem both for themselves and for the country.

Thus the heavy unemployment emphasis of the poverty coalition does not seem to accurately reflect the priorities of the non-black welfare pool. Nor can it be said to reflect members policy preferences. For example it is a clear implication of the poverty coalition's view that prices should be controlled and government spending somewhat expanded. As we can see in table 26, a majority of welfare pool members do favor price controls—more so than most other groups. But an overwhelming 81.3 percent think reducing government spending to fight inflation is a good idea and only 9.2 percent disagree, less than in any other occupational group. This does not necessarily mean that welfare pool members would object to greater government spending on themselves—only that they object to the probable overall increase in spending resulting from such action.

The best summary of these findings is that, taken as a whole, fixed income recipients consider the effects of inflation on them to be worse than do the groups who represent them. Their expressed policy preferences however, are considerably less contrary to the position taken by the poverty coalition.

What of the division between the groups? Does the greater stress on inflation by groups representing the aged than by groups representing other poverty categories[61] result from different opinions held by their respective constituencies? Table 32 divides welfare pool members into two categories—those under sixty-five and those over sixty-five. This provides very little support for the different emphases of old people's and other groups. Although marginally more of the aged claim to be "very much" hurt by inflation, this is more than offset by the greater number of the younger welfare pool members claiming to be "much" hurt.

Since they are still potentially in the labor market, there would seem to be good reason to expect the younger people to place a greater relative stress on unemployment than their older compatriots. Table 37, taken from the 1969 Michigan Survey of Consumer Finances, indicates this may be the case. It shows the percentage giving inflation as the major reason for their lower incomes. Whereas more than 60 percent of those over-sixty-five blamed their lower income on inflation, less than 30 percent of

Table 37   Inflation Given as Major Reason for Decrease in Income in 1969

Occupational category	Reason for lower real income		
	Inflation	Other	N
Shareholders	51.7%	48.3%	(29)
Self-employed	30.0	70.0	(20)
Farmers	12.5	87.5	(16)
Professionals/technicians	46.3	53.7	(41)
Managers/officials	47.8	52.2	(23)
Clerks/sales workers	37.0	63.0	(54)
Craftsmen/foremen	53.4	46.6	(73)
Operatives	40.0	60.0	(60)
Laborers/service workers	51.1	48.9	(47)
Fixed income under 65	29.3	70.7	(58)
Fixed income over 65	60.8	39.2	(79)

Raw chi-square = 27.758 Significance = 0.002

Source: *Survey of Consumer Finances* (Ann Arbor: University of Michigan), Fall 1969.

those under-sixty-five gave this as the primary reason. This indicates other factors are much more important for this latter group.[62] Hibbs's finding that those not in the labor force are more likely than the employed to lose faith in the president when inflation is high and less likely to do so when unemployment is high, also supports this view.[63]

However, this does not seem to be strongly borne out by Harris data asking people to evaluate the effects of rising prices and high unemployment. A February 1979 poll showed that 91 percent of those over-sixty-five thought inflation was the more important problem for them and their family, while only 3 percent thought unemployment was the more important problem. Of those under sixty-five, 88 percent thought inflation was the more important problem, versus 7 percent who thought unemployment was. This small difference was, at least, in the right direction. But when the same poll asked which problem was more important for the country as a whole, 18 percent of those under sixty-five thought unemployment more important as against 19 percent of those over sixty-five. Further, while 71 percent of those under sixty-five thought inflation was the more important problem, only 61 percent of those over sixty-five did.[64]

Looking finally at the policy emphases of the two groups shown in table 35, we find, as we might expect, the price controls are equally emphasized by both groups. But we also find that, although both groups support reductions in government spending, the under-sixty-five group is slightly less inclined to seek reductions than the over-sixty-five group.

Taken as a whole these figures reveal a mild tendency for opinions among younger and older welfare pool members to differ in ways which are consistent with the different emphases of the groups representing them. But the differences in opinions seem very small, are not statistically significant, and do not seem sufficient to explain the different emphases of old people's groups and other poverty groups.

We have seen that it is difficult to explain the overall position of the poverty coalition by examining the opinions of welfare pool members. Likewise, we have seen that the small differences in opinion between those welfare pool members over and under sixty-five seem insufficient to account for the observed differences in emphases between old people's and other poverty groups. Can we find better explanations by looking at the raw data?

The fit to our short-term figures is indeed somewhat better. We saw in tables 1 and 2 that inflation does not, as commonly supposed, have major negative short-term effects on the rate of change of either OASI or AFDC payments, and that what effect there is tended to decrease over time. Only unemployment benefits show a reliable negative effect from inflation in both the short and long-term, but it seems implausible that inflation would be more important than unemployment to the unemployed. It could be objected that OASI payments are not the only source of income for the elderly poor and that both savings and fixed pensions are eroded by inflation. But it must be remembered that for most of our period only a minority of the elderly received fixed pensions or had substantial savings and that the larger numbers that owned their own homes benefitted from the fact that housing prices outpaced inflation.[65] In addition, as Phelps and Hollister and Palmer point out, the long-term effects of inflation on the poor do not seem very negative.[66]

Thus it seems possible to view the emphasis of welfare pool groups as rational on the assumption that they are leadership rather than representative groups. This however would be misleading. While union leaders seem to have correctly estimated that unemployment hurts their members more than inflation, this does not seem to be true of most welfare pool group leaders. Rather, they seem to share their follower's beliefs as to the harm inflation causes, but fail to convert those beliefs into an appropriate policy response.[67]

What of the differences in emphases between old people's and other groups, particularly those representing blacks? Can this be explained by the aggregate data? The answer here seems to be affirmative. It must be remembered that black groups represent working people to a much greater extent than old people's groups. Thus more of their constituents have incomes with some flexibility in the face of inflation. Indeed disproportionate numbers of blacks are employed in that low wage sector particularly responsive to demand forces that, as we saw in chapter 3, is particularly resistant to inflation. At the same time, blacks have unemployment rates double those of whites, while the elderly are generally retired and hence unlikely to feel direct negative effects from increased unemployment. This combination of forces makes an expansionary view very rational for black groups and a deflationary or compensatory approach rational for old people's groups.

If this view is true it becomes easier to explain the overall position of the poverty coalition. Blacks have been much better organized than old people since at least the mid-1960s and as their relative strength waxes, their views tend to predominate. Therefore, their expansionary position has tended to become the position of the entire poverty coalition. Furthermore, the process of coalition points in the same direction. In order to lend force to their views, poverty groups have allied themselves with the AFL-CIO—a group which, as we have seen, tends to take a strongly expansionary position.[68]

As we have seen, welfare pool members do not seem to fit the pluralist-democratic mold any better than the other sectors we have examined. There is no single group, as there should be, that represents their distinctive combined interests. The objective evidence on the degree to which inflation harms them in both the short and long-term does not appear consistent with their perceptions of its effects. These perceptions in turn do not seem consistent with the policies they demand. Their unwillingness to raise taxes, which fall mainly on others, or to increase government spending, which mainly benefits the poor, is particularly noticeable. As in other sectors, it is not clear that the policy emphases of welfare pool members bear much relation to the actions of the groups that represent them. Furthermore these groups, representing a substantial section of the population, are almost entirely excluded from macroeconomic policy making—something that is not entirely consistent with an efficient pluralist-democratic system.

Again the Marxist model seems more plausible, prima facie. Viewing the sector as a part of the working class, makes both their overall position and their active alliance with labor more explicable. Furthermore, some of the contradiction between their policy views and their views on how they are harmed by inflation is explained by viewing them as that part of the population particularly susceptible to false consciousness.

An elitist model would view this group as part of the mass to be manipulated by the elite. Here, as in the Marxist explanation, the emphasis on compensation and the exclusion from power are both ways by which the elite controls the mass. The contradictions in beliefs, and the inability of constituents to make their leaders responsive to their wishes, are a natural result of elite manipulation.

Overall then, although it is not impossible to make sense of what is happening in this sector in terms of a very loose pluralist-democratic model that emphasizes leadership rather than representation, it seems more economical to look to the activity in terms of other models.

Political Parties

There seem to be four major ways of characterizing the relation between parties and their supporters. In one view, springing from the work of Downs and more recently found in work by Nordhaus and MacRae, parties are seen as collections of political entrepreneurs, whose major motivation is the collection of the votes necessary to achieve and retain political office.[69] Those in this rational-voter tradition maintain that parties will structure their economic policies in such a way as to secure re-election. Although they do not emphasize this, the model clearly implies that both parties will have similar economic policies as there is only one maximizing function.

A second way of characterizing the relation, consistent with Page and Pomper, but perhaps best exemplified in the work of Hibbs and Beck, is to view parties as representatives of different social groups with different underlying economic interests.[70] In this view, consistent both with pluralist democracy and structuralist Marxism, the Democratic party, because of its blue-collar base, is seen as having a semi-permanent interest in redistributive economic policy and in stimulative policies to reduce unemployment. The Republican party, because of its predominantly white-collar and capitalist constituency, is seen as having a semi-permanent interest in reducing redistribution and in restrictive economic policies aimed at reducing inflation and increasing unemployment. This model implies clear policy differences between the parties that correspond to similar differences among their supporters.

A third way of characterizing the relation, found to some degree in the work of Domhoff and Edelman, is to view parties as a way in which an elite or ruling class co-opts, diffuses and controls actual or potential pressure from below.[71] From this viewpoint, most consistent with traditional Marxism and elitism, parties symbolically represent the major groups in the population, while permitting actual policies to be controlled by the elite. This would lead us to expect differences between the rhetoric of the two major parties, particularly that rhetoric aimed at activists, accompanied by similar policies, and claims from both parties that their policies benefitted the masses. We would expect some consistency between the parties' rhetoric and the biases of their supporters, but little between the actions and the real interests of most of their supporters.

A last possibility, most consistent with O'Connor,[72] is that the two parties could represent different sides in an intra-elite or intra-ruling class struggle. In the elite struggle version it might be reasonable to see the Democratic party as representing the interests of the information based technocrats whose major desire is to increase state control of the economy and economic planning, and the Republicans as representing the interests of capitalists whose major interest lies in preserving as much as possible of the "free" market. In this view we would expect the economic policies of the two parties to differ while in office, but not in ways that represented the real interests of the mass of their supporters. One would expect the rhetoric of both parties to be similar, as both seek support among the masses by purporting to represent their real interests.

For purposes of assessing which of these views is right, it is necessary to adjudge the degree of long-term consistency in the public statements, private ideology and policy actions of the two parties and the degree to which each of these is dictated by a need to represent or attract their core constituency. It is also important to look at shorter-term change in the parties' positions in and out of power in order to see whether they act in ways consistent with the entrepreneurial, representative, co-optive or competing elite models. In doing so it is wise to remember that American parties are not monolithic and that any generalization about their economic policy positions should be understood as a main tendency surrounded by exceptions.

Looking first at the public statements of the two parties, one is more struck by the similarities than the differences. Both parties usually publicly support reducing unemployment and inflation, increasing economic growth, personal income and productivity, and maintaining exports and the value of the dollar.[73] Both parties support reduced government spending, decreased taxes and a balanced budget. Both parties claim to represent the interests of the average man and/or the little man and/or the truly needy and/or small business. Both support the American enterprise system. While there are differences on the relative emphasis placed on these goals and on the means of best achieving them, the public goals system seems consensual.

When we move from the area of public statements to semi-public ideology the difference between the two parties widens considerably.[74] The Republicans have always placed primary emphasis on controlling inflation.[75] Growth and high employment are also deemed desirable, but only so long as they do not cause inflation. Although the Republican party has always believed in the inevitability of the business cycle, in the desirability of balanced budgets and in minimal government control of the economy,[76] more recent Republican presidents and their advisers have been a little more willing to accept some minimal government planning and small rather than non-existent deficits.[77] Less likely than Democrats to approve the use of wage-price policy or manpower policy, Republicans prefer to place more emphasis on monetary policy and less on fiscal policy.[78] If they had control over all branches of government the Republicans would generally choose to reduce taxes—particularly the more progressive corporate and income taxes—and reduce government spending.[79] It should be noted however that government spending has in fact expanded under most Republican presidents.

While the Republican party has a generally deflationary emphasis, the Democratic party has a generally expansionary one. Although the party's optimal trade-off point between inflation and unemployment is somewhat conservative by the standards of leftist parties in other countries,[80] the Democrats are much more biased toward solving unemployment than the Republicans.[81] Most of the thrust behind wage-price policy comes from the Democrats[82] and, while they are a little less enthusiastic than the unions about manpower policy, they consider it a useful addition to other policies.[83] Fiscal policy is preferred by Democrats for economic manipulation, with monetary policy seen more as a useful auxiliary for small short-term changes in the economy.[84] Within fiscal policy the Democrats prefer to use tax policy to manipulate the economy while maintaining a steady expansion in government spending.[85] They have been much more willing than Republicans to accept the Keynesian revolution and much less willing to accept the monetarist one. They generally accept the necessity of deficit spending when unemployment exceeds the full employment level—a level that they place lower than Republicans do.[86]

This outline of Democratic party preferences must be modified when we look at southern Democrats. Although southern Democrats are not as far from the positions of northern Democrats on economic as on social issues, they are nonetheless more conservative. They place a greater stress than other Democratic leaders on restraining inflation and a little less on solving the unemployment problem.[87] This difference in stress is manifested chiefly in their much greater desire to restrain government spending—particularly non-defense spending.[88] On other macroeconomic policy measures their position is either near to that of other Democrats or they are prepared to trade votes on these measures for measures of greater salience to them.[89] In Congress this difference in economic ideology has sometimes led southern Democrats to combine with Republicans in a Conservative Coalition, which has been particularly instrumental in restraining spending by northern Democrats.

It must be emphasized that although there are discernible party ideologies the variance in opinion on economic policy between elected officeholders of the same party is greater in the United States than in most other Western democracies. In addition American parties lack strong institutional substructures capable of forcing the party line on unwilling officeholders. These circumstances allow room for other influences on the actions of officeholders to assume greater importance and make it possible for quite large changes in party power in Congress or the executive to result in rather small changes in the economic policy making balance. Pomper for example, in an attempt to show that party change is *more* important than commonly thought, generates figures showing that the party winning the presidency redeemed 84 percent of its platform pledges on economic issues in the 1944–1966 period and 75 percent in the 1968–1978 period. But he also shows the party that lost the presidential election was able to fulfill 53 percent of its economic platform pledges in the 1944–1966 period and a full 66 percent in the 1968–1978 period.[90] It is worthwhile then to look at what has actually been the effect of changes in party strength in the two elected branches of government on economic policy and economic outcomes.

It should be clear from my earlier description of the process of economic policy making that the most plausible interpretation of the effects of such changes is that they alter the relative strength of the two coalitions which, through choice or necessity, make marginal changes within a consensual economic framework. It also follows from my earlier description of the clumsiness of policy making and the long lags involved that we would expect a change in party strength to work its way through to economic outcomes in a slow, erratic and somewhat unpredictable manner.

Despite this, it is clearly possible for even quite careful observers to feel that party change makes a great difference. Three things mislead people in this regard. First, and least important, the incoming party will typically portray itself as about to make major improvements, while the losing party will typically claim the proposed changes are too extensive, drawing attention to what does happen and away from what does not.[91] Second, it is easy for the observer to see the American economy in local rather than international context, making what are, in international terms, rather small departures from existing practice seem large when compared to the pre-existing situation.[92] Last, it is easy to overstate because party power changes more frequently and abruptly than the power of other elements and because changes in party power are more visible and quantifiable than changes in the power of those elements.[93]

The general point that party change does not have major immediate effects but does nonetheless have an effect is borne out by the data presented in table 38. Looking first at the general economic variables it

Table 38   Mean Rates of Change in Key Economic Variables under Democratic and Republican Presidents, 1947–1977

Economic variables	Whole period	Democratic presidents	Republican presidents
Aggregate indicators			
Unemployment Rate	5.14%	4.93%	5.35%
Change in Unemployment rate	4.17	−4.16	12.51
Inflation rate	3.80	3.72	3.88
Change in per capita disposable income	2.16	2.51	1.81
Market incomes			
Wages and salaries	1.17	1.29	1.05
Wages	1.33	1.34	1.31
Profits	4.55	5.81	3.30
Dividends	3.17	3.97	2.38
Farm	0.14	0.95	−0.66
Small business	1.28	2.68	−0.12
Transfer incomes			
OASDI	4.71	5.30	4.13
AFDC	1.42	1.96	0.87
Unemployment compensation	1.42	0.83	2.01
Aggregate transfers	6.42	3.86	8.98

Farm and small business income is pre-tax. Transfer income is not on a per capita basis and hence measures both increases in the rates and in the number of recipients. I recalculated lagging one year to allow for the fact that economic policy may be "locked in" for the first year of a term, but results were little altered.

is evident that the differences in outcome under presidents of the two parties do not accord closely with the parties' ideologies.[94] While unemployment rates are lower under Democratic presidents, the difference is clearly not great.[95] Further inflation, far from being lower under Republican presidents, is actually significantly higher. Nor is there evidence to support the idea that administrations have been able to manage the distributive impact of these major variables in such a way as to ensure that their own supporters gain the most in terms of incomes. When we look at the income changes of major groups we find for example that profit receivers and small businessmen do worse than all other income receivers during the terms of Republican presidents and better than most during the terms of Democratic presidents.

Although these results do show that party change, at least in the executive branch, does not result in immediate major changes in line with party ideologies, they do not show that parties do not try to change policy to fit their ideologies, or that they do not eventually achieve some of the desired results. This comes out clearly in the figures for change in unemployment, where the differences are large and in the expected direction, a result consistent with recent work by Hibbs and Beck.[96] And while the inflation figures can not be dealt with so readily, if we remember that booms typically trigger off inflation near their end and that recessions do not immediately lower it, it is possible to see the figures as a Republican inheritance from spendthrift Democratic predecessors.

A number of recent works have sought to portray the parties as more entrepreneurial and/or more powerful than the above account indicates. As these works have been quite influential, it is necessary to briefly review them and show why I place little faith in them as descriptions of what actually happens.

Perhaps most influential, and certainly most intriguing, has been the work of Nordhaus and MacRae.[97] Following a suggestion by Lindbeck, they constructed a model of the political process which took advantage of the government's supposed ability to manipulate the timing of the business cycle.[98] They argued that if society is at the natural rate of unemployment near election time, it is in the interest of the party in power to disturb the equilibrium. Because in the short term it is possible to have lower unemployment without incurring substantial inflationary costs, and because (they assume) people vote only on the basis of what the economy does in the year preceding the election, the party in power has an incentive to reduce unemployment in the year preceding the election and pay the costs of higher inflation and unemployment during the three years that don't count, thus forming a regular political business cycle. On the assumption, disputed by Frey and Ramser among others,[99] that parties seek to maximize their short-run rather than long-run electoral success, and on the assumption that parties act like selfish entrepreneurs, Nordhaus and MacRae are, in my view, successful in establishing that parties have an incentive to manipulate the economy.

However, neither they nor others have in my opinion been successful in establishing that parties in power actually manipulate the economy in the way indicated. Nordhaus is clearly more interested in propounding the theory than in testing it. MacRae finds that the predicated behavior occurred in only two of the four election periods he examines, although he goes to elaborate lengths to explain this away. McCallum, using a more elaborate though not entirely satisfactory test, which compares the variance explained by the political business cycle theory with that explained by more conventional economic theories, finds no effect.[100] My own view is that the theory may well explain the first Nixon term, but is not a particularly good explanation for any other presidential term. Indeed the Carter presidency, the first in a position to take MacRae and Nordhaus's advice, operated in exactly the reverse fashion with a three-year expansion followed by an election year recession.[101]

A more inductive and confused version of the basic model, assuming satisfising rather than maximizing behavior, is put forward by Tufte.[102] He uses two somewhat contradictory sets of assumptions about how parties behave in election years. One set says that if there is a highly visible economic problem, such as inflation in 1948, 1952 and 1976, presidents alter policy to solve that problem, but that otherwise they change policy to fit the emphasis of their platform—anti-inflation for Republicans, anti-unemployment for Democrats.[103] The other set simply says, "The greater the electoral stakes, the greater the economic stimulation."[104] If one follows the first assumption set, presidents should have slowed the economy before seven of the nine postwar presidental elections, and accelerated it in two. Following the second assumption set, they should have speeded it up in all nine. Tufte presents evidence to support both sets of assumptions. The reader will not be surprised to find that I, together with other observers such as Winters, find this evidence weak and inconclusive.[105] There is nonetheless a kernel of truth in Tufte's formulations. Presidents, like more ordinary mortals, do like job security, do want to solve the nation's most pressing problems and do like to follow their beliefs. Therefore they try fairly often to change economic policy to fit one or another of these sometimes contrary goals, and sometimes, like Nixon in his first term, even succeed. However, it is more common, as with Johnson's efforts to pass a surtax, for the president to be but one factor in a larger political balance, itself constrained to act within certain bounds.

How does this general policy thrust of the two parties fit with the economic interests, the perceived economic interests and the policy views of their supporters? To what extent do the two parties represent rallying points for those most for and against inflation and unemployment respectively? The general answer to these questions is that the policy differences do correspond to some marginal differences between their supporters, but do not do so in such a way that parties can be viewed as always representing the economic needs and opinions of the bulk of their supporters.

When we examine the relation between objective interest and party policy, the degree of isomorphism clearly varies with the economic indicator we choose to look at. Looking first at the most congruent case, Hibbs and Tufte are correct in thinking that more Democrats than Republicans will benefit from reductions in the unemployment rate.[106] As we saw in figure 34, blue-collar workers—and, it might be noted, blacks—are far more likely to become unemployed and these two groups are disproportionately likely to identify with the Democratic party.[107] But this must be tempered by our knowledge that around 60 percent of those in the groups most subject to unemployment do not vote or otherwise participate politically and by evidence indicating those actually unemployed are likely to reduce rather than increase their political participation.[108] Further, it is doubtful whether those with the worst personal experience with unemployment automatically rally around the Democratic party. In the eight Harris polls asking people whether they personally had worse problems with unemployment or inflation which were summarized in table 29, marginally more independents (12.2 percent) than Democrats (11.5 percent) reported that unemployment was the worst problem for them and their family, and 9.1 percent of Republicans saw unemployment as having worse effects on them or their families. Further, while Schlozman and Verba in their 1976 survey show a slightly greater tendency for the unemployed to desert the Republican party, more of the deserters became Independents than Democrats.[109]

Moving to inflation, we have seen that on neither a long-term nor a short-term basis is there evidence that inflation causes redistribution away from groups most likely to be members of one party toward groups most likely to be members of another. There remains the possibility that individuals within the occupational groups we examined who benefit or lose from inflation might rally around different parties, a possibility that we will look at shortly using opinion data.

Finally there is the possibility that different groups have different income increases, whether for inflationary or other reasons, under administrations of the two parties, and that that leads them to give the parties their support. The data in table 38 seems only partly consistent with this interpretation. It is true that people in all groups do absolutely better under the Democrats and this certainly fits with the fact that more people in all occupational groups—with the possible exception of profit receivers—identify with the Democrats than the Republicans. But it is clearly hard to reconcile the fact that profit receivers and small businessmen do relatively better under Democratic administrations and wage earners and transfer recipients relatively better under Republican administrations with actual party composition.

Actual impacts are not always the criterion for pluralists however. As Sorauf reminds us, "Americans develop what appear to be SES sympathies that are not necessarily congruent with their own SES. . . . So the relationship is not always between socioeconomic characteristics and party identification; it may also be between attitudes and party. And in politics, after all, it is the operational attitude, not the origin, that is important."[110] In table 29 we looked at the weight placed on solving inflation by those in different parties. We looked at responses to questions on whether the respondent was worse affected by inflation or unemployment, which was felt to be the worse problem for the country as a whole and whether they would accept a lower pay raise in order to reduce inflation. In each case, it will be recalled, there was a slight but noticeable tendency for Republicans to give the more anti-inflationary response.

Yet the fact that responses to at least the first two of these questions are biased by the necessity of giving a dichotomous response when one of the alternatives is unemployment make it difficult to judge whether negative effects from inflation alone induce people to gather around the Republican party. Fortunately, evidence is available to test this latter point that does not force a dichotomous response. I took the responses to a Gallup question asked thirteen times between 1975 and 1980 on what was the most important problem facing the country, and for each poll found the percentage of Democrats and Republicans naming inflation or unemployment as the most important problem. I then took the mean figures for each party over all thirteen polls. The results do show the expected difference on unemployment. Whereas 13.9 percent of Republicans saw unemployment as the most important problem, a full 20.2 percent of Democrats thought it was the most important problem.[111] But there seemed absolutely no tendency for those who most opposed inflation to rally to the Republicans. The mean percentage of Republicans thinking inflation was the most important problem was 56.7 as compared to 56.3 percent of Democrats. Further it is worth noting that in a period when President Carter was following mildly inflationary policies most of the time, more than twice as many Democrats were worried about inflation as were worried about unemployment.

However, as Sorauf's words (just quoted) indicates, it might well be people's policy views rather than their economic priorities that influence party leaders and cause people to change parties. To what degree does the thrust of the two parties accord with their followers' policy views?

The answer would seem to be not very well. As we saw at the beginning of this chapter, both parties attempted to control inflation primarily through higher interest rates and tax changes. Neither party, at least until very recently, seems to have tried very hard to reduce government spending to curb inflation. Although I do not have party breakdowns of the public's attitudes to these policies, it will be recalled from table 23 that overwhelming numbers favor using spending reductions to control inflation and oppose using tax or interest rate increases. I do however have party breakdowns of the open ended question on which policy would best deal with inflation, shown in table 39. As can be seen, the marginal figures are in the "right" direction, but the overall figures are not. While Democrats were more likely to see wage-price policy as the answer than Republicans, and Republicans were more likely to see government spending cuts as the answer than Democrats, Republicans were more likely to propose some form of wage-price policy than spending cuts and neither set of partisans supported the policies actually resorted to.

A final question is whether people, despite all the above, accurately perceive the differing emphases of the two parties. This can be broken into whether people see a difference and, if so, what that difference is. Table 40 shows that only 41 percent see Republicans and Democrats in their area as having different positions on inflation and only 39 percent see them as having different positions on unemployment. Despite this, much larger numbers see "their" parties as best able to solve these problems. It will be recalled that in table 26 we saw 46 percent of Republicans saying their party was best able to deal with inflation and 61 percent of Democrats thinking their party could best handle the problem. Taken

Table 39   Preferred Anti-inflation Policies in September 1974 by Party, Open-ended

	All	Republicans	Democrats	Independents
Wage-price controls	12%	8%	13%	13%
Price controls	13	12	13	16
Wage controls	3	2	3	4
Government control businesses	4	2	3	6
Cut government spending	8	12	6	9
Consumers spend less	8	11	5	10
Cut foreign aid	5	7	6	4
Others	23	23	24	20
Don't know	36	35	38	31

The question was "How, in your opinion, should inflation be dealt with?" Totals exceed 100 percent due to multiple responses.

Source: *Gallup Opinion Index,* October 1974.

Table 40   Perceived Degree to Which Party Positions Differ on Inflation and Un-
                employment in June 1978

	Parties differ	Don't differ	No opinion
Rising prices	41%	46%	13%
Unemployment	39	45	16

The question was, "Do you think Republicans and Democrats in your area have different
positions on (read each), or don't they differ?"

Source: *Public Opinion*, February/March 1980. CBS-NYT Poll June 19–23, 1978.

together these two sets of figures seem more consistent with the view
that partisans automatically support the policy positions of "their" party,
than with the view that people perceive actual economic policy differences
and choose their party on the basis of these.

Conclusion

In this chapter we looked at groups representing profit receivers, the
self-employed, blue-collar workers, white-collar workers and transfer recipients, as well as looking at the two political parties. Essentially our
interest here was in the degree of consistency between the views and
actions of the leaders of groups supposedly representing those sectors
and the opinions and objective interest of the members of those sectors.
We were most interested in showing the broad consistency between objective interest and opinions and between opinions and the actions of
representatives that a pluralist-democratic model would lead us to expect.
We did not find a clear pattern of this type, although parts of the patterns
we looked at seemed consistent with parts of the pluralist-democratic
model. Often, as we looked at the patterns revealed, it seemed as though
a Marxist or elitist interpretation would give a more economical explanation of the patterns than the pluralist-democratic one, although space
prevented us from examining these alternative interpretations in the same
depth.

8   The Political Economy of Inflation

At the beginning of this book I set out to do three things. First I hoped to describe the processes associated with the making of inflation policy, looking at a wide variety of data. Second, I intended to cast some illumination upon a number of commonly held assumptions on the distributive effects of inflation under varying conditions, on the reactions of people to inflation and on their reasons for reacting as they do. Last, I wanted to use the knowledge of the policy process thus uncovered to test whether pluralist, Marxist or elitist models best described that process. In this chapter I will briefly review the degree to which these aims have been realized, before concluding with some more general observations on the potential usefulness of these findings.

A Description of the Process

In attempting to describe the political process we first examined the effects of inflation on individuals, with the expectation that examination of these effects would show the policy choices that would be in the interests of the polity as a whole and of various of the groups within it.

Looking first at the work on the long-term effects of inflation, we found that even when the effects were considered in isolation from the economic process, the adverse effects of inflation were very mild for the population as a whole and there was little of the redistribution between groups that some economic theory might lead us to expect. Most interesting was the fact that the expected strong redistribution away from welfare recipients, the aged and the poor was not found. Almost as interesting was the finding in the more sophisticated works that there was the mild redistribution away from the top 5 percent of income earners, casting doubt on the widely held belief that the wealthy are the prime beneficiaries from inflation. When we looked also at the place of inflation in the business cycle and related it to changes in unemployment and GNP, the general opinion seemed to be that everyone tended to gain absolutely during inflationary periods while deprived groups also gained relatively.

Hypothesizing that opinions on inflation are likely to be based on observed short-term correlations rather than long-term relations we also looked at the short-term effects of inflation on the real income of different groups. We expected to find that in the short term inflation had positive effects on profits and self-employment income and negative effects on wage and salary and transfer incomes. The effects of inflation on wage and salary, transfer and farm incomes were much as expected. But non-farm self-employment income and profits both proved to be negatively affected by inflation in the short run. Thus it seemed that all groups except farmers might be expected to perceive inflation as being against their interest, assuming that they did look at short-term rather than long-term effects and that they did not see inflation as something to be traded off against growth or employment.

We next looked at four special situations. Looking at an industry by industry breakdown we concluded that while workers and owners in different industries might find their incomes affected a little differently by inflation, on the whole, short-term effects of inflation on wages and profits in the different industries were roughly similar. Looking at the effects of concentration and unionization, we found the effects of inflation on wages and profits did not seem to vary along these dimensions, except that in those industries identified by Galbraith as the demand sector, inflation had markedly less adverse effects. Looking at the difference made by having policy controlled by administrations of different parties, we found some interesting differences in the mean rate of increase of different types of income and saw that most incomes grew faster under Democratic administrations. However we also saw that the short-term relation between inflation and incomes was similar under administrations of both parties, except that the relation with profits seemed negative under Republican presidents and positive under Democratic ones. Finally we saw that the short-term negative effects of inflation on federal expenditures seemed larger than the short-term positive effects on federal revenues.

When we turned to look at public opinion we found, as expected, that attitudes toward inflation were more consistent with its short-term than its long-term effects, though the short-term effects seemed insufficient to account for the degree to which inflation was disliked. The attitude of the general public was highly negative. Over three-quarters of the public saw themselves as harmed by inflation although only about a quarter thought they were severely harmed. This perceived harm has led to highly negative attitudes toward inflation on the part of most people, even if those people think that others are more severely harmed than they are. These figures changed little over time and there was evidence that inflation has been seen as one of America's major problems for most of the postwar period. However the public's already negative attitude became even more negative as the rate of inflation increased in the post-Vietnam war period.

When we turned from the aggregate figures to the breakdowns by group, the most outstanding feature of the figures was that inflation was unpopular with all groups, even those like homeowners and farmers, whom inflation seems to benefit in the short term. There were variations in the degree to which inflation was feared, but these did not seem to follow so much from actual harm as from long-standing public beliefs on who was harmed by inflation. We found that the general public thought that the poor, the aged and those on fixed incomes were the most harmed and the rich and businessmen least harmed. Self-reported harm seemed to follow these opinions, with the welfare pool most likely to report being harmed, blue-collar workers the next most likely and well-off professionals and profit receivers least likely to feel inflation harmed them.

Because the short-term effects on individuals seemed insufficient to explain why inflation has been seen as such a major problem, I looked at a variety of alternative explanations for Americans' great fear of inflation. Four alternatives were explored; real income effects, income illusion, demand transference, and non-income effects. Though all of these alternatives seemed to have at least some effect, income illusion, the idea that people see inflation as taking away real gains in earnings, and demand transference, the idea that people blame price rises for losses actually due to reductions in the relative demand for their services, seemed to best explain the highly negative view of inflation that we found.

Having looked at attitudes toward inflation we turned to look at what the public saw as the best policies to deal with inflation. Here we were immediately struck with the fact that the causes of inflation cited by the public, insofar as they were able to name them, were markedly different from the causes cited by most professional economists. This difference seemed partly explained by cognitive dissonance, with causes such as low taxes being rejected in favor of things such as consumer spending. As a result of this the public supported a policy mix very different from that of most economists, with reductions in government spending, price controls and lower consumer spending being emphasized at the expense of higher taxes and increased interest rates. It was interesting to note that, for most of the groups we examined, the policies recommended seemed to have little to do with their real long- or short-term interests and seemed unlikely to combat inflation as effectually as their attitudes toward inflation indicated was desired. This was particularly true of the lower-income groups, with the strong opposition of the welfare pool to government spending being especially ironic. But even the better-educated, higher-income groups did not have opinions that coincided either with those of economists or, in most cases, with their own income interests, though a case could be made that the policy opinions held by the public would aid this group to maintain relative dominance.

We also examined evidence for the two propositions that political parties represent the interests of those most opposed to inflation and unemployment and that people control economic policy through their use of the vote. Looking at the first of these propositions we found that while the two parties' policy positions on unemployment do correspond with real, albeit small, differences in their constituencies, the same was not true for inflation. People's views on policy seemed, at best, only very loosely related to what their parties did. Taken as a whole the data indicated that people do not use either party to represent their intense feelings about inflation.

Looking at the second of these propositions we found that the evidence that people even attempted to use the vote to register their reaction to economic policy was weak and that the bulk of it indicated that there was usually a small effect on the presidential vote and an even smaller, probably counterproductive, one on congressional voting.

When we turned from public opinion to look at the immediate political processes surrounding macroeconomic policy making we entered a different world, a world in which the prejudices of group leaders have to be translated into the language of economics to be persuasive, and where the process of translation often alters the content of the messages. The information costs attendant upon this process separate the group leaders from their followers in two ways. First they allow leaders who disagree with their followers to advocate the policies they themselves prefer with less risk of being sanctioned. Second they encourage them to "lead" rather than "represent" their followers, which greatly increases the possibility that they may advocate policies they consider in their followers' long-term interests, but which their followers would not if they possessed the same information. Thus information costs serve to insulate the policy making process from public opinion, although public opinion may well set limits to the range of policy choice and provide some reinforcement to advocates of more conservative policies.

Within this closed world of policy makers, power over macroeconomic policy is largely determined by access to the institutionalized positions that immediately control policy. The occupants of top bureaucratic positions in the Treasury, Office of Management and Budget, Council of

Economic Advisers, White House and Federal Reserve have the most immediate power, but are constrained by Congress and the leaders of the major producer groups. The two parties also play a role, chiefly through their socializing influence on the holders of administrative positions, though it should be noted that these latter have often also been socialized through elite education and exposure to the legal and business communities.

We saw that these participants are usually encountered as two rather loose but opposing coalitions. The liberal coalition is mainly composed of Democratic administrations, northern Democratic congressmen and big labor, with some aid more recently from the public interest groups. The conservative coalition is mainly composed of Republican administrations, Republican and some southern Democratic congressmen, business and financial groups and the major farm groups. Both coalitions have allies in the bureaucracies and the universities, though both these institutional bases are more inclined toward the liberal position. Over time there has been a power shift toward the liberal coalition as increasing urbanization has decreased the power of the farm bloc and the numbers of rural-based congressmen and as an increasingly educated population has elected more liberal congressmen and combined into public interest groups. However, periodic cycles often obscure this long term shift.

By the standards of other developed Western nations both coalitions are somewhat conservative in terms of the rates of growth, inflation and unemployment they consider proper, but, when compared with one another, the liberal coalition is considerably more expansionary and is prepared to trade off somewhat higher inflation rates for lower unemployment and faster and steadier growth. Furthermore there are different emphases on which policy tools are most suitable, with the conservative coalition placing primary reliance on monetary policy and the more interventionist liberal coalition placing more emphasis on fiscal and wage-price policy.

Debate between those in the two coalitions is conducted in the language of public interest. Spokesmen for both sides publicly claim that their solutions are in the public interest and will benefit the people as a whole. Beneath this surface it seems fair to say that, while those on both sides do seem to have generally convinced themselves that the aggregate would benefit on balance from their solution, they also see the benefits as differentially weighted. Thus those on the conservative side see primary benefits from their policies as accruing to business, although it seems fair to say both that they see secondary benefits to other groups and that they consider alternative positions unrealistic. Liberals on the other hand tend to see wage earners, the poor, and minorities as the primary beneficiaries of their policies, although they also claim that because their policies are more economically sophisticated they will also benefit business. Thus, on the surface, the debate is over the public interest, while, in the minds of policy makers, it is in part a conflict between groups with different interests.

But there is a third possible level of analysis, the examination and interpretation of the participants' patterns of behavior and the actual policy outcomes. At this level it is possible to interpret what is happening in a number of ways. One is a modified pluralist model in which the policy makers provide leadership for their respective constituencies, although, as we have seen, the policy outcomes secured by the different coalitions are often less favorable to the interests of their constituencies than those advocated by opposing groups. Another is that relative power, rather than absolute income change, is the key and that the policy process is largely an intracapitalist debate over whether to repress or co-opt the vanguard of the proletariat. A third is that the process represents a struggle between a dominant capitalist elite rooted in the ownership of the means of production and an emergent technocratic elite based on its control of the information necessary for planning an increasingly interdependent economy. I will come back to these themes later. Here I mention them merely to show that description of the policy process can lead us beyond the seemingly obvious.

Lastly it might be mentioned that not only has the balance of power between the coalitions changed over time, but the content of their policy proposals and the policies enacted have also changed. In general the trend has been toward acceptance of greater government control of the economy—as President Nixon said, "We are all Keynesians now"—together with a somewhat greater willingness to use direct controls. However, the combination of the Reagan administration with a Republican Senate has led to at least a temporary reversal of the trend.

When we turn to look at the way our earlier data on the real effects of inflation and on public opinion toward it relates to the policy processes described above, we are struck with three primary impressions.

The first is that many groups in the population have no obvious representation in the networks that make economic policy. This we found to be particularly true of fixed income recipients, salaried workers and the self-employed. Although some influential policy makers claim to speak for these groups, their own interest groups play little part in the policy process.

Second, as can be seen in table 41, there is little consistency between the different groups' real interests, short-term interests, perceived interests, preferred policies and the policies advocated in their name. This is true to some extent of all groups but seems particularly true for fixed income recipients and for farmers.

Last, it seems worthwhile to point out that despite the strong anti-inflation emphasis both of the general public and of the policy making

Table 41   Congruence of Actual Effects, Perceived Effects and Policy Preferences

		Fixed incomes	Wage earners	Salary earners	Farmers	Non-farm self-employed	Profit receivers
Long-term actual effects		Slight loss	None	Slight gain	None	None	Slight loss
Short-term actual effects							
1948–79	*b*	−1.23	−0.44		1.19	0.51	−1.43
	B	−0.30	−0.73		0.21	0.40	−0.25
1962–77	*b*	−0.20	−0.50	−0.52	2.74	−0.66	−4.20
	B	−0.09	−0.72	−0.96	0.34	−0.39	−0.62
Perceived harm to family							
Strong		40.0%	32.0%	21.5%	27.3%	21.2%	17.5%
Weak		49.6	56.6	65.2	56.8	63.6	57.0
None		10.4	11.4	13.3	15.9	15.2	25.5
Policy view: percent in favor							
Raise income taxes		7.2	6.3	15.8	10.9	11.8	15.5
Raise interest rates		10.7	9.4	14.5	10.9	10.3	17.8
Reduce govt. spending		82.8	78.5	75.3	87.0	80.9	83.8
Consumers spend less		69.8	63.7	61.0	73.9	70.6	77.6
Consumers borrow less		76.5	78.0	79.2	80.4	82.4	87.9
Govt. controls prices		50.0	47.1	36.4	28.9	55.9	29.3
Govt. controls wages		44.3	27.4	36.4	26.7	52.9	27.4

In looking at the short-term actual effects of inflation on fixed incomes above I have used the figures for old age payments per recipient as these figures cover far more members of the welfare pool than the other results on a per capita basis. To judge the degree of distortion introduced one can re-examine the more extensive figures in tables 1 and 2.

Source: The opinion data is from *Survey of Consumer Finances* (Ann Arbor, University of Michigan), 1969.

elite, inflation has increased rather than decreased over the postwar period. Though this is in part due to international influences and in part due to the increasing influence of the liberal coalition, it may also in part be a comment on the cumbersomeness of available policy instruments and the need for continued institutional reform in this area.

Some Important Findings

As well as having a descriptive aim, this book also aimed to throw some light on a number of commonly held assumptions and theories about the impact of inflation, about public attitudes toward it and about the processes surrounding inflation policy making.

If we look first at the analysis of the aggregate data, it seems worthwhile to make a few brief comments on the findings on the longer-range effects of inflation, even though these are not original to this book. It is clear, as can be seen in chapter 4, that the prevailing opinion among the general public is that inflation is harmful for the entire economy and that it has adverse distributional effects in that it transfers income from the poor to the rich. Some economists share a more sophisticated version of these opinions, holding that so-called "welfare" effects reduce total GNP and that inflation is likely to lead to redistribution away from the poor, particularly fixed-income recipients, and toward better-off profit receivers and self-employed.

The studies mentioned in chapter 3 throw considerable doubt on both these propositions. We saw there that the "welfare" effect is likely to be minuscule and its effects on GNP are likely to be outweighed by positive employment effects, given any but a vertical Phillips curve. Indeed, even in this case, the training considerations advanced by Phelps may be more than sufficient to outweigh the "welfare" effects on GNP.

Furthermore, the distributional effects in practice do not seem to fit the theoretical model. When inflation was looked at in isolation, some of the studies, particularly the simulations, found some slight evidence to support the idea of a redistribution against the fixed-income poor (though some of the other articles found either no effect or a positive effect), but what evidence there was seemed to show downward rather than upward movements in the incomes of the very rich, with any benefits accruing to middle-income people. Most striking of all, however, was the virtually unanimous finding of the various studies that any redistributional effects of inflation are very mild. Moreover, when inflation was looked at in the context of the business cycle and the Phillips curve trade-offs, there was almost complete agreement that the increase in employment and business activity that accompanied inflation was likely to result in considerable gains for the poor, as these are most subject to cyclical income fluctuations. Thus, all in all, the examination of the findings produced little support for the popular model of the effects of inflation and little evidence that reducing a moderate current rate of inflation was worth paying real costs for.

Our examination of the short-term distributional effects of inflation also produced a few surprises. One was the strong negative short-term effect of inflation on profits and self-employment income. It seemed reasonable to expect that while other incomes would lag behind inflation, real profit income should increase with higher prices in the short term, and self-employment income might hold its own. As we have seen however, this did not seem to be the case for properly adjusted profit income, and non-farm self-employment income also seemed negatively affected by inflation. It should be noted that this makes more sense in the context of defensive cost-induced price rises than in that of demand inflation.

Amongst the public opinion findings perhaps the most interesting were the degree to which inflation is perceived as a problem for the individual and the reasons for the highly negative view. What at first seemed the most reasonable explanation, that people were responding to actual effects on their incomes, had little support from the long-term aggregate data, and while the short-term correlations did show a negative relation, neither the variations by group nor the degree of perceived harm seemed justified by the results. We found that people paying off mortgages, who clearly benefit from inflation, showed little perception of this and that farmers, whose incomes showed a positive short-term correlation with inflation, liked it less than most other groups. Further, when we looked at alternative reasons for the negative attitudes, we found that those based on real effects, such as the asymmetric utility loss effect and the increased activity explanation, seemed much less well supported by the data than those not based on real effects, such as income illusion, demand transference and irrational uncertainty.

In the course of this book we have also examined much empirical material relevant to the proposition that expectations have effects on inflation and policy outcomes. It will be recalled that there are basically two versions of expectations theory. Extrapolationist theory holds that people come to expect what has happened in the near past to continue and base their future actions on this assumption. Rational expectations theory holds that people can project the effects of policy changes and other "shocks," and alter their expectations accordingly. In general the material we have looked at in this book confirms parts and disconfirms other parts of the extrapolationist view. Almost all of it, on the other hand, seems contrary to the implications of rational expectations theory.

The material on the relation between current inflation and future expectations of inflation appeared partly in agreement with the extrapolationist view. It will be recalled that there seemed to be a reasonably strong relation between actual changes in prices and expectations of future inflation, with price changes over the past year yielding a higher R^2 than price change over the past three months. Further, the R^2 probably understates the actual relation as the expectations data included predicted points, was converted to means in a rough manner and embodied the margin of error normal in survey data. On the other hand it will be recalled that the mean expected rate seemed in general to be considerably below the actual rate and that the gap widened in periods of rapid inflation. These seem to imply that to the degree that future inflation depends on present expectations, those expectations might be expected to exert a downward influence on inflation, rather than the upward one extrapola-tionists typically postulate.

Perhaps more important as negative evidence is the fact that most people feel unable to respond to inflation and that the predominant response of those who do feel able to do something is to reduce spending, something which should reduce rather than increase inflation. It is also interesting, although by no means conclusive, that most people do not immediately see income raises as a way of protecting themselves against inflation. All three of these response patterns seem to cast some doubt on the picture of masses of people acting to protect themselves against future inflation as soon as they expect it, and suggest instead that most people lack the knowledge or the means to protect themselves. Indeed even today, when means and knowledge have expanded, far more people have their money in low yielding savings accounts than in money market funds paying two to three times as much.

Rational expectations theory is far less supported by the data in this book than extrapolationist theory. First, although it is implied rather than directly shown by my findings, the average person finds it hard to absorb economic data, in part because he or she has no coherent framework that can be used to integrate it, and hence often avoids economic news. More important, as the data clearly demonstrates, there is little understanding among the general public what the implications of a given policy are. It seems unrealistic, for example, to expect the 85 percent who think in-creasing taxes will not reduce inflation to react to a tax cut by expecting future inflation and acting upon that expectation. Indeed perceptions are so muddy that it seems hard to predict how people might behave if they predicated their actions on the effects they expected policy changes to have on the economy. Further it must be remembered that here too evi-dence is lacking that people have the knowledge and the freedom from institutional constraints to act upon such perceptions.

Although the opinion data we have looked at does not accord very well with either version of expectations theory, another thrust of this book may be more compatible. It will be recalled that we found that policy makers seemed both to have different and superior information and to be relatively unconstrained by their purported constituents' opinions in their attempts to affect policy. It therefore seems possible to this observer that one could reconstruct versions of expectations theory on a Marxist or an elitist base with economic impact attributed only to a severely restricted set of relatively well-informed actors, although on balance I am skeptical.

What have we learned in this book about the political business cycle? It will be recalled that this theory had three elements. People were sup-posed to vote for or against incumbents on the basis of economic con-ditions; incumbents should respond by attempting to stimulate demand

223

The Political Economy of Inflation

near election time; and elected incumbents should have the power to successfully achieve their object. We have not found much evidence to support this theory.

We spent most time on the first part of the theory, the one in my view with the most initial plausibility. We saw that there was some evidence to indicate that economic conditions influenced political popularity and electoral outcomes, especially in presidential elections. However we also saw that there was good reason to think that the effect was not a large one, and some reason, especially for congressional elections, to doubt that many of the postulated effects exist. We also saw that to the extent that there was an effect on congressional voting it would give the Democratic party good reason to obstruct any Republican president seeking election-year stimulation. Finally we saw, especially at the presidential level, much evidence to indicate that reducing inflation might be as important or more so to electoral success as increasing income or reducing unemployment.

Turning to intentions, while it is true, ceteris paribus, that elected officials usually seek re-election, three of the nine postwar presidential elections did not feature incumbents and most economic policy makers in Congress were rarely in danger of electoral defeat. Nor is re-election the only motivation of elected officials, with other considerations such as the health of the economy in the long term also having some weight. We saw in the last two chapters that one of the two major parties has a long-term aversion to sudden stimulation, as do many of its allies in business and elsewhere. Further, many elected officials believe that low inflation is also conducive to re-election, a belief that we saw to have considerable empirical support. However, it is my own impressionistic view that many legislators are more likely to think stimulative policies will aid them than the evidence warrants.

Neither our examination of the policy making system nor our review of the successes and failures of economic theory in guiding public policy led us to confirm the idea that elected officials can obtain the policies they want when they want them. We saw that many non-elected groups such as the Federal Reserve, bureaucrats, business groups and labor unions hold considerable power. Further, we saw that a fragmented governmental structure embodying many veto points makes it hard for any elected official, even the president, to obtain the changes he desires and that even when the changes are secured it is hard to ensure that the benefits will be felt at the intended time. Last, it should be remembered that, particularly at the beginning and end of our period, the economy did not always respond to economic policy in the anticipated manner, or with the anticipated lags.

Perhaps the most unexpected of our public opinion findings is the public's views on the party most likely to solve inflation. To anyone that has looked even casually at the policies proposed and adopted by the two parties it is clear that the Republican party places a far higher emphasis on solving inflation and is much more prepared to make sacrifices to achieve that goal. Furthermore this has been true throughout the postwar period. Yet the responses from the public show little tendency to consider the Republicans as more likely to solve inflation. Indeed, the admittedly scanty evidence points to the opposite conclusion, that the public generally sees the Democrats as the party best able to solve inflation. This is largely due to the combination of party loyalty and larger numbers of avowed Democrats, though one of the two sets of broken down figures available shows independents also favoring the Democratic party.

The discussion on the behavior of those actually responsible for making policy contained far fewer surprises. But two findings do seem worthy of mention in this context. One is the fact that many of the group's leaders have positions on inflation that are not in accord with either the objective interests or the wishes of their constituents. The other is that groups with important interests in the rate of inflation, such as those representing consumers and fixed income recipients, not only are not substantially involved in the policy making process, but show little interest in becoming involved.

Testing the Models

The third aim of this book was to see whether the models used by pluralist, Marxist or elitist theories best described the relation between economic changes, public opinion and policy making. We looked at three variants of the pluralist model—a group model, a pluralist-democratic model and a rational-actor model. We also looked at a traditional Marxist model and a structuralist one, as well as two variants of the elitist model, one with a single controlling elite and the other one with a dominant elite being challenged by a new rising elite. These various models were specified in some detail in chapter 1 and we need not repeat that description here.

Our primary concern throughout this book has been to test the pluralist-democratic model, and the book was designed to make it easier to test the linkages in that model. This was done because of the dominance of the pluralist-democratic model in contemporary political science. Therefore the comments I will make on the degree to which the group, rational-actor, Marxist and elitist models fit the data must necessarily be taken somewhat more tentatively than my comments on the degree of fit to the pluralist-democratic model.

It will be recalled that the chief feature of the group model was the fact that organization followed interest and that formal groups and institutions were essentially empty shells to be used by somewhat more fluid groupings around particular interests. There were aspects of the data that were consistent with this picture. Opinions on inflation were strong, were not strongly stratified along other dimensions such as class and showed little tendency to view inflation as an interest in a trade-off relation with other interests. And at the leadership level we found coalitions that bound together somewhat disparate formal groups and institutions. But the central feature of the model was not replicated. There seemed no explicit organization around the interest, despite the fact that people considered it one of the two most important domestic problems. In addition, not only have strong anti-inflation groups not arisen, but there is little evidence that the political parties have served as rallying points for those most for and against inflation. Furthermore, the alliances at the leadership level were between united groups, rather than cutting across them as the group model would predict, and the disparities between real interest, perceived interest and proposed policy were much greater than this model would lead us to expect.

The rational-actor model, while more plausible in our area than the group model, also seems to have irretrievable flaws as a complete description of our findings. It is succesful in having answers for the failure of a group to form around the inflation issue, and for the lack of involvement of some groups in economic policy making: high information costs, the competitive advantage of producer groups and the lower costs of a compensation strategy. It is also consistent with the activities of union and business groups with regard to unemployment and with the mild tendency for people to vote against incumbent presidents when the economy does badly. However the model does not have easy answers for people's tendency to overstate the importance of inflation as a problem, for their failure to understand the appropriate policy solutions, and for failure of most to perceive the real differences between the parties on the issue. It does not explain the weakness of the voting link nor why congressional voting punishes the president's party rather than the majority party. Nor does it seem very consistent with the power of non-elected groups and their failure to represent their constituencies, with the power of elite opinion, or with the difficulty elected officials seem to have in enforcing their mandates. Finally it is not obvious, given this explanation, why inflation, perceived by most as the most important problem of the 1970s, increased greatly over the 1970–1980 period.

The pluralist-democratic model has as its basis the effective representation of interests. It is usually assumed that people have real interests in a given area and that they are aware of those interests and calculate a solution to them. As in the group model it is assumed that they will organize around their most salient interests but that this organization can be expressed through existing groups where these are organized in a way roughly coincident with the interest, particularly where start-up costs are high. In the variants with political parties, these are viewed as aggregating the interests of broadly defined, usually class-oriented, groups. Ideally the groups and parties should be democratically organized, with the followers able to sanction the leaders, but, at a minimum, the groups and parties should represent the real interests of their constituents. At the leadership level a process of bargaining, log-rolling and coalition formation is envisaged in which leaders trade their votes on matters not salient to their constituents for votes on matters of greater salience to them.

This model, particularly the variant with political parties aggregating interests, has a better fit to the data we have examined than the group or rational-actor models. This is particularly true at the leadership level where, as we have seen, many of the group leaders see themselves as representing the interests of their constituents. Furthermore the bargaining, log-rolling and coalition formation predicted by the model clearly takes place. When we move back a stage and look at the links between leaders and followers, some of the linkages proposed by the pluralist-democratic model seem to exist. Parties do seem to serve an aggregation role, both in aggregating the groups into coalitions and in aggregating and expressing two very distinct views as to optimal demand management. And some of the groups also have proper linkages, with unions acting in a "leadership" role and representing their members' real interests and business groups acting in a "representational" role and expressing their members' opinions.

But despite these points of congruity the pluralist-democratic model seems a very inadequate description of the total activity in the area. The primary defect of the model as a representation of reality in this area is the assumption that interests are accurately perceived and represented. Comparing our findings with the first stage of the model, we saw that there was little similarity between the real long-term interests of the public and their views on the importance of inflation and the degree to which it was affecting them. Even when we compared the opinions with the short-term effects of inflation, we only found reasonable agreement by isolating the effects of inflation from simultaneous effects of unemployment and growth, something which, while it is proper for the group model, is more dubious for the pluralist-democratic model. Furthermore, even when we looked at the short-term effects in isolation, there seemed little correspondence between those groups whom inflation affected most adversely in absolute terms and the degree to which those groups opposed inflation.

At the next stage of the model there seems little correspondence between the strength of the desire to stop inflation and the efficacy of the means chosen to halt it. Nor does the public seem to have an accurate idea of which party they can rely on to control inflation. Thus the pluralist-democratic assumption that perceived harm can be converted into effective demands does not seem to have been met.

Turning to the third stage of the model, it is evident that, despite our earlier observations on unions and business groups, the system of representation bears little resemblance to that in the pluralist-democratic model. We saw that many population groups, including the fixed income group which the opinion data identified as most adversely affected by inflation, have virtually no representation in the inflation process. And, to the degree that their leaders do take part in the process, they often do not represent their constituents, with the fixed-income recipients' leaders, for example, clearly giving unemployment priority over inflation. Even when we focused only on the representative groups that appear to have influence on the process, we found that while a reasonable case can be made that pluralist-democratic linkages hold for business groups and possibly for the Republican party, it is much more difficult to find such linkages for unions or the Democratic party. Thus, taken all in all, the pluralist-democratic model does not fit well, despite some congruence for some groups at some points of the model.

If pluralist models do not fit our data well, do Marxist and elitist models do any better? The answer seems, on the whole, to be positive. I will look first at the findings in this book that generally support both Marxist and elitist models, before looking at contrary evidence and seeing which of the four models appears best supported.

One supportive finding is the failure of most people to perceive their own interests accurately, something consistent with the false conciousness or general ignorance seen as normal by these models. Particularly noticeable was the universality of the tendency to overstate the negative effects of inflation upon the individual. The reader will recall that when we pursued this, the most plausible reasons for this view—income illusion and demand transference—seemed to require the systematic misdirection that Marxist and elitist theory postulate. In a similar vein, the fact that different real effects on different groups did not lead to different views about inflation also points to people's opinions being formed by means other than their direct experience.

Also consistent was the confusion in people's economic policy opinions and the fact that after three decades during which inflation had been perceived as one of the most important problems facing the country and the most important one facing the individual, people had not developed any grasp of which policies would increase it and which would decrease it. Moreover it was interesting, though not conclusive, that people could perceive that the conservative solution of reduced government spending would reduce inflation, but not perceive that the liberal solution of increasing taxes would.

When we moved from people's opinions on what is happening, and what should be done about it, to their demands, the evidence also accorded with Marxist and elitist theories. We saw that people feel helpless to do very much to protect themselves directly from inflation, something that fits the elitist view particularly well. We saw that this is allied with a considerable degree of skepticism about the ability of the political system to solve economic problems. When we looked at the use of the vote to influence policy we saw that voters seem as likely to vote to control the largely illusory problems caused by inflation as the real ones caused by slow growth, unemployment and limited redistribution. In addition we saw both that voting on economic grounds does not explain much of the variance in the vote and that the limited amount of economic voting that does occur is based not on what is happening to people but what they think is happening to the country, something clearly more easily manipulated.

At the next stage, the wide difference between the views of those involved in policy making and the general public clearly fits. The number of business-related non-elected actors also fits. Also consistent is the fact that few of the groups and parties seemed to have "representative" leaders, with the actual patterns better fitting the "leadership," "statesmanship" and "organizational maintenance" patterns that are more consistent with Marxist and elitist theory. Further, the major exceptions to the generalization that groups do not reflect both the views and interests of their members, i.e. business groups and possibly the Republican party, are exactly the exceptions that Marxist and elitist theories would lead us to expect.

Despite these impressive consistencies, none of the theories account for all our findings. Three parts of the pattern do not fit any of these theories well. The fact that none of the long-term studies indicate that inflation benefits the well-off, as it seems to for example in Brazil, and that most see it as harming them, is not very consistent with any of the theories given the actual increases in inflation. The number of actors and the degree of independence of the actors is also greater than most people would see as implied by these theories. Last, while it is consistent that profit receivers feel less harmed by inflation than others, at the same time that their representatives lead the fight against it, the fact that most higher-income people genuinely think inflation is a major problem points away from those versions of Marxist and elitist theory where a cynical elite manipulates policy in their selfish interest and toward versions where these people are genuinely able to convince themselves that they are acting in the best interests of the country.

Of the four theories I find the single elite model the least convincing. Aside from the fact that I have some trouble visualizing a military-industrial-political elite that would shrink the share of GNP going to the military from the 10.9 percent of 1955 to the 4.9 percent of 1980, it is not very clear why this theory would lead us to expect inflation to increase, and it is not clear why the liberal position gained force over time or indeed why there are competing coalitions on economic policy. Nor is it clear why the unions take a position in opposition to that of profit receivers rather than becoming co-opted by them. It is hard to explain the reasonably independent role of technocrats, bureaucrats and academicians and the fact that these elements seem more inclined to oppose than support profit receivers. Finally, some elements of the public-opinion and voting evidence, such as the congruity between actual rates of inflation and unemployment and people's perceptions of them and the fact that the vote sometimes does appear to be affected by economic considerations, and does have policy effects, are not entirely consistent with this theory.

Many of these problems are less pressing for an elite theory that incorporates a competing technocratic elite. The expansion of government spending combined with the decline in the percentage spent on defense and the periodic attempts to reverse the trend, clearly fit the picture of a battle between an old and a challenging elite, as do the existence and the ideologies of the two coalitions, and the fact that they agree on many basics. More importantly, looked at from this perspective inflation can be seen as an outcome with payoffs for both competing elites. The old elite can use it to pursue policies that keep workers in place, while the new elite can use it to aid the expansion of government and justify economic planning. Further, on this view one can see unions as constrained to support a liberal coalition some of whose policies, such as wage-price policy, seem more likely to expand government and planning than help unions or workers. It obviously fits the independent policy role of technocrats, bureaucrats and academicians. Finally, on the assumption that the two elites would compete for the support of the masses, it makes sense to expect some limited input from the public into the policy process. However the problems of definition of the elites and their unidimensional motivation, which have always bedeviled elite theory, do not seem to be dealt with by my data.

The evidence also seems broadly consistent with my traditional Marxist model. Aside from the supporting evidence we considered earlier, the "leadership" role of the unions and the false consciousness exhibited by workers seem to fit this model particularly well, as does the fact that the representatives of the welfare pool tend to ally themselves with the unions.

However some aspects of the evidence do not fit the the model as well. The complexity and lack of unity of the policy making process does not fit well with traditional Marxism, although the fact that there is considerable agreement among policy makers on goals, methods and taboo approaches does. The independence of the technocrats from business interests also does not fit well. Nor is it clear why the long-term shift appears to be toward the liberal coalition and why government has expanded so much, although the Reagan reaction is what the theory might lead us to expect.

Some of these problems are resolved when we switch to the structuralist variant of Marxism. The independence of the technocrats fits the structuralist emphasis on the role of the state, even though I feel compelled to add that I have never fully understood what structuralists mean by "the state." The division among policy makers partly fits the structuralist notion of conflict between the co-optive and repressive sections of the ruling class and between small and large business, while the fact that there is a liberal coalition and that it has made gains fits with their assertion that the working class is becoming more self-conscious and harder to co-opt. This also explains why inflation is necessary to the system and hence why capitalist price setters might encourage it; it simultaneously restricts the real gains of workers and provides a rationale for conservative policies. On the other hand some evidence seems more consistent with traditional Marxism than structuralism. There seems far less class consciousness than the theory would lead us to expect. Union membership, strikes and less formal protest seem to be decreasing rather than increasing. And far from a gathering legitimacy crisis there at least appears to be a conservative reaction against earlier gains.

What can we say overall about the degree to which the different models explain the findings of this book? While it seems that none of the theories explains all that we have seen perfectly, it is clear that the Marxist and elitist theories perform better than the pluralist ones. Of these former the competing elites version of pluralism seem the most consistent with the evidence, but a case could also be made for the two variants of Marxism.

One final observation seems in order before we consider the generalizability of these findings. Theories in political science are loose and overlapping, sometimes containing incongruous elements cheek by jowl with one another; and political scientists, like other social scientists, often prefer to complicate their basic theory rather than to discard it when it fails to adequately account for some aspect of the real world. It is, I think, natural to feel that facts that do not fit one's preferred model can be adequately explained by that model given a few additional assumptions. I invite the reader at least to entertain the possibility that it is their basic model that is wrong, and in any case to ask whether the added assumptions necessary to achieve a "fit" are consistent with the underlying premises of their model.

Generalizing the Findings

It is obviously of interest what the processes involved in the formation of macroeconomic policy are, as it is interesting what the policy processes are in the formation of any policy. But it is also reasonable to ask what the contribution of this study is to the larger task of mapping the political processes characteristic of societies. In this connection four questions inevitably arise. One is the question of comparability: Are the processes surrounding the making of inflation policy the same in all countries? Are they the same in some subset of nations such as developed Western nations, or are they peculiar to the United States? Another is the question of relevance: Is this a suitable policy area for testing the major theoretical frameworks we have looked at in this book? A third is the question of importance: How important are the policies made in the area for society as a whole and how much difference does it make if they are made one way or another? Last is the question of typicality: How generalizable are the findings in this area to political processes in other policy areas?

This book is obviously not set up to deal with the question of comparability. However it does seem fair to say that some of the features characteristic of the area in the United States such as complexity, poor information flow, and the dominant position of technocrats and producer groups in policy making seem to also hold in other countries. Thus there do seem prima facie reasons for expecting similar policy processes to obtain. There is however an obvious need for comparative research aimed at discovering whether inflation is dealt with in a similar way in other countries.

The question of relevance can be answered more definitely. Here the answer is clearly affirmative. When one looks at the postwar literature that has emerged from American Marxists, elitists and pluralists, it is clear that there are few policy areas that all three claim are characterized by the processes specified by their models. Macroeconomic policy is clearly central to the claims of all three camps. If the pluralist model cannot describe the activity in this area, at a minimum we must question its generality, while at a maximum one is led to C. Wright Mills's description of pluralist processes as characterizing only secondary policies. It is important to the elitists because it seems clearly one of that limited number of central policies setting societal parameters to which their description must apply if it is to be more than an idiosyncratic description of some aspects of foreign policy. Last, to the Marxists, with their general belief in eventual economic determinism, control of the economy is clearly the central policy area. In this context my partial confirmation of the Marxist and elitist models lends some additional weight to their claims and renders less plausible pluralist claims to generality.

The question of the area's importance can also be clearly answered. Macroeconomic policy is clearly one of the most important kinds of policy both for its direct and for its indirect effects. Directly, its effects in terms of the scope and salience of the results to the public are clearly very great, with only decisions on peace or war being more important. Indirectly, its results have strong effects on what is possible in other policy areas, both because it largely determines the resources available for division and because different outcomes can have strong effects on particular areas, as for example with unemployment and civil rights. Thus, even if the results observed here applied only to this area, they would be important in a depiction of the entire policy process.

This observation leads naturally to consideration of the last of our questions. To what extent do the conditions determining policy processes in this area obtain in other areas? How far can our findings be generalized? While all policy areas have some unique features, it is my opinion that our results are generalizable, but not to all other policy areas.

Figure 36 shows a simple, three-dimensional model of some determinants of policy processes. The general model would separate policies according to three criteria—their importance, the information level of the people affected by the policy and the degree of divergence of group interests in the different policy outcomes. Group divergence, which is a measure of the differences between the cost benefit ratios for the affected groups, can also be thought of as a combination of the zero-sum or non-zero-sum nature of policy outcomes, combined with the size of the payoffs in N individual cells. Information level is determined by the ratio of the costs to the citizen of gathering policy information and the individual payoff to him from acquiring such information. The costs in turn are affected by the complexity of the policy and knowledge on the consequences of alternative outcomes. Importance is seen as a combination of the number of people affected by decisions in a given policy area and the degree to which they feel affected.

When we restrict this model to two dimensions by assuming the policy to be important, as we have done in the lower part of the figure, we emerge with four quadrants, defined by group divergence and public information. I would argue that policies that fall into the corners of these quadrants would exhibit rather different policy processes. The ideal type for high-information, high-divergence policies would be the "conflictual" process similar to the redistributional category of Lowi. Here well-organized groups representing constituent interests battle for dominance. The ideal type for high-information, low-group-divergence policy is the

GENERAL POLICY PROCESS MODEL

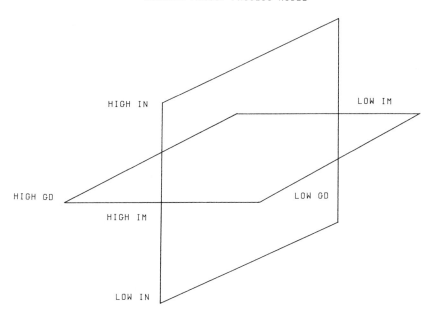

POLICY PROCESS MODEL FOR HIGHLY
IMPORTANT POLICIES

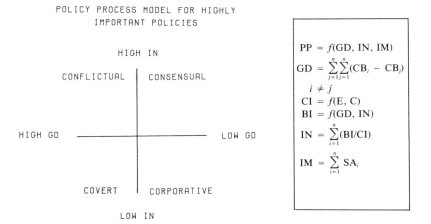

Figure 36   A model of the policy process.
Legend: PP = Policy process; GD = Group divergence; IN = Information level of af-
fected population; IM = Importance of policy; CI = Cost of obtaining information; BI
= Individual's benefit from information; C = Complexity of policy; E = Education;
SA = Salience to affected individuals; CB = Cost/benefit ratio

"consensual" process marked by agreement between groups, acting in the interests of their constituents. The ideal type for low-information, high-divergence policies is the "covert" process, similar to the distributive category of McConnell and Lowi, where small well-organized groups are able to gain benefits for themselves at the expense of the public interest. Finally the ideal type for low-information, low-divergence policies is the "corporative" process, where elites rule in the public interest.

In terms of this model, macroeconomic policy falls near the border of the corporative and covert sectors. Policy seems generally aimed at maintaining a politico-economic system that appears to give the greatest rewards to the groups from which policy makers come. However, within these distributive boundaries, policy makers do try to maximize the general welfare as they perceive it. The placement of the policy in this quadrant also answers the earlier question of how far we can generalize our findings. We would expect to find similar processes in important policies characterized by low public information and low group divergence.

Last, it is worth asking into which of the quadrants most important policies fall. It is my own opinion that important policies are distributed with some evenness throughout the quadrants, possibly with some bias toward the covert sector. But with the increasing complexity and interdependence of public policies, the cost of accurate policy information is likely to rise steadily in all areas. Unless this trend is offset by education and information-processing gains, "corporative" and "covert" processes will probably become more characteristic of American public policy than is currently the case.

Conclusion

The picture that has emerged in this book is one that cannot be entirely pleasing to those who believe in the virtues of a democratic process. It appears that most people have little idea of the true impact of economic variables upon themselves and others, and tend to overstate or misperceive the negative effects of inflation. There appears to be increasing uncertainty about what to do with the economy accompanied by resistance to many of the more plausible means of managing it. There appears little correlation between the expressed desires of people and the actions and beliefs of their leaders. As Demetrius Phalereus once put it, "Men having often abandoned what was visible for the sake of what was uncertain, have not got what they expected, and have lost what they had, being unfortunate by an enigmatical sort of calamity."

Notes

Chapter One

1. Many economists, it must be pointed out, would hold that, because of the quality of available data, the difficulty of separating the income effects of inflation from the income effects of other variables and the uncertain lags involved, a deductive approach is likely to be more fruitful.

2. Robinson G. Hollister and John L. Palmer, "The Impact of Inflation on the Poor," in Kenneth Boulding and Martin Pfaaf, eds., *Redistribution to the Rich and the Poor* (Belmont, Ca.: Wadsworth, 1972), 240–70; Jeffrey G. Williamson, " 'Strategic' Wage Goods, Prices and Inequality," *American Economic Review*, 67 (March 1977): 29–41; Neil W. Swan, "Inflation and the Distribution of Income" (PhD. dissertation, University of Pennsylvania, 1969); Edmund S. Phelps, *Inflation Policy and Unemployment Theory* (New York: Norton, 1972).

3. George L. Bach and James B. Stevenson, "Inflation and the Redistribution of Wealth," *Review of Economics and Statistics* 56 (February 1974): 1–13 ; Edward N. Wolff, "The Distributional Effects of the 1969–1975 Inflation on Holdings of Household Wealth in the United States," *Review of Income and Wealth* 25 (June 1979): 195–207; Edward Budd and David F. Seiders, "Micro-Aspects of Macro Performance: The Impact of Inflation on the Distribution of Income and Wealth," *American Economic Review* 61 (May 1971): 128–38 ; William D. Nordhaus, "The Effects of Inflation on the Distribution of Economic Welfare," *Journal of Money, Credit and Banking* 5 (February 1973): 465–508 ; Joseph J. Minarik, "The Size Distribution of Income During Inflation," *Review of Income and Wealth* 25 (December 1979): 377–92. Two methodologically less satisfactory works that attempt a comprehensive review are Albert E. Burger, "The Effects of Inflation (1960–1968)," *Federal Reserve Bank of St. Louis Monthly Review* 51 (November 1969): 25–36; and Andrew F. Brimmer, "Inflation and Income Distribution in the United States," *Review of Economics and Statistics* 53 (February 1971): 37–48.

4. Examples are George Katona, *Price Control and Business* (Bloomington: University of Indiana Press, 1945), *Psychological Analysis of Economic Behavior* (New York: McGraw-Hill, 1951); and the annual issues of George Katona and Associates, *Survey of Consumer Finances* (Ann Arbor: University of Michigan), and its successor publication *Surveys of Consumers* (Ann Arbor, University of Michigan).

5. The earliest work I know of to make serious use of this data was S.J. Turnovsky, "Empirical Evidence on the Formation of Price Expectations," *Journal of the American Statistical Association* 65 (December 1970): 1441–

54. The most recent and careful use is in Rodney L. Jacobs and Robert A. Jones, "Price Expectations in the United States," *American Economic Review* 70 (June 1980): 269–77.

6. George L. Bach, *Making Monetary and Fiscal Policy* (Washington, D.C.: Brookings Institution, 1971) and *The New Inflation* (Providence: Brown University Press, 1973); Aaron Wildavsky, *The Politics of the Budgetary Process*, 3d ed. (Boston: Little, Brown, 1974); Lawrence C. Pierce, *The Politics of Fiscal Policy Formation* (Pacific Palisades, Ca.: Goodyear, 1971); John F. Manley, *The Politics of Finance* (Boston: Little, Brown, 1970); Arnold R. Weber, *In Pursuit of Price Stability: The Wage-price Freeze of 1971* (Washington, D.C.: Brookings Institution, 1973); John Sheahan, *The Wage Price Guideposts* (Washington, D.C.: Brookings Institution, 1967); Grant McConnell, *Steel and the Presidency 1962* (New York: Norton, 1963); Garth L. Mangum, *The Emergence of Manpower Policy* (New York: Holt, Rinehart & Winston, 1969); Rodger Davidson, *The Politics of Comprehensive Manpower Legislation* (Baltimore: Johns Hopkins University Press, 1972).

7. The reasons are discussed in Martin J. Bailey, "The Welfare Cost of Inflationary Finance," *Journal of Political Economy* 64 (April 1956): 93–110.

8. See for example Phelps, *Inflation Policy*, especially chapter 6.

9. This seems the general conclusion of most of the readings mentioned in notes 2 and 3 above.

10. See for example Phelps, *Inflation Policy*; and Hollister and Palmer, "Impact of Inflation."

11. The Gallup organization asked the question "What do you think is the most important problem facing the country today?" around 100 times between 1946 to 1979 inclusive. The number of problems reported varied between three and twelve. During this period inflation was mentioned as one of the most important problems all but four times, and was the most important problem thirty-six times, the second most important twenty-two times and the third most important ten times. See George H. Gallup, *The Gallup Poll*, 3 vols. (New York: Random House, 1972) and various issues of *The Gallup Opinion Index*.

12. The classic article is John F. Muth, "Rational Expectations and the Theory of Price Movements," *Econometrica* 29 (July 1961): 315–35. Reasonable surveys of the field are Brian Kantor, "Rational Expectations and Economic Thought," *Journal of Economic Literature* 17 (December 1979): 1422–41; and Bennett T. McCallum, "The Significance of Rational Expectations Theory," *Challenge* (January-February 1980): 37–43.

13. Bennett T. McCallum and John K. Whitaker, "The Effectiveness of Fiscal Feedback and Automatic Stabilizers under Rational Expectations," *Journal of Monetary Economics* 5 (April 1979): 171–86.

14. There is no generally accepted definition of what a pluralist-democratic system should look like but rather a list of overlapping definitions inconsistent in one respect or another. The most influential books in the development of this theory, generally referred to in the literature as pluralist rather than pluralist-democratic, are David B. Truman, *The Governmental Process* (New York: Knopf, 1951), Robert A. Dahl, *A Preface to Democratic Theory* (Chicago: University of Chicago Press, 1956), Gabriel A. Almond and James S. Coleman, *The Politics of Developing Areas* (Princeton, N.J.: Princeton University Press, 1960) and Earl Latham, *The Group Basis of Politics* (New York: Octagon Books, 1965). The approach outlined below does not follow any of the writers literally but rather seeks to fit the general approach to the known facts in the area so as to avoid producing a "straw man" that could be easily and misleadingly disproved.

15. See Mancur Olson, *The Logic of Collective Action* (Cambridge, Mass.: Harvard University Press, 1965), for the reasons underlying this assumption.

16. The classic statements of the group model are found in James Madison, "The Federalist No. 10"; and Arthur F. Bentley, *The Process of Government: A Study of Social Pressures* (Chicago: University of Chicago Press, 1908). Since Bentley's rediscovery by Truman the approach has been very influential. Though few today would adopt all aspects of it, many use parts of it. Earl Latham, *Group Politics*, is the current theorist giving most emphasis to this approach.

17. James M. Buchanan and Gordon Tullock, *The Calculus of Consent* (Ann Arbor: University of Michigan Press, 1962); William H. Riker and Peter Ordeshook, *An Introduction to Positive Political Theory* (Englewood Cliffs, N.J.: Prentice-Hall, 1973); Norman Frolich

and Joe A. Oppenheimer, *Modern Political Economy* (Englewood Cliffs, N.J.: Prentice-Hall, 1978); Anthony Downs, *An Economic Theory of Democracy* (New York: Harper, 1957); Norman Frolich, Joe A. Oppenheimer and Oran Young, "A Test of Downsian Voter Rationality: 1964 Presidential Voting," *American Political Science Review* 72 (March 1978): 178–97; V.O. Key, *The Responsible Electorate: Rationality in Presidential Voting 1936–1960* (Cambridge, Mass.: Harvard University Press, 1966); Benjamin I. Page, *Choices and Echoes in Presidential Elections: Rational Man and Electoral Democracy* (Chicago: University of Chicago Press, 1978); Gerald Pomper, "From Confusion to Clarity: Issues and American Voters, 1956–1968," *American Political Science Review* 66 (June 1972): 415–28; Benjamin I. Page and Calvin C. Jones, "Reciprocal Effects of Policy Preferences, Party Loyalty and the Vote," *American Political Science Review* 73 (December 1979): 1071–89. Interesting evaluations of the rational-voter hypothesis are Michael Margolis, "From Confusion to Confusion: Issues and the American Voter (1956–1972)," *American Political Science Review* 71 (March 1977): 31–43; and Edward G. Carmines and James A. Stimson, "The Two Faces of Issue Voting," *American Political Science Review* 74 (March 1980): 78–91.

18. Gerald Kramer, "Short-term Fluctuations in U.S. Voting Behavior, 1896–1964," *American Political Science Review* 65 (March 1971): 131–43; Edward R. Tufte, *Political Control of the Economy* (Princeton: Princeton University Press, 1978); William Nordhaus, "The Political Business Cycle," *Review of Economic Studies* 42 (April 1975): 169–89.

19. The one variant of Marxism that I have omitted that does purport to describe current American society and does subject itself to empirical tests is finance capitalism. I have not dealt with it both because the tests left me unconvinced of its plausibility and because I wished to restrict the theoretical alternatives.

20. Ralph Milliband, *The State in Capitalist Society* (New York: Basic Books, 1969).

21. Nicos Poulanzas, *Political Power and Social Classes* (London: New Left Books, 1975); *State, Power, Socialism* (London: New Left Books, 1978); Claus Offe, *Strukturprobleme des kapitalistischen Staates: Aufsätze zur politischen Soziologie* (Frankfurt am Main: Suhrkamp, 1972); James O'Connor, *The Fiscal Crisis of the State* (New York: St. Martin's Press, 1973).

22. Two recent articles postulating rather different implicit bargains between the working class and capitalists are David M. Gordon, "Capital-Labor Conflict and the Productivity Slowdown," *American Economic Review* 71 (May 1981): 30–35; and Adam Przeworski and Michael Wallerstein, "The Structure of Class Conflict in Democratic Capitalist Societies," *American Political Science Review* 76 (June 1982): 215–38.

23. C. Wright Mills, *The Power Elite* (New York: Oxford University Press, 1956); G. William Domhoff, *The Powers That Be: Processes of Ruling-class Domination in America* (New York: Random House, 1978); Vilfredo Pareto, *Sociological Writings* (New York: Praeger,1966); Gaetano Mosca, *The Ruling Class* (New York: McGraw, 1939); Daniel Bell, *The Coming of Post-industrial Society: A Venture in Social Forecasting* (New York: Basic Books, 1976).

24. C. Wright Mills, *Power Elite;* Mosca, *Ruling Class;* Bell, *Post-industrial Society;* Suzanne Keller, *Beyond the Ruling Class: Strategic Elites in Modern Society* (New York: Random House, 1963).

25. Robert Michels, *Political Parties: A Sociological Study of the Oligarchical Tendencies of Modern Democracy* (New York: Free Press, 1966); G. William Domhoff, *Who Rules America?* (Englewood Cliffs, N.J.: Prentice-Hall, 1967); Olson, *Collective Action.* I view Olson and other public choice theorists writing in the same vein as elitists rather than pluralists, because their primary contribution has been to largely solve a major problem associated with elite theory, namely why the masses are politically apathetic and the elite is not. Their answer, that participation is not in the rational interest of the individual unless that individual receives direct extrinsic rewards for participation, bases apathy firmly in a theory of individual self-interest.

26. This is in large part due to the fact that Marxist theory can be regarded as a special case of elite theory, with power based on the control of the means of production being only one of a number of possible bases for elite power. In addition some elitists have consciously incorporated Marxist elements—e.g. Domhoff.

27. C. Wright Mills, *Power Elite;* Thomas R. Dye, *Who's Running America?: Institutional Leadership in the United States* (Englewood Cliffs, N.J.: Prentice-Hall, 1976).

28. Mosca, *Ruling Class;* James Burnham, *The Managerial Revolution* (Harmondsworth, Middlesex: Penguin, 1962); Bell, *Post-industrial Society;* Robert Alford, *Health Care Politics: Ideological and Interest Group Barriers to Reform* (Chicago: University of Chicago Press, 1975).

29. Frances Fox Piven and Richard A. Cloward, *Regulating the Poor* (New York: Vintage, 1971); Samuel Bowles, Herbert Gintis and Peter Meyer, "The Long Shadow of Work: Education, the Family and the Reproduction of the Social Division of Labor," *The Insurgent Sociologist* 5 (Summer 1975): 3–22; Domhoff, *Powers That Be*; Murray Edelman, *Politics as Symbolic Action: Mass Arousal and Quiescence* (Chicago: Markham, 1971); Theodore Lowi, "American Business, Public Policy, Case Studies and Political Theory," *World Politics* 16 (July 1964): 677–93; Grant McConnell, *Private Power and American Democracy* (New York: Vintage, 1966).

30. Kenneth Prewitt and Alan Stone, *The Ruling Elites* (New York: Harper & Row, 1973): 120–22.

Chapter Two

1. Good surveys of the literature are Martin Brofenbrenner and Franklyn D. Holzman, "Survey of Inflation Theory," *American Economic Review* 53 (September 1963): 593–661; Harry G. Johnson, "A Survey of Theories of Inflation," in *Essays in Monetary Economics* (Cambridge, Mass.: Harvard University Press, 1967); Helmut Frisch, "Inflation Theory 1963–1975: A Second Generation Survey," *Journal of Economic Literature* 15 (December 1977): 1289–1317; Anthony M. Santomero and John J. Seater, "The Inflation-Unemployment Trade-off: A Critique of the Literature," *Journal of Economic Literature* 16 (June 1978): 499–544.

2. Some good examples of this statement are found in the papers written for a symposium on "The Future of U.S. Wage-Price Policy," in *Review of Economics and Statistics* 54 (August 1972): 213–34.

3. P. Streeten, "Productivity Inflation," in R.J. Ball and Peter Boyle, eds., *Inflation* (Bungay, Suffolk: Penguin, 1972).

4. Frisch, "Inflation Theory": 1308–9.

5. Walter S. Salant, "International Transmission of Inflation," in Laurence B. Krause and Walter S. Salant, eds., *Worldwide Inflation: Theory and Recent Experience* (Washington, D.C.: Brookings Institution, 1977), p. 198.

6. ibid., p. 197.

7. A.W. Phillips, "The Relationship Between Unemployment and the Rate of Change of Money Wage Rates in the United Kingdom 1861–1957," *Economica* 25 (November 1958): 283–99.

8. Richard G. Lipsey, "The Relation Between Unemployment and the Rate of Change of Money Wage Rates in the United Kingdom 1862–1957: A Further Analysis," *Economica* 27 (February 1960): 456–87; Paul Samuelson and Robert M. Solow, "The Problem of Achieving and Maintaining a Stable Price Level: Analytical Aspects of Anti-Inflation Policy," *American Economic Review* 50 (May 1960): 177–94.

9. For a summary of the Phillips curve literature in both its static and natural rate forms see Santomero and Seater, "Inflation-Unemployment Trade-off."

10. Ibid., pp. 525–32.

11. See for example Alex Cukierman, "A Test of the 'No Trade-off in the Long Run' Hypothesis," *Econometrica* 42 (November 1974): 1069–80; Edward M. Gramlich, "Macro Policy Responses to Price Shocks," *Brookings Papers on Economic Activity* no. 1 (1979): 125–66. However for a contrary view from a mainstream Keynesian see Robert Gordon, *Macroeconomics* (Boston: Little, Brown, 1978).

12. See for example Stephen A. Ross and Michael L. Wachter, "Wage Determination, Inflation and the Industrial Structure," *American Economic Review* 63 (September 1973): 675–94.

13. See for example Bent Hansen, "Excess Demand, Unemployment, Vacancies and Wages," *Quarterly Journal of Economics* 84 (February 1970): 1–23; Robert J. Barro and Herschel I. Grossman, "Suppressed Inflation and the Supply Multiplier," *Review of Economic Studies* 41 (January 1975): 87–104.

14. See for example Charles C. Holt, "How Can the Phillips Curve be Moved to Reduce both Inflation and Unemployment?," in Edmund S. Phelps et al., *Microeconomic Foundations of Employment and Inflation Theory* (New York: Norton, 1970); Charles C. Holt, Duncan C. MacRae, Stewart O. Schweitzer and Ralph E. Smith, *Manpower Programs to Reduce Inflation and Unemployment* (Washington, D.C.: Urban Institute, 1971); Paul Samuelson, *Economics*, 9th ed. (New York: McGraw-Hill, 1973), p. 836.

15. Good reviews of the controversy over this assertion are contained in John M. Peterson and Charles T. Stewart, Jr., *Employment Effects of Minimum Wage Rates* (Washington, D.C.: American Enterprise Institute, 1969); Finis Welch, *Minimum Wages: Issues and Evidence* (Washington, D.C.: American Enterprise Institute, 1978); and Donald O. Parsons, *Poverty and the Minimum Wage* (Washington, D.C.: American Enterprise Institute, 1980).

16. For empirical tests of these effects see Joseph A. Pechman and P. Michael Timpane, eds., *Work Incentives and Income Guarantees: The New Jersey Negative Income Tax Experiment* (Washington, D.C.: Brookings Institution, 1975); Michael C. Keeley et al., "The Labor Supply Effects and Costs of Alternative Negative Income Tax Programs," *Journal of Human Resources* 13 (Winter 1978): 3–36; Stephanie Wilson, Danny Steinberg and Jane C. Kulik, "Guaranteed Employment, Work Incentives and Welfare Reform: Insight from the Work Equity Project," *American Economic Review* 70 (May 1980): 132–37.

17. Dale T. Mortensen, "A Theory of Wage and Unemployment Dynamics," in Phelps, et al., *Microeconomic Foundations*; Charles C. Holt, "Job Search, Phillips' Wage Relation and Union Influence," in Phelps et al., *Microeconomic Foundations*; S.C. Salop, "Systematic Job Search and Unemployment," *Review of Economic Studies* 40 (April 1973): 191–202.

18. Milton Friedman, *Dollars and Deficits: Inflation, Monetary Policy and the Balance of Payments* (Englewood Cliffs, N.J.: Prentice-Hall, 1968); Robert E. Lucas, "An Equilibrium Model of the Business Cycle," *Journal of Political Economy* 83 (December 1975): 1113–44; Thomas J. Sargent, "Rational Expections, the Real Rate of Interest and the Natural Rate of Unemployment," *Brookings Papers on Economic Activity* no. 2 (1973): 429–72. A recent test of this model found little evidence to support it in the United States however. See Anders Bjorklund and Bertil Holmlund, "The Duration of Unemployment and Expected Inflation: An Empirical Analysis," *American Economic Review* 71 (March 1981): 121–31.

19. Salop, "Model of Natural Rate."

20. Hyman B. Kaitz, "Analysing the Length of Spells of Unemployment" *Monthly Labor Review* 93 (November 1970): 11–20; George Perry, "Unemployment Flows in the U.S. Labor Market," *Brookings Papers on Economic Activity* no. 2 (1975): 245–78; Robert E. Hall, "Turnover in the Labor Force," *Brookings Papers on Economic Activity* no. 3 (1972): 709–56; Martin S. Feldstein, "Lowering the Permanent Rate of Unemployment," (Washington, D.C.: U.S. Congress, Joint Economic Committee, 1973).

21. George A. Akerlof and Brian G.M. Main, "Unemployment Spells and Unemployment Experience," *American Economic Review* 70 (December 1980): 885–93.

22. Robert E. Lucas, "Econometric Testing of the Natural Rate Hypothesis," in *The Econometrics of Price Determination: Conference* (Washington, D.C.: Board of Goverors of the Federal Reserve System, 1972); Yoram Weiss, "On the Optimal Lifetime Pattern of Labor Supply," *Economic Journal* 82 (December 1972): 1293–1315.

23. The best article is Martin Feldstein, "The Effect of Unemployment Insurance on Temporary Layoff Unemployment," *American Economic Review* 68 (December 1978): 834–46.

24. See for example James L. Sundquist, *Politics and Policy: The Eisenhower, Kennedy, and Johnson Years* (Washington, D.C.: Brookings Institution, 1968), chap. 3. Samuelson, *Economics*, p. 836; Lloyd Ulman, ed., *Manpower Programs in the Policy Mix* (Baltimore: Johns Hopkins Press, 1973) (though this tends to devalue the skills approach); and U.S. Congress, Senate, Committee on Labor and Public Welfare, *Hearings on the Nation's*

Manpower Revolution, 10 vols., 89th Cong., 1st sess., 1965. The ten volumes are probably the best single source for the early period.

25. See for example Milton Friedman, *Capitalism and Freedom* (Chicago: University of Chicago Press, 1962), pp. 191–94; Henry J. Aaron, *Why is Welfare so Hard to Reform* (Washington, D.C.: Brookings Institution, 1972).

26. See for example Holt et al., *Manpower Programs*; and Holt, "Can Phillips Curve be Moved."

27. Gramlich, "Macro Responses," p. 125.

28. More precisely "Full employment . . . means having always more vacant jobs than unemployed men, not slightly fewer jobs." William H. Beveridge, *Full Employment in a Free Society* (New York: Norton, 1945), p. 18.

29. See Gordon, *Macroeconomics*, pp. xv–xxi, for a recent estimated series of full employment points.

30. See Garner Ackley, "An Incomes Policy for the 1970s," *Review of Economics and Statistics* 54 (August 1972): 218–23 for a fairly pure version of the theory.

31. For a clear if somewhat simplified statement of the position see Abba P. Lerner, "Inflationary Depression and the Regulation of Administered Prices," in U.S. Congress, Joint Economic Committee, *The Relationship of Prices to Economic Stability and Growth* (Washington, D.C.: Government Printing Office, 1958); and more recently Abba P. Lerner, *Flation* (New York: Quadrangle Books, 1972), chaps. 6 and 10.

32. Charles P. Schultze, "Recent Inflation in the United States," in U.S. Congress, Joint Economic Committee, *Employment Growth and Price Levels, Hearings before the Joint Economic Committee* 86th Cong., 1st sess., 1959, pp. 4–10.

33. Frisch, "Inflation Theory," p. 1304.

34. Odd Aukrust, "PRIM 1: A Model of the Price and Income Distribution Mechanism of an Open Economy," *Review of Income and Wealth* 16 (March 1970): 51–78; Gosta Edgren, Karl-Olaf Faxen and Clas-Erik Ohdner, *Wage Formation and the Economy* (London: Allen and Unwin, 1973).

35. Aubrey Jones, *The New Inflation: The Politics of Prices and Incomes* (London: Andre Deutsch, 1973).

36. Alfred S. Eichner, ed., *A Guide to Post-Keynesian Economics* (White Plains, N.Y.: M.E. Sharpe, 1979); James R. Crotty, "Post-Keynesian Economic Theory: An Overview and Evaluation," *American Economic Review* 70 (May 1980): 20–25.

37. Lester C. Thurow, *The Zero-Sum Society: Distribution and the Possibilities for Economic Change* (New York: Basic Books, 1980).

38. Radford Boddy and James Crotty, "Class Conflict and Macro-Policy: The Political Business Cycle," *Review of Radical Political Economics* 7 (Spring 1975): 1–19.

39. The classic statements of the position are Milton Friedman, "The Role of Monetary Policy," *American Economic Review* 58 (March 1968): 1–17, and his earlier *A Program for Monetary Stability* (New York: Fordham University Press, 1960). A simpler and more closely worked through presentation can be found in Samuel A. Morley, *The Economics of Inflation* (Hinsdale, Ill.: Dryden Press, 1971). A basically similar view that uses the same assumptions but argues that even so there might be a case for reducing unemployment below the natural rate, is found in Phelps, *Inflation Policy*.

40. The most extreme statement of the equilibrium model approach is probably Thomas J. Sargent and Neil Wallace, " 'Rational' Expectations, the Optimal Monetary Instrument and the Optimal Money Supply Rule," *Journal of Political Economy* 83 (April 1975): 241–54. An overall exposition is Robert E. Lucas and Thomas J. Sargent, "After Keynesian Macro-economics," *Federal Reserve Bank of Minneapolis Quarterly Review* 3 (Spring 1979): 1–16.

41. It is important to note that while both demand-pull and monetarist economists focus on the money supply, the demand-pull economists generally see the money supply as a variable policy tool, while the monetarists feel that because of uncertain lag structures and political factors the money supply should not be varied in response to short-term changes in the economy.

42. See Paul Samuelson, *Economics*, 10th ed. (New York: McGraw-Hill, 1976), pp. 356–57.

43. More precisely the argument has involved four magnitudes, split between two basic approaches. One approach has argued that one should watch either the level of free reserves available for lending or else the interest rate. In the pre–1960 period the major emphasis within this general orientation was on the level of free reserves with a gradual switch to the interest rate as the criterion after this date. The other approach has stressed either the money stock or the monetary base (member bank reserves plus currency outstanding) as the measure to be adopted. Generally policy makers in the United States tended to agree with the first school of thought until the mid–1960s. Since then however there has been a pronounced swing toward using one of the measures of the quantity of money as an alternative criterion. A good discussion can be found in Bach, *Monetary Policy*, especially p. 107 and pp. 138–43.

44. Thus Milton Friedman and Anna Schwartz, *in A Monetary History of the United States 1867–1960* (Princeton: Princeton University Press, 1963), go to some lengths to point out that the depression did not come about despite correct monetary policies but because of incorrect ones. At full employment levels however, the proponents of monetary policy split, with some, such as J.P. Cooper and Stanley Fischer, arguing for a discretionary policy and others like Milton Friedman asking for some constant rate of expansion.

45. See Sheahan, *Guideposts*; and George P. Shultz and Robert Z. Aliber, eds., *Guideposts, Informal Controls, and the Market Place: Policy Choices in a Full Employment Economy* (Chicago: University of Chicago Press, 1966), for varying assessments of the value of guideposts in the American context, and McConnell, *Steel*, for a clear account of how pressure was applied.

46. Brief accounts of the American experience can be found in Roger L. Miller and Raburn M. Williams, *The New Economic Policy of Richard Nixon* (New York: Harper & Row, 1972); Harry B. Yoshpe, John F. Allums, Joseph E. Russell and Barbara A. Atkins, *Stemming Inflation* (Washington, D.C.: Office of Emergency Preparedness, Government Printing Office, 1972); and Weber, *Freeze of 1971*. An assessment of the effectiveness of controls in this period is Robert J. Gordon, "The Response of Wages and Prices to the First Two Years of Controls," *Brookings Papers in Economic Activity* no. 3 (1973): 765–80.

47. The next few paragraphs generally follow J.S. Flemming, "The Economic Explanation of Inflation," in Fred Hirsch and John Goldthorpe, eds., *The Political Economy of Inflation* (Cambridge, Mass.: Harvard University Press, 1978): 13–36.

48. William Nordhaus, "Inflation Remedies: Real and Make Believe," *New York Times* Sunday, 25 January 1981, p. F2

49. See Jude Wanniski, "Taxes, Revenues and the 'Laffer Curve'," *Public Interest* 50 (Winter 1978): 3–18, for a simple presentation. For an attack by a conservative economist see Herbert Stein, "Some 'Supply-Side' Propositions," in *The AEI Economist* (April 1980): 1–3. The basic idea that at some point people reduce work effort in the face of higher taxes, normally referred to as the "substitution effect," goes back to at least the eighteenth century and is usually balanced against an "income effect" working in the opposite direction. For discussions of tax based incomes policies (TIPS) see Arthur Okun and George L. Perry, eds., *Curing Chronic Inflation* (Washington, D.C.: Brookings Institution, 1978).

50. For an argument that wage-price policy may be best seen as a form of symbolic action see J. Murray Edelman and R.W. Fleming, *The Politics of Wage-Price Decisions, A Four Country Analysis* (Urbana, Ill.: University of Illinois Press, 1965).

51. See George L. Perry, "Stabilization Policy and Inflation," in Henry Owen and Charles L. Schultze, eds., *Setting National Priorities* (Washington, D.C.: Brookings Institution, 1976).

52. See ibid.; Walter N. Heller, *New Dimensions of Political Economy* (New York: Norton, 1967); and Arthur M. Okun, *The Political Economy of Prosperity* (New York: Norton, 1970).

53. See Perry, "Stabilization Policy."

54. See Sundquist, *Politics and Policy;* and Okun, *Political Economy.*

55. See Pierce, *Fiscal Policy*, for an example of the effects of a long "inside lag" on legislation on taxation, and Davidson, *Manpower Legislation*, for the effect on manpower legislation.

56. See Okun, *Political Economy,* and Heller, *New Dimensions.*

57. See Perry, "Stabilization Policy," p. 276.
58. See Pierce, *Fiscal Policy*, pp. 88–93.
59. See Pierce, *Fiscal Policy;* and Manley, *Politics of Finance*.
60. Robert H. Haveman, "Unemployment in Western Europe and the United States: A Problem of Demand, Structure or Measurement?," *American Economic Review* 68 (May 1978)· 44–50.

Chapter Three

1. Bailey, "Welfare Cost," pp. 93–110.
2. Reuben A. Kessel and Armen A. Alchian, "Effects of Inflation," *Journal of Political Economy* 70 (December 1962): 532.
3. Phillip Cagan, "The Monetary Dynamics of Hyperinflation," in Milton Friedman, ed., *Studies in the Quantity Theory of Money* (Chicago: University of Chicago Press, 1956); Kessel and Alchian, "Effects of Inflation."
4. Phelps, *Inflation Policy*, chap. 6. Phelps goes so far as to argue that it might be desirable to have an inflationary tax on liquidity, because it makes stabilization easier and because moderate inflation may have lower costs than alternative taxes.
5. For a good listing of possible effects see Stanley Fisher and Franco Modigliani, "Toward an Understanding of the Real Effects and Costs of Inflation," *Weltwirtschaftliches Archiv* 114 no. 4 (1978): 810–33.
6. See Henry Aaron, ed., *Inflation and the Income Tax* (Washington, D.C.: Brookings Institution, 1976).
7. See American Enterprise Institute, *Does the Government Profit from Inflation: A Roundtable Discussion* (Washington, D.C.: n.p.), (cassette).
8. From 1973 to 1977 newly retiring elderly also gained because social security was double indexed.
9. For a typical list with typical implicit contradictions, see Garner Ackley, "The Costs of Inflation," *American Economic Review* 68 (May 1978): 149–54.
10. Phelps, *Inflation Policy*.
11. For a recent reformulation in terms of downside risk see C. Menezes, C. Geiss and J. Tressler, "Increasing Downside Risk," *American Economic Review* 70 (December 1980): 921–32.
12. Ronald G. Bodkin, "Real Wages and Cyclical Variations in Employment: A Re-examination of the Evidence," *Canadian Journal of Economics* 2 (August 1969): 353–74; Lester C. Thurow, "Analyzing the American Income Distribution," *American Economic Review* 60 (May 1970): 261–67; Charles Metcalf, *An Econometric Model of the Income Distribution* (Chicago: Markham, 1972); Phelps, *Infaltion Policy;* Douglas A. Hibbs, Jr., *Economic Interest and the Politics of Macroeconomic Policy* (Cambridge, Mass.: Center for International Studies, MIT, 1975).
13. Briefly the argument is that when unemployment temporarily drops below the natural rate, people who would not normally be sufficiently attractive for employers to train get drawn into the work force. With their value enhanced by this training they remain a part of the work force thereafter, thus permanently lowering the natural rate. It should be noted that this argument is open to two objections: that most jobs in this range need little training and that the reverse phenomenon should occur when the inevitable adjustment of expectations leads to the unemployment rate moving temporarily above the natural rate.
14. T. Paul Schulz, "Secular Trends and Cyclical Behavior of Income Distribution in the United States: 1964–65," in Lee Soltow, ed., *Six Papers on the Size Distribution of Wealth and Income*, NBER Studies in Income and Wealth, no. 33 (New York: NBER, 1969); Charles E. Metcalf, "The Size Distribution of Personal Income During the Business Cycle," *American Economic Review* 59 (September 1969): 657–68; Edwin Kuh, "Income Distribution and Employment over the Business Cycle," in James Duesenberry et al., eds., *The Brookings Quarterly Econometrics Model of the United States* (Chicago: Rand McNally, 1965), pp. 277–88; Thad W. Mirer, "The Effects of Macroeconomic Fluctuations on the Distribution of Income," Institute for Research on Poverty Discussion Paper, University of Wisconsin, Madison, January 1972; and Radford Boddy and James Crotty, "Class Conflict."

15. Hollister and Palmer, "Impact of Inflation."

16. Jeffrey G. Williamson, " 'Strategic' Wage Goods."

17. Gwen A. Fountain, "The Distributional Impacts of Inflation: Evidence from a Panel Study" (PhD. dissertation, University of Michigan, 1972); Brimmer, "Inflation and Income."

18. Swan, "Inflation and Income."

19. Bach and Stephenson, "Inflation and Wealth," pp. 1–13.

20. Edward N. Wolff, "The Distributional Effects of the 1969–1975 Inflation on Holdings of Household Wealth in the United States," *Review of Income and Wealth* 25 (June 1979): 195–207.

21. Budd and Seiders, "Impact of Inflation"; Nordhaus, "Political Business Cycle"; Joseph J. Minarik, "Who Wins, Who Loses from Inflation," *Challenge* (January-February 1979): 26–31; "The Size Distribution of Income During Inflation," *The Review of Income and Wealth* 25 (December 1979): 377–92.

22. Budd and Seiders, "Impact of Inflation," p. 138.

23. Kristen R. Monroe, "Economic Influences on Presidential Popularity," *Public Opinion Quarterly* 42 (Fall 1978): 360–69; "God of Vengeance and of Reward?: The Economy and Presidential Popularity," *Political Behavior* 1 (Winter 1979): 301–29.

24. The Pearsons *r* between GNP and unemployment is −.11, that between inflation and GNP is .11 and that between inflation and unemployment is .19 with this yearly data in the 1948–1979 period.

25. Paul Peretz, "The Political Economy of Inflation" (PhD. dissertation, University of Chicago, 1978).

Chapter Four

1. The data is from George Katona et al., *1964 Survey of Consumer Finances* (Ann Arbor: University of Michigan, 1965): p. 184. Responses broken down in this way for the entire 1957–1965 period can be found in Paul Peretz, "Political Economy," p. 109.

2. The data is from *Public Opinion,* 1 (September-October 1978): 22. It is the mean response of those estimating that prices will go up and thus excludes responses from those who thought that inflation would go down or remain the same.

3. An interesting graph comparing social issues, energy, economic issues and foreign affairs issues in the 1969–1979 period can be found in *Public Opinion* 3 (December-January 1980): 40.

4. See *The Gallup Opinion Index* (June 1976): 25; and *The Gallup Opinion Index* (May 1977): 24, for Gallup data broken down by occupation and income, and table 29 in this volume for a party breakdown of Harris data similar to the Michigan data used above.

5. See Donald R. Kinder and D. Roderick Kiewiet, "Economic Discontent and Political Behavior: The Role of Personal Grievances and Collective Economic Judgements in Congressional Voting," *American Journal of Political Science* 23 (August 1979): 495–527.

6. The data is from *Public Opinion* 2 (January-February 1979): 23.

7. The data was supplied to the author by Harris polls.

8. *The level* of inflation was a little high however and that of unemployment a little low during this period, so it is possible that the combination of level and rate of change could have resulted in a similar degree of emphasis on each in a neutral press.

9. It should be noted that the larger absolute number of replies citing news items on unemployment or business conditions is probably not a reflection either of greater interest in those items or of more items on that topic, but of the way the questions were asked.

Chapter Five

1. See F. Thomas Juster, "Uncertainty, Price Expectations and the Personal Saving Rate: Some Preliminary Results and Some Questions for the Future," in Burkhard Strumpel et al., *Surveys of Consumers 1972–73* (Ann Arbor: University of Michigan, 1975), pp. 5–30.

2. *The Gallup Opinion Index* (October 1974): 10–13.

3. See Muriel Converse et al., "Coping with Inflation," *Economic Outlook USA*, Spring 1980, p.37.

4. See Adam Clymer, "The President Inspired High Expectations; Now the Test," *New York Times* 15 February 1981, sec. 4, p. 4.

5. *The Harris Survey*, October 23, 1975.

6. *Survey of Consumer Finances* (Ann Arbor: University of Michigan, Fall 1969).

7. *The Washington Post*, 27 February 1967.

8. George Gallup, *The Gallup Poll 1935–1971* (New York: Random House, 1972), pp. 652 and 674.

9. *The Gallup Opinion Index* (September 1974), p. 31; *Public Opinion* (December-January 1980), p. 41.

10. Douglas A. Hibbs Jr., "The Dynamics of Political Support for American Presidents Among Occupational and Partisan Groups," *American Journal of Political Science* 26 (May 1982): 312–32.

11. See for example Tufte, *Political Control*, pp. xi, xiv.

12. The percentage of the voting-age population voting for a presidential candidate dropped from 62.8 in 1960 to 51.8 in 1980, with voting rates for U.S. representatives in presidential years around 5 percent lower than this, and in non-presidential years about 15 percent lower. A good article is V. Lance Tarrance, "Suffrage and Voter Turnout in the United States: The Vanishing Voter," in Jeff Fishel, ed., *Parties and Elections in an Anti-Party Age* (Bloomington, Ind.: Indiana University Press, 1978), pp. 77–85.

13. The classic work is Angus Campbell, Phillip E. Converse, Warren E. Miller and Donald Stokes, *The American Voter* (New York: Wiley, 1960).

14. The personality variables appear most important at the presidential level while incumbency is most important for representatives, with senators occupying an intermediate position. For reasons for the incumbency effect see Morris Fiorina, "The Case of the Vanishing Marginals: The Bureaucracy Did It," *American Political Science Review* 71 (March 1977): 177–81; and Richard F. Fenno, Jr., *Home Style: House Members in Their Districts* (Boston: Little, Brown, 1978), chaps. 6 and 7. In recent years personal characteristics appear to have increased in importance. See Robert Agranoff, "The New Style of Campaigning: The Decline of Party and the Rise of Candidate-Centered Technology," in Fishel, ed., *Anti-Party Age*, pp. 230–40.

15. Morris P. Fiorina, "Short- and Long-term Effects of Economic Conditions on Individual Voting Decisions," in Douglas A. Hibbs, Jr. and Heino Fassbender, eds., *Contemporary Political Economy* (Amsterdam: North Holland, 1981). With regard to the latter point, as Oppenheimer demonstrates, with only three issues with only two solutions each it is possible to get cyclic majorities given coalitions of minorities. See Joe A. Oppenheimer "Some Political Implications of 'Vote Trading and the Voting Paradox: A Proof of Logical Equivalence,'" *American Political Science Review* 69 (September 1975): 963–66.

16. When different parties hold Congress and the presidency it is not even clear which is the incumbent party.

17. For a first attempt at sorting out these effects see Paul Peretz, "The Effect of Economic Change on Political Parties in West Germany," in Hibbs and Fassbinder, eds., *Contemporary Political Economy*. For evidence that American voters may vote for the party with the "correct" policy, rather than simply against the incumbent see D.Roderick Kiewiet, "Policy-Oriented Voting in Response to Economic Issues," *American Political Science Review* 75 (June 1981): 448–59.

18. Bruno Frey and Friedrich Schneider, "On the Modelling of Politico-Economic Interdependence," *European Journal of Political Research* (3, 1975): 339–60.

19. Two articles which give helpful summaries of the literature in this area in more depth than is possible here are Kristen Monroe, "Econometric Analyses of Electoral Behavior: A Critical Review," *Political Behavior* 1 (Summer, 1979): 137–73; and Richard Winters et al., "Political Behavior and American Public Policy: The Case of the Political Business Cycle," in Samuel Long ed., *Handbook of Political Behavior* (New York: Plenum Publishing, 1981). I found the latter especially useful.

20. Gerald Kramer, "Short-Term Fluctuations in U.S. Voting Behavior, 1896–1964," *American Political Science Review* 65 (March, 1971): 131–43.

21. George Stigler, "Micropolitics and Macroeconomics: General Economic Conditions and General Elections" *American Economic Review* 63 (May 1973): 160–67.

245   Notes to Pages 137–40

22. Gerald Kramer, *Short-Term Fluctuations in U.S. Voting Behavior, 1896–1964*, Bobbs-Merrill Reprint. An error made by Kramer's research assistant in the original APSR article was corrected for the reprint.

23. Francisco Arcelus and Allen H. Meltzer, "The Effect of Aggregate Economic Conditions on Congressional Elections," *American Political Science Review* 69 (December 1975): 1232–39.

24. Saul Goodman and Gerald H. Kramer, "Comment on Arcelus and Meltzer, The Effect of Aggregate Economic Conditions on Congressional Elections," *American Political Science Review* 69 (December, 1975): 1255–65.

25. Howard S. Bloom and H. Douglas Price, "Voter Response to Short-Run Economic Conditions: The Asymetric Effect of Prosperity and Recession," *American Political Science Review* 69 (December, 1975): 1240–54.

26. Richard P. Y. Li, "Public Policy and Short Term Fluctuations in U.S. Voting Behavior: A Reformulation and Expansion," *Political Methodology*, 3 no. 1 (1976): 49–70.

27. Tufte, *Political Control*.

28. Jeffrey W. Wides, "Self-Perceived Economic Change and Political Orientations," *American Politics Quarterly* 4 (October 1976): 395–411.

29. Ricardo Klorman, "Trend in Personal Finances and the Vote," *Public Opinion Quarterly* 42 (Spring 1978): 31–48.

30. Morris P. Fiorina, "Economic Retrospective Voting in American National Elections: A Micro-Analysis," *American Journal of Political Science* 22 (May 1978): 426–43.

31. Donald R. Kinder and D. Roderick Kiewiet, "Economic Discontent and Political Behavior," *American Journal of Political Science* 23 (August 1979): 504.

32. In a later work, dealing with pro-party rather than anti-incumbent voting, Kiewiet finds exactly the opposite, that the vote is affected more by thinking unemployment is a problem for oneself than for the nation. D. Roderick Kiewiet, "Policy-Oriented Voting in Response to Economic Issues," *American Political Science Review* 75 (June 1981): 448–59.

33. J.W. Wides and M. Kuechler, "Economic Perceptions and the '76 Presidential Vote: A WLS Analysis," unpublished manuscript, Edwardsville, Illinois.

34. Dana Levenson et al., "The Political Economy of the Vote," unpublished manuscript, Dartmouth, New Hampshire, September 1977.

35. James Kuklinski and Darrell M. West, "Economic Expectations and Voting Behavior in United States House and Senate Elections," *American Political Science Review* 75 (June 1981): 436–47.

36. Stanley Feldman, "Economic Self-Interest and Political Behavior," *American Journal of Political Science* 26 (August 1982): 446–66. The data adduced by Feldman to support his position is however capable of more than one interpretation.

37. James E. Pierson, "District Economic Conditions and Congressional Elections," paper presented at the annual meeting of the Midwest Political Science Association, Chicago, April 21–23, 1977.

38. John R. Owens and Edward C. Olson, "Economic Fluctuations and Congressional Elections," *American Journal of Political Science* 24 (August 1980): 469–93.

39. John R. Hibbing and John R. Alford, "The Electoral Impact of Economic Conditions: Who is Held Responsible?" *American Journal of Political Science* 25 (August 1981): 423–39.

40. This last observation, based on Hibbing and Alford and tables in Owen and Olson, implies that the aggregate vote could be substantially affected by economic conditions, with a few or no congressmen losing their seats as a result. This seems consistent with the fact that incumbents very seldom lose, and that in the 1970s, when economic conditions became more volatile, incumbency became more, not less, important.

41. Attempts to show the majority party is hurt have been universally unsuccessful. See for example Owens and Olson, "Economic Fluctuations." Ray Fair makes a similar observation in "The Effects of Economic Events on Votes for President", *Review of Economics and Statistics* 60 (May 1978): 165.

42. Kramer "Short-Term Fluctuations," pp. 140–41. Stigler, "Micropolitics."

43. Fair, "Economic Events."

44. Tufte, *Political Control*. Tufte's results hold only if one uses his unusual and somewhat arbitrary reconstruction of the dependent variable and includes presidential popularity in the equation. If for example one runs the actual mid-term vote against inflation, unemployment and change in real disposable income, one gets t scores of -2.19 for inflation, -1.64 for unemployment and 1.03 for disposable personal income change, with the equation accounting for 84 percent of the variance and a Durbin Watson of 2.25.

45. Fair, "Economic Events," p. 171. Or, as Tufte puts it in another book, "The real difficulty is in deciding when the extrapolation beyond the range of the variables is warranted and when it is merely naive." Edward R. Tufte, *Data Analysis for Politics and Policy* (Englewood Cliffs, N.J.: Prentice-Hall, 1974), p. 32.

46. John Mueller, "Presidential Popularity from Truman to Johnson," *American Political Science Review* 64 (March 1970): 18–34.

47. Douglas A. Hibbs, Jr., "Problems of Statistical Estimation and Causal Inference in Time-Series Regression Models," in H.L. Costner, *Sociological Methodology 1973–1974* (San Francisco: Jossey-Bass, 1974), pp. 284–89.

48. Henry C. Kenski, "The Impact of Economic Conditions on Presidential Popularity," *Journal of Politics* 39 (August, 1977): 764–73.

49. One should note however that this does not just take out the serial correlation. It also transforms the substantive meaning of the inflation variable.

50. Samuel Kernell, "Explaining Presidential Popularity," *American Political Science Review* 72 (June, 1978): 506–22.

51. Kristen R. Monroe, "Economic Influences on Presidential Popularity," *Public Opinion Quarterly* 42 (Fall 1978): 360–69; Kristen R. Monroe, "God of Vengeance and Reward?: The Economy and Presidential Popularity," *Political Behavior* 1 (Winter 1979): 301–29.

52. Monroe, "God of Vengeance," p. 323.

53. Maurice D. Levi and Kristen R. Monroe, "Economics Expectations and Presidential Popularity," unpublished manuscript, New York 1979.

54. Robert J. Michaels, "Reinterpreting the Role of Inflation in Politico-Economic Models," unpublished manuscript, Fullerton, Ca.

55. Bruno S. Frey and Friedrich Schneider, "An Empirical Study of Politico-Economic Interaction in the United States," *Review of Economics and Statistics* 60 (May 1978): 174–83.

56. Douglas A. Hibbs, Jr., "Why Are U.S. Policy Makers So Tolerant of Unemployment and Intolerant of Inflation," in Leon Lindberg and Charles Meier, *The Politics and Sociology of Global Inflation*, (Washington, D.C.: Brookings Institution, forthcoming).

57. Douglas A. Hibbs, Jr., et al., "On the Demand for Economic Outcomes: Macroeconomic Performance and Mass Political Support in the United States, Great Britain and Germany," unpublished manuscript, Harvard University, January 1980.

58. Douglas A. Hibbs, Jr., "The Dynamics of Political Support for American Presidents Among Occupational and Partisan Groups," *American Journal of Political Science* 26 (May 1982): 312–32.

59. Wides, "Political Orientations," p. 406

60. Morris P. Fiorina, "Short- and Long-Term Effects of Economic Conditions on Individual Voting Decisions," in Hibbs, ed., *Contemporary Political Economy*.

61. Fiorina, "Long-Term Effects."

62. Wides, "Political Orientations."

63. Stephen Weatherford, "Economic Conditions and Electoral Outcomes: Class Differences in the Political Response to Recession," *American Journal of Political Science* 22 (November 1978): 917–38.

64. Douglas A. Hibbs, Jr., "Political Parties and Macro-economic Policy," *American Political Science Review* 71 (December, 1977): 1467–87.

65. Hibbs, "Tolerant of Unemployment"; Hibbs, "Dynamics of Political Support."

66. This is not in fact shown unambiguously in either article. In the first the results are in the expected direction for inflation and unemployment but are in the wrong direction for income. However, his use of popularity depreciation variables in this work, for reasons explained in Kernell, "Explaining Popularity," p. 506, make it less plausible than the second article. But the results in the second article can also be read in more than one way. The

short term b's show that there is no difference between the two groups on unemployment and a small difference in the wrong direction on income. It is only when these are divided by $1 - g$ that the "correct" results appear. But it is a necessary assumption of the technique used that g, the lagged effect of the independent variables, be the same for every variable in the equation. As he himself notes with regard to the non-economic variables, this assumption, while necessary, is not plausible.

67. Though it is less obvious, this may also hold true for the congressional literature relying on opinion polls. These typically show self-reported turnout as around 55 percent, when we know actual turnout to be nearer 35 percent. Further, it makes good sense to expect that people who fail to vote because of the temporary strains imposed by unemployment or worsened finances might be the most likely to falsely claim they voted.

68. Steven J. Rosenstone, "Economic Adversity and Voter Turnout," *American Journal of Political Science* 26 (February 1982): 25–46. The evidence seems stronger for the financial variable and weaker for unemployment. Although the artificial construction of the financial situation variable, possible multi-collinearity and the weak significance levels of most of the unemployment variables should induce caution, there is a wealth of independent supportive evidence for the negative effect of unemployment on turnout, most of which is summarized at the beginning of the article.

Chapter Six

1. See, for example, the Full Employment Act of 1946, which directed the federal government to use all "means consistent with its needs and obligations . . . in a manner calculated to foster and promote free competitive enterprise . . . to promote maximum employment, production and purchasing power." Although not stated explicitly in this passage, price stability is also a central economic goal of contemporary economists and policy makers.

2. "Besides having this special role in the troika process, the Treasury technicians tend to add a conservative, anti-inflationary bias to the troika exercise . . . considering the department's responsibility for debt management, the balance of payments, and keeping the business community happy." Pierce, *Fiscal Policy*, pp. 48–49. It should be noted that this has not always been the case. Under the Roosevelt and Truman administrations, particularly before the accord on interest rates between the Federal Reserve and the Treasury on March 3, 1951, the Treasury was a somewhat more liberal agency. For an account of the change see Edward L. Flash, *Economic Advice and Presidential Leadership* (New York: Columbia University Press, 1965), especially p. 76–85.

3. "The Federal Reserve authorities have consistently sought to maintain stable, even-keel conditions in national financial markets, mainly through defensive open market operations. As a bank supervisory authority, the Fed has shown consistent concern for the welfare of banks." Bach, *Monetary Policy*, p. 176. In fact it can be observed that the Board of Governors is mainly composed of those with a banking background, reinforcing the conservatism of the body and emphasis on monetary policy.

4. Nominally the Council of Economic Advisers is run by neutral people who are "not affiliated with particular interest groups . . . they have no programs to run and no responsibilities or power that they can exercise on their own." Okun, *Political Economy*, pp. 25–26. In fact as can be seen both in the Okun book and in Walter Heller's *New Dimensions*, CEA chairmen and members tend to have a very liberal manifesto.

5. For example the appointment of Arthur Burns in 1953 gave the CEA much more influence in the numerous interagency disputes with the Treasury, the Bureau of the Budget and the Federal Reserve. The replacement of Burns by Saulnier in late 1956 led to "somewhat less close relations with the White House," and hence less CEA power. See Flash, *Economic Advice*, especially p. 172.

6. The best work on the House Ways and Means committee remains Manley, *The Politics of Finance*. The best work on the House Appropriations Committee remains Richard Fenno, *The Power of the Purse* (Boston: Little, Brown, 1966). More recent works are Thomas J. Reese, *The Politics of Taxation* (Westport, Conn.: Quorum, 1980); and Lance LeLoup, *The Fiscal Congress: Legislative Control of the Budget* (Westport, Conn.: Greenwood Press,

1980). The ability of the House and Senate Appropriations committees to control spending has declined as "uncontrollable" spending has risen from 54 percent of the budget in 1970 to 77 percent in 1980. This is primarily due to the increase in the number, and share of the budget, of entitlement programs such as Medicare and Social Security.

7. See Lance LeLoup, "The Impact of Congressional Budget Reform: The House Budget Committee," paper presented at the Midwest Political Science Association meeting, April 1978; and Mark W. Huddleston, "Thraining Lobsters to Fly: Assessing the Impacts of the 1974 Congressional Budget Reform," paper presented at the Midwest Political Science Association meeting, April 1979. Huddleston sees the impact of the Budget Committee as chiefly symbolic while LeLoup claims a small but real substantive impact on co-ordination and appropriations.

8. The House Rules and Administration Committee had a lot more influence, generally in a conservative direction, before the various enlargements of the committee from 1961 onward. Since that time its power has waned considerably, to the point where one member describing its powers could say, "We're traffic cops, that's what we are. We grant rules on the timing of debate, the kinds of amendments that can be offered. The rules are flexible." From Robert L. Peabody, "The Enlarged Rules Committee," in Robert L. Peabody and Nelson W. Polsby, eds., *New Perspectives on the House of Representatives* (Chicago: Rand McNally, 1963), p. 137. For a comprehensive description of the use of these powers from 1937 to 1962, see James A. Robinson, *The House Rules Committee* (Indianapolis: Bobbs-Merrill, 1963).

9. See Manley, *Politics of Finance*, pp. 98–150, for a complete explanation of Wilbur Mills's rise to power and domination.

10. "Taken as a whole, these measures [subcommittee reforms on the House] struck directly at the powers of the committee chairmen . . . Control over subcommittee jurisdictions, chairmen, activities and powers now rests with subcommittee chairmen instead of [full] committee chairmen, as previously." Norman J. Ornstein, "Causes and Consequences of Congressional Change: Subcommittee Reforms in the House of Representatives, 1970–73," in Norman J. Ornstein, ed., *Congress in Change: Evolution and Reform* (New York: Praeger, 1975), p. 110.

11. For a summary of the powers of the leadership, see Robert L. Peabody, *Leadership in Congress: Stability, Succession and Change* (Boston: Little, Brown, 1976), pp. 27–65.

12. For an account of the Senate Budget Committee see Lance LeLoup, "Budgeting in the Senate: Old Ways of Doing New Things," paper presented at the Midwest Political Science Association meeting, April 1979. For an explanation of why the Senate Committee is more influential see John W. Ellwood and James A. Thurber, "The New Congressional Budget Process: The Hows and Whys of House-Senate Differences," in Lawrence C. Dodd and Bruce I. Oppenheimer, *Congress Reconsidered* (New York: Praeger, 1977).

13. For a good description of the working of the Senate around the middle of the period we are concerned with, see Donald R. Matthews, *U.S. Senators and Their World* (New York: Random House, 1960). For more recent assessments, see Randall B. Ripley, *Power in the Senate* (New York: St. Martin's Press, 1969); and *Congress: Process and Policy* (New York: Norton, 1975).

14. For comparisons of committees in the two bodies, see Jeffrey L. Pressman, *House v. Senate* (New Haven: Yale University Press, 1966), chap. 3, pp. 28–52. Also see Lewis A. Froman, Jr., *Congressmen and Their Constituencies* (Chicago: Rand McNally, 1963), chaps. 6 and 7, pp. 69–97.

15. For a brief introduction to the role of the Joint Economic Committee, see Harvey J. Mansfield, "The Congress and Economic Policy," in David B. Truman, ed., *The Congress and America's Future* (Englewood Cliffs, N.J.: Prentice-Hall, 1965), pp. 146–49.

16. A good index of input into the process of macroeconomic policy making is the number of times a group has testified before the annual hearings of the Joint Economic Committee. Of the thirteen hearings between 1959 and 1971 the AFL-CIO testified in thirteen, the UMW in six, the UAW in five, the National Federation of Independent Unions in five and the Communication Workers and Railway Executives in one each. All except the independents and the auto workers essentially echoed the AFL-CIO line and the auto workers did not depart very far.

17. The Committee for Economic Development is not a peak organization in the same sense as the other two. It does not, like them, aggregate smaller interest groups. But, if one thinks of the major corporations as groups in themselves, the CED and the Business Council can both be seen as peak groups.

18. Note that small business organizations have never been very successful. In terms of political power to influence policy decisions, the small business organizations appear to be disproportionately weaker, in comparison to big business, than their numbers in the population suggest. Harmon Ziegler says, "There is no small business interest. The way the small business associations conceive of their clientele suggests they do not perceive small business as a separate segment of the business population having unique interests and goals." L. Harmon Ziegler, *The Politics of Small Business* (Washington, D.C.: Public Affairs Press, 1961), p. 66. Groups that aim to specifically represent *small* business have never been able to acquire much power or many resources possibly because they have had to compete with the Chambers of Commerce.

19. Monetary policy is largely the responsibility of the Federal Reserve, a quasi-independent agency. The Federal Reserve is actually made up mainly of individuals from the commercial banking system, therefore the influence of the financial sector is quite direct. See Bach, *Monetary Policy*, for a description of the influential others in monetary policy making.

20. During the thirteen times there has been testimony before the JEC in the 1959–1971 period, Chase Manhattan, Morgan Guaranty and the First National City Bank all testified once, the Independent Bankers Association testified three times, the National Association of Mutual Savings Banks testified six times, the National League of Insured Savings Associations two times, and the American Bankers Association four times, in addition to testimony by various insurance associations. This is a heavy involvement for a single industrial sector, particularly as its major influence is upon monetary policy rather than fiscal policy (with which the JEC is more concerned).

21. See R. Joseph Monsen, Jr., and Mark W. Cannon, *The Makers of Public Policy: American Power Groups and Their Ideologies* (New York: McGraw-Hill, 1965), chap. 4, pp. 96–128, for details.

22. The people in these bodies may most nearly approach Mannhein's disinterested intellectuals within this policy arena. See Karl Mannhein, *Ideology and Utopia: An Introduction to the Sociology of Knowledge* (New York: Harcourt, 1936), for a description of the role of the intellectual.

23. See Aage R. Clausen, *How Congressmen Decide: A Policy Focus*, (New York: St. Martin's Press, 1973).

24. This was an inaccurate label because the doctrine was in fact relatively new. The "old time" for Republicans was balancing the budget. The phrase is that of Herbert Stein while he was chairman of the Council of Economic Advisers during the Nixon administration.

25. Although I refer to the alliances described below as coalitions, the reader should be careful not to impute to this word the more exact meaning of the term as it is used in the extensive literature on coalition formation. The coalitions described here are both more weakly specified and more important than those in the literature.

26. Priorities also vary according to an individual's institutional and ideological affiliations. "Democrats and liberals, who are generally considered to be left of the political center, usually place a greater emphasis on full employment and economic growth. This ordering of priorities is also shared by . . . the C.E.A. Republicans and conservatives tend to place a higher priority on price level stability and balance of payments equilibrium. These priorities are also dominant . . . in the Department of the Treasury." Pierce, *Fiscal Policy*, p. 24.

27. For a description of the Conservative Coalition over time see John F. Manley, "The Conservative Coalition in Congress," in Lawrence C. Dodd and Bruce I. Oppenheimer, eds., *Congress Reconsidered* (New York: Praeger, 1977).

28. This is because it not only helps stabilize the economy but also redistributes purchasing power and allocates between private and public goods. We should recall however that many economists now feel that monetary policy is more important than fiscal policy for dealing with inflation.

29. Council of Economic Advisers, *Economic Report of the President, January 1980* (Washington, D.C.: Government Printing Office, 1980), p. 288. State and local governments account for a much higher percentage of purchases of goods and services, 51.4 percent in 1950 and 65.1 percent in 1979.

30. For diagrams showing the policy flow in the executive and in Congress see Wildavsky, *Budgetary Process*, Appendix. Diagrams showing the policy process prior to 1974 can be found in the Appendix of the second edition of the same book.

31. Useful figures showing the policy making flow can be found in Pierce, *Fiscal Policy*, pp. 37 and 47.

32. According to the CED, the new budget process to date has had a favorable impact on the character and quality of congressional debates on budgetary, economic and financial issues. See Committee for Economic Development, *The New Congressional Budget Process and the Economy* (n.p., 1975).

33. See Lowi, "Public Policy," for a description of the two kinds of process.

34. See Pierce, *Fiscal Policy*, p. 37.

35. For example, in 1966 Carl Madden of the Chamber of Commerce was disappointed that the CEA economic report gave "little searching consideration . . . to the logic of budget surpluses in periods of full employment," and in 1970 the NAM stated, "We know that [inflation] never occurs unless it is initially fueled by federal deficits and exessive monetary expansion." The quotes are from testimony before the Joint Economic Committee on the annual CEA report.

36. An example of the view of fiscal policy decisions as outcomes of a complex organizational process was President Johnson's tax surcharge proposal of 1967. "The Labor Department wanted and insisted that the business community carry its share of the tax increase, so the surtax was applied to both personal and corporate incomes. Businessmen are generally opposed to big government and tax increases. Consequently, they insisted on making the tax surcharge a temporary measure." Pierce, *Fiscal Policy*, p. 202. The tax surcharge first proposed to the president by his economic advisers in January 1966 (ibid., p. 8) was not sent to Congress until August 1967 and did not become law until June 1968.

37. An example of the resistant-to-change nature of tax laws can be seen in the so-called Tax Reform Act of 1976. While the act banned deductions for "non-recourse" financing in oil and gas drilling syndications, these deductions were still permitted for coal mine leasing syndications.

38. Usually several of the seven governors are from the banking community, and there is a Federal Advisory Council which represents the views of bankers to the Board. Benjamin Beckhart, *Federal Reserve System* (New York: American Institute of Banking, 1972), pp. 36, 38–39. In addition the twelve Reserve banks are formally owned by the banks in their area and at least one-third and usually at least one-half of the directors of the twelve banks are from the banking community (pp. 44–47). Although the powers of bankers over the Fed have declined since the 1920s, "some observers still question the close relationships between the Federal Reserve officials and commercial bankers. While they acknowledge that private bankers do not formally control the Federal Reserve, they agree that in practice the Reserve, like other regulatory agencies has come, albeit subconsciously, to protect the interests of the banking industry." Bach, *Monetary Policy*, p. 178.

39. See Bach, *Monetary Policy*, p. 212.

40. Wooley holds that the Federal Reserve is even more subservient to the executive than we would expect on the basis of these limited powers, though he does not provide a completely satisfactory explanation for this putative phenomenon. See John Wooley, "Central Banks: Influence and Independence," in Lindberg and Maier, *Global Inflation*.

41. See Flash, *Economic Advice*, pp. 76–85.

42. The reasons for this are neither obvious nor clear. A discussion of the point together with some evidence on the relationship can be found in Wooley, "Central Banks."

43. For an account, see Bach, *Monetary Policy*, pp. 256–68 and 122–25.

44. Given a choice between a policy option over which it has effective sovereignty and one which other societal groups have some control over, a rational government should always prefer the former, ceteris paribus, as using it will reduce the inside and outside lags and minimize the necessity for bargaining. Despite the fact that the Federal Reserve is formally independent of the president, monetary policy is much more controllable than the

other kinds of policy used to control the economy. The degree to which fiscal policy making can be vetoed by non-executive groups is aberrant in international terms.

45. The first occasion was in 1950 when congressional pressure led to the inclusion of a wage-price control measure in the Defense Production Act signed by Truman in September 1950. See Flash, *Economic Advice*, pp. 42–45. The second occasion was in 1970 when Congress passed the Economic Stabilization Act, signed by Nixon in August 1970, despite the fact that he did not ask for it or want it. See Yoshpe et al., *Stemming Inflation*.

46. During World War II wage-price controls were handled by the Office of Price Administration. They were handled by the Economic Stabilization Agency during the Truman administration and by the Cost of Living Council during the Nixon administration. The Kennedy-Johnson guidelines were mainly handled inside the White House and the CEA.

47. See McConnell, *Steel 1962*, for a clear account of how pressure was applied.

48. During World War II the 4,000 Industrial Advisory Committees attached to the Office of Price Administration filled this role. During the Nixon freeze the Pay Board and the Price Commission tried to fill the role, although labor resignations from the Pay Board reduced its effectiveness.

49. Wage-price policies appear, at least in their strong form, to have reduced inflation in the short term. However, a surge in wages and prices after controls are lifted typically wipes out the temporary gains. Since political pressures have invariably led to wage-price policy being tried at exactly the wrong time, i.e. when demand pressure was high, it is not certain whether it would fail under more benign circumstances. For an assessment of the Nixon controls see Robert Gordon, "Response to Controls."

50. This first pattern holds fairly well for the wage-price controls imposed by Nixon and Truman. It is also a common pattern in other countries such as Britain.

51. The Kennedy-Johnson guidelines policy followed this pattern, though it never reached a stage of strong enforcement.

52. See Theodore Lowi, "Decision Making vs. Policy Making: Toward an Antidote for Technocracy," *Public Administration Review* 30 (May 1970): 314–25.

53. See Stanley H. Ruttenberg, *Manpower Challenge of the 1970s: Institutions and Social Change* (Baltimore: Johns Hopkins Press, 1970): p. 2. In the 1970s the increasing emphasis on public service jobs has led to a continuance of this view, together with an increasing tendency to see manpower programs as also a kind of counter-cyclical revenue sharing program or welfare for cities. See William Mirengoff et al., *CETA: Assessment of Public Service Employment Programs* (Washington, D.C.: National Academy of Sciences, 1980) for an assessment of the new programs.

54. See Davidson, *Politics of Manpower Legislation*.

55. See Ruttenberg, *Manpower Challenge*, for a discussion of some of these problems in the late 1960s.

56. "For instance, until the opposition of labor unions and employment service lobbies was overcome in 1969, three separate bureaus shared responsibility for various manpower programs and often operated at cross purposes. Each defended its prerogatives as if it were an independent body, even though all these were in the Labor Department." Sar A. Levitan and Robert Taggart, *Social Experimentation and Manpower Policy: The Rhetoric and the Reality* (Baltimore: Johns Hopkins Press, 1971), p. 54. This competition has continued into the post-CETA era. "Central to the problems confronting ES . . . has been the duplication and competition that has developed between the Employment Service and other manpower agencies. This refers particularly to the administration of the Comprehensive Employment and Training Act 1973 (CETA), but includes many other programs as well." Bernard Gladieux, "In Search of Harmony in Manpower Services," p. 24.

57. "Behind the scenes was a bureaucratic struggle for territorial rights [to manpower program control]. At the national level the Office of Economic Opportunity, the Department of Health, Education, and Welfare and the Department of Labor vied with one another for control of those programs." At the local level, "the lack of coordination occasionally bordered on chaos . . . state governments against local agencies, community groups against city hall." Levitan and Taggart, *Social Experimentation*, pp. 53–54.

58. Using past and current manpower programs as a guide, "a third of the enrollees will drop out of the programs, and more than half will show no benefits in employment and earnings. Improvements for those who are helped cover the initial costs only over the long

run, and these improvements might be only slightly greater than would have been achieved by spending the manpower funds some other way." Ibid., p. 90.

59. Despite the public emergence of numerous consumer groups in recent years, they have been conspicuously absent from macroeconomic policy making sessions such as the Joint Economic Committee hearings. There is a difference between the old-line consumers' organizations such as Consumers Research, Consumers Union of the United States and the National Consumers League and the newer consumer-oriented groups such as Common Cause and Ralph Nader's Public Citizens Inc. The newer institutions have been attempting since the early 1970s to influence economic policy, generally in an expansionary direction. The attitude of the older groups is typified by the 1951 testimony of C.E. Wayne of the Consumers Union before the Joint Economic Committee, which essentially said that the Consumers Union had neither the resources nor the time to testify on macroeconomic policy matters. See U.S. Congress, Joint Economic Committee, *Economic Report of the President, Hearings before the Joint Economic Committee*, 82d Cong., 1st sess., 1951.

60. See Monson and Cannon, *Makers of Policy*, pp. 46–48.

61. More fully these are the American Federation of State, County and Municipal Employees (650,000), the American Federation of Government Employees (300,000), the American Federation of Musicians (300,000), the American Postal Workers Union (300,000), the Retail Clerks International Association (605,000), and the American Federation of Teachers (205,000). Numbers refer only to the unions' white-collar membership in 1970.

62. See Olson, *Collective Action*, pp. 143–44, for a generalization of this argument.

63. See ibid. for the meaning of this phrase.

64. See Sidney Verba and Norman Nie, *Participation in America* (New York: Harper & Row, 1972), especially chap. 20, for an analysis of the impact of socio-economic factors upon political participation.

65. In 1970, 9.8 percent of white-collar workers were unionized as compared to 39.3 percent of blue-collar workers. For further details on unionization rates see U.S. Department of Labor, Bureau of Labor Statistics, *Selected Earnings and Demographic Characteristics of Union Members, 1970*, Report 417 (Washington, D.C.: Government Printing Office, 1972).

Chapter Seven

1. It should be noted that all four of the names I have used carry positive emotional connotations. They could have been respectively called "mob rule," "rule by elite," "betrayal" and "corruption." I chose the positive mode because that is the ordinary language choice made in the United States for all except the last of the categories. It should be noted that the choice of positive names for "leadership" and "statesmanship" could be interpreted as an attempt to retain a pluralist-democratic analytical framework in the face of elitist phenomena.

2. See Murray Edelman, *The Symbolic Uses of Politics* (Urbana: University of Illinois Press, 1964).

3. See Grant McConnell, *Private Power and American Democracy* (New York: Random House, Vintage Books, 1970), chap. 8, for an account of the history of the Business Council, a group that generally tries to avoid the harsh glare of publicity.

4. See Monsen and Cannon, *Makers of Policy*, pp. 26, 46. The two groupings have also been described as an old capital sector and a new capital sector but this seems a less accurate division for our present purposes.

5. "The historical record is clear that inflation can be controlled only by reducing excessive demand . . . for business it may mean slowdown in sales, build-ups in inventories, profits squeezes . . . for labor, curbing excessive demand means some rise in unemployment." Carl H. Madden of the U.S. Chambers of Commerce, testifying before the Joint Economic Committee in 1970. See U.S. Congress, Joint Economic Committee, *Economic Report of the President, Hearings before the Joint Economic Committee*, Part 3, 91st Cong., 2d sess., 1970, p. 531.

6. In addition to the priority of balance of payments in international trade, business groups also believe that "the United States should pursue a constructive and realistic tariff policy which seeks to encourage a high level of international trade and investment, while affording

reasonable protection for United States business interests." Chamber of Commerce of the United States, *1963–64 Policy Declarations* (Washington, D.C., 1963), p. 55.

7. Note that both groupings, business and corporate, make an exception to their distaste for rapidly increasing government spending when it is for defense purposes.

8. This preoccupation with growth can be noted in the corporate funded publication, *Economic Growth in the United States.* "This universal drive to expansion in search of profit, animating each one of millions of economic teams, has undoubtedly been the great generating force for the cumulative economic growth that has taken place in the whole society." Committee for Economic Development, Research and Policy Committee, *Economic Growth in the United States* (New York, 1958), p. 20.

9. This discontent may be expressed in terms of a call for more government control of corporations and increased corporate income tax rates. Both of these are obviously contrary to corporate group preferences.

10. See Martin Feldstein, "Inflation and the Stock Market", *American Economic Review* 70 (December 1980): 839–47.

11. See Monsen and Cannon, *Makers of Policy*, pp. 28–56.

12. See Francis X. Sutton et al., *The American Business Creed* (Cambridge, Mass.: Harvard University Press, 1956), p. 172.

13. *Public Opinion*, May-June 1978, p. 27.

14. "In other words, consonant with the Grange ideology of moderation in both domestic and international policy, the Grange is less liberal than the Farmers Union and less conservative than the Farm Bureau." Monsen and Cannon, *Makers of Policy*, p. 130.

15. The National Grange demands, "a balanced budget . . . except during periods of extreme emergency." National Grange, *Summary of Legislative Policies and Programs, 1963* (Washington, D.C.: National Grange, 1963), p. 26.

16. "The National Grange believes that government can curtail expenditures through greater efficiency, economy in purchasing and the elimination of many nonessential services." Ibid., p. 26.

17. "The Employment Act of 1946 should be amended to make it clear beyond any doubt that it is national policy to stabilize the purchasing power of the dollar as well as to maintain a high level of employment." American Farm Bureau Federation, *Farm Bureau Policies, 1963* (Atlanta, Ga., 1963), p. 52.

18. The NFU has called for increased government spending and has stated that "the problem of the public debt is grossly exaggerated." *Statement of the N.F.U. in Regard to Proposals by the President for Tax Reduction and Reform*, presented by Angus McDonald to the House Committee on Ways and Means, March 12, 1963, pp. 1–2.

19. "To the small businessman the best government is the one that has the least to do and say." John H. Bunzel, "General Ideology of Small Business," *Political Science Quarterly* 70 (March 1955): 95–96.

20. See U.S. Department of Commerce, *Business Statistics 1977*, pp. 11 and 41. The pattern of income drop has been somewhat different from that of other groups. In the 1945–1970 period the major drop came about a year or so before the onset of the recession with income stabilizing in the recession period. Since 1970 the drop-off in income has become more nearly synchronized with that in other sectors.

21. Though it is not clear that this is the direction of causation, particularly in view of the inconsistencies in the opinions of the self-employed noted above.

22. Since being founded in 1955, the AFL-CIO legislative division has been headed by Andrew Biermiller.

23. The research division of the AFL-CIO was headed by Nathaniel Goldfinger for most of the period since 1955.

24. The United Auto Workers (UAW) have been frequently represented in testimony before the Joint Economic Committee by Leonard Woodcock. I.W. Abel of the United Steelworkers has also been actively involved in economic policy discussions such as the Labor Conference on Inflation, September 11, 1974, in Washington, D.C.

25. Despite this defection in 1968, George Meany of the AFL-CIO and Leonard Woodcock of the UAW expressed publicly their willingness to work in harmony for the labor

movement and its ideological positions. In 1981, shortly after Lane Kirkland succeeded Meany, the UAW re-affiliated.

26. "Adequate economic growth is the only road to maximum employment, production and purchasing power." Walter Reuther, testifying before the JEC in 1962. See U.S. Congress, Joint Economic Committee, *Economic Report of the President, Hearings before the Joint Economic Committee*, 87th Cong., 2d sess., 1962, p. 758.

27. "We want to fight inflation; we're the victims of inflation; our members are the victims of inflation; and we will join and cooperate in any program that is equitable, completely equitable." George Meany, testifying at the Labor Conference on Inflation. See Executive Office of the President, *The Labor Conference on Inflation, September 11, 1974*, p. 13. Labor pictures its wage demands as merely an attempt to keep up with the inflation caused by the business sector.

28. Government in the AFL-CIO ideology, is "to play a dynamic economic role designed to stimulate employment through liberal fiscal policies." The AFL-CIO encourages government spending to promote welfare and lower rates of unemployment in the low-income groups, even at the risk of huge deficits. See Monsen and Cannon, *Makers of Policy*, pp. 75–76.

29. The AFL-CIO agrees with the business sector that major tax reform is necessary. Labor and business disagree on what the objectives of this reform should be. Organized labor argues that "the objective of tax reform is to increase tax revenues by eliminating loopholes and to decrease rates on lower-income groups." "If and when such a tax increase is imposed . . . the levy on corporate income should be much higher than on individual income" and "it should obviously exempt the lower income taxpayers." Nathaniel Goldfinger, testifying before the Joint Economic Committee for the AFL-CIO, July 2, 1967. See U.S. Congress, Joint Economic Committee, *Economic Report of the President, Hearings before the Joint Economic Committee*, Part 2, 90th Cong., 1st sess., 1967, p. 692.

30. Labor dislikes emphasis being put on curbing inflation through monetary policy. "Inflation certainly does not stem from easy money or low interest rates. In fact, this country grew, to a large extent, on the basis of a general easy availability of credit at relatively low interest rates." Lane Kirkland, testifying at the Labor Conference on Inflation. See Executive Office of the President, *Labor Conference*, p. 62.

31. Thus in the debate in early 1977 over the form that economic stimulus should take in the Carter administration, labor advocated more emphasis on job creation than on tax reduction.

32. "We recommend that price controls be imposed as soon as possible." But "it goes without saying that it would be the height of injustice to impose wage stabilization." William Green, then president of the AFL, testifying before the Joint Economic Committee, July 2, 1951. See U.S. Congress, Joint Economic Committee, *Economic Report of the President, Hearings before the Joint Economic Committee*, 82d Cong., 1st sess., 1951, p. 477. This reflects once again labor's insistence that inflation is caused by business.

33. As we saw in chapter 5, the blue-collar worker does not perceive the trade-off and may even see inflation and unemployment as linked.

34. Kinder and Kiewiet, "Economic Discontent."

35. They are also a little less likely to stress inflation, with more workers than others volunteering that both are equally important problems. This evidence appears to contradict in part the evidence offered by Hibbs in "Political Parties," p. 1470, and elsewhere. My tentative explanation is that Hibbs looked only at responses to the question asking the perceived effect on the country and that his data was drawn from an atypical period, although some of the differences between his data and that in figure 33 may be due to the different definitions and methods of the Michigan Consumer Survey and the Harris Poll.

36. This latter figure is included to indicate that the unemployment rates shown in figure 34 understate the number of people directly affected by unemployment, as they only look at the cross section of those unemployed on a given day, not at those suffering from unemployment at some point during the year. Furthermore, as very large numbers leave the work force during economic downturns and return during booms (during upturns, for every person taken off the unemployment figures two and one-half people are added to the ranks of the employed), even the figures in figure 35 leave out some unemployed. On the other

hand it must be recalled that in a normal year voluntary unemployment is only a little less than involuntary employment, and that there is considerably less unemployment for male heads of household than for women and teenagers.

37. We should note that this is typically the claim of unions. In criticizing the Nixon administration's policy of economic restraint Nathaniel Goldfinger of the research department of the AFL-CIO pleaded for all blue-collar workers by saying, "much of the weight of this burden of rising unemployment," from anti-inflation oriented policy, "will fall on blue-collar workers, particularly those with the least work experience, the least skill and education." Nathaniel Goldfinger, testifying before the Joint Economic Committee, July 2, 1970. See Congress, *Hearings*, Part 3, 91st Cong., 2d sess., p. 496. It should be noted that marginal workers are typically not in the unions.

38. Monsen and Cannon think that the ideology espoused by "corporate" groups such as the Business Council and the Committee for Economic Development is best described by the term "managerial ideology." See Monsen and Cannon, *Makers of Policy*, pp. 46–56.

39. Jerry Wurf of AFSCME has typically been a non-conformist spokesman in the AFL-CIO. Also, as previously stated, government employees are typically more liberal than other white-collar workers. For an account of Wurf's disagreement with craft union leadership, see Haynes Johnson and Nick Kotz, *The Unions* (New York: Simon & Schuster, 1972), pp. 52–54.

40. Literally, "freischwebende-Intelligenz," the English edition of *Ideology and Utopia*, translates this as "socially unattached intellegentsia." The term is originally from Weber. For a development of the concept see Mannhein, *Ideology and Utopia*, especially pp. 154–64. Also see Karl Mannhein, *Essays on the Sociology of Culture* (London: Routledge & Kegan, 1956), pp. 91–171. The basic idea is that the intellegentsia from a "relatively classless stratum" is better able to conceptualize the public interest.

41. Professional economists are the outstanding example, with their influence being strongest in the Council of Economic Advisers but with individual economists being powerful in the other economic agencies, on congressional staffs and in research groups within the major interest groups.

42. It should be noted however that professional groups have evolved means of protecting their members from market competition through devices such as imposing barriers to entry, limiting price competition, preventing advertising and making their members' services mandatory. The American Medical Association, the American Bar Association and the National Funeral Directors Association have been particularly successful in this regard.

43. It is worth noting that the lack of organization of salaried workers may also depress their wages relative to those of unionized workers. Further to the extent that we view inflation as a way to redistribute in an environment where monetary decreases would cause conflict or where income is legally fixed in monetary terms it is likely to be particularly effective against unorganized workers.

44. A 1976 Gallup poll with a sample of 23,086 found around 32 to 35 percent of white-collar workers were independents compared with around 30 to 34 percent of blue-collar workers and 29 percent of service workers. The most Democratic white-collar group is clerical workers (45 percent Democratic, 23 percent Republican) and the least Democratic is sales workers (36 percent Democratic, 29 percent Republican). See Everett Carll Ladd with Charles D. Hadley, *Transformations of the American Party System*, 2d ed. (New York: Norton, 1978), p. 296.

45. See C. Wright Mills, *The New Middle Class* (New York: Oxford University Press, 1951) pp. 63–76.

46. Fixed-income groups such as the elderly, the disabled and welfare recipients are typically the least mobile and the most financially constrained. These two things sharply deter the costly, time-consuming process of interest group organization.

47. See Swan, "Inflation and Income," for a description of the pre-1972 process.

48. "Indeed, our emphasis here must be on insisting that every possible protection be given the poor, the disabled and the elderly who are bearing the greatest hardships in the current depressed and inflated economy. This means improvements—not cutbacks—in the income security and social service programs." Bert Seidman, testifying for the AFL-CIO at the Conference on Inflation. See Executive Office of the President, *Health, Education*

and Welfare, Income Security, Social Services Conference on Inflation, September 19–20, 1974, p. 114.

49. Most significant representation of racial minorities is done by the NAACP, the National Urban League, the Congress on Racial Equality, the Southern Christian Leadership Conference, Operation Breadbasket and the Black Caucus. The power of these groups, while still minor, has increased greatly over our period.

50. Charitable groups such as Lions International, Kiwanis International, Rotary International, the Salvation Army, Volunteers of America, the YMCA and the Easter Seal Society tend to eschew the political arena. Although they do much to help many fixed-income recipients, especially the handicapped and the aged poor, their "private" orientation, the implicit competition with government welfare programs and the middle-class character of their membership make them poor representatives of the interests of the poor.

51. Some of these are the National Association of Catholic Charities, the American Jewish Committee, the National Council of Churches of Christ, the National Council of Churches and the American Friends Service Committee. Churches tend to feel special responsibility for needs of poor people of their faith.

52. The Ford Foundation with assets of over $3.5 billion is easily the most important. Next in order of importance are the Johnson, Rockefeller, Duke, Lily, Pew, Kellogg and Mott Foundations. Not all of these feel any special responsibility for the poor but some do, including the Ford Foundation. They are more willing than charities or churches to lobby for the poor, but their tax-exempt status makes them vulnerable and in recent years they have been more restrained than in the 1960s.

53. The three major representative groups are the American Association of Retired Persons, the National Council on the Aging and the National Council of Senior Citizens. Two younger groups, The Gray Panthers and the National Alliance of Senior Citizens, seek an active part in policy making, albeit from opposite ends of the ideological spectrum.

54. "Poor and low income persons are already making the major sacrifices in the inflationary period. Thus, it is essential that funds for human services programs for poor and low income persons be substantially increased." Resolution D, signed by representatives of virtually all national organizations participating in the HEW Conference on Inflation. See Executive Office of the President, *Income Security Conference*, pp. 70–72.

55. At the Conference on Inflation, September 19, 1974, all prominent old people's groups including the AARP, the Gerontological Society and the National Council on Senior Citizens viewed inflation as the priority issue, with employment a weak second and growth virtually unmentioned. See ibid., pp. 76–183.

56. Employment is of some importance to old people's groups. At the Conference on Inflation, September 19, 1974, the National Retired Teachers Association and the AARP called for removal of labor market barriers which preclude the elderly from earning income to supplement their inflation-ridden fixed income. Ibid., pp. 164–66.

57. The NRTA and the AARP also called for a separate aged index because of their different expenditure patterns. Ibid., pp. 161–64.

58. The complexity of the issues involved leads even groups which are heavily involved in the process of economic policy making, such as business groups, unions and political parties, to occasionally make inconsistent statements on the issues. It is therefore hardly surprising that groups with only marginal involvement make statements that are not economically consistent. The groups tend to focus on narrow issues and ignore the larger implication of those positions.

59. This is due in large measure to the concentration of unemployment among minorities living in central cities. The fact that welfare is partly funded and largely administered at the local level also makes urban governance easier during periods of high employment. Urban groups such as the U.S. Conference of Mayors, the National Urban Coalition and the Urban Institute combine expertise and political clout and their mutual interest in lowering unemployment leads them to cooperate closely with the more economically inclined civil rights groups such as the National Urban League.

60. It should be noted that the inflationary implications of the policies recommended by these groups are not publically admitted by the groups and in many cases are not perceived.

61. "Today we are confronted by both inflation and unemployment. While the problem of inflation is certainly the more serious of the two, our Associations recognize that the continued pursuit of drastically restrictive monetary and fiscal policies may push the rate of unemployment far above its already unacceptable level." John Martin, Consultant to the National Retired Teachers Association and American Association of Retired Persons. "The traditional views of fighting inflation by balanced federal budgets, high interest rates and artificially-deflated methods has already brought us to the edge of economic disaster . . . Instead of the unworkable methods we need to have tax reforms that cut taxes for low income families while closing loopholes for the better off. Also, we need a massive federal public employment program accompanied by necessary cuts in the swollen defense budget." Alexander Allen, Deputy Executive Director of the National Urban League. Both quotes are from Executive Office of the President, *Income Security Conference*, pp. 147 and 232, respectively.

62. It should be noted that this result could be due to age and/or generation effects instead of, or in addition to, the attitudes engendered by being in a retirement situation. Thus it seems reasonable that people could become more risk-averse with age and it is possible that the inflation rates of the 1960s might seem particularly threatening to a generation brought up in a period of near stable prices.

63. Hibbs, "Dynamics of Political Support."

64. Those between fifty and sixty-five could be expected reasonably to have a greater dislike of unemployment than those over-sixty-five. The elderly may however place more weight on unemployment because of their experiences during the 1930s.

65. In 1950 about 22 percent of the private workforce was covered by private pensions. This had increased to 44 percent by 1974. Less than 30 percent of retirees in 1974 received private pensions and only 32 percent of those receiving such pensions got more than $3,000 per annum. See Alicia Munnell, *The Future of Social Security* (Washington D.C.: Brookings Institution, 1977), pp. 19–24.

66. See Phelps, *Inflation Policy*; and Hollister and Palmer, "Impact of Inflation."

67. "Inflation, while adversely affecting everyone, is not nondiscriminatory. It imposes an unequal burden upon those least able to endure—the poor." Rev. E. Lowry, Chairman, Southern Christian Leadership Conference. "While inflationary food prices have affected the upper and middle classes, the effect has been even more devastating on the poor." J. L. Tillman, executive director, National Welfare Rights Organization. Both quotes are from Executive Office of the President, *Income Security Conference*, pp. 235 and 242, respectively. It should be noted that the inflation of the early 1970s was somewhat different from the earlier inflation looked at by Hollister and Palmer in that food prices increased faster, rather than more slowly, than the rest of the Consumer Price Index.

68. See ibid., pp. 269–70. From the point of view of the poverty groups this is a matter of necessity, though they have some moral weight and some support from the bureaucracy, and within Congress and some administrations they need the resources of the AFL-CIO to overcome any but the weakest opposition. The AFL-CIO has been particularly important for the aged. As Derthick shows, it has long been the strongest ally of the social security program and the National Council of Senior Citizens was virtually created by them. See Martha Derthick, *Policy Making for Social Security* (Washington, D.C.: Brookings Institution, 1979), pp. 197–98.

69. Downs, *Economic Democracy*; Nordhaus, "Political Business Cycle"; C. Duncan MacRae, "A Political Model of the Business Cycle," *Journal of Political Economy* 85 (April 1977): 239–63.

70. Benjamin Page, *Choices and Echoes in Presidential Elections* (Chicago: University of Chicago Press, 1978); Gerald M. Pomper with Susan Lederman, *Elections in America: Control and Influence in Democratic Politics*, 2d ed. (New York: Longman, 1980); Hibbs, "Political Parties."

71. Domhoff, *Powers That Be*; Jacob Murray Edelman, *Political Language: Words that Succeed and Policies that Fail* (New York: Academic Press, 1977).

72. O'Connor, *Fiscal Crisis*.

73. For example in the 1980 presidential election, which offered candidates with more than normally different economic philosophies, the Democratic platform promised, "We

will continue to pursue the fight against inflation in ways not designed or intended to increase unemployment." *C Q Weekly Report* 38 (August 16, 1980): 2390. Compare this with the Republican platform's assertion that "our foremost goal here and at home is simple: economic growth and full employment without inflation." *C Q Weekly Report* 38 (July 19, 1980): 2030.

74. Tufte provides a fascinating analysis of differences in emphasis between mentions of inflation and mentions of unemployment in the platforms of the two parties and in issues of *Economic Report of the President* put out under Democratic and Republican administrations. See Tufte, *Political Control*. I would however differ from Tufte in assessing the significance of these differences. As the documents in question are read thoroughly only by strong party activists, political scientists and professional economists, I would regard them as semi-public rather than public statements. Further, as footnote 70 above illustrates, the difference in emphasis does not mean that the two parties clearly claim one goal and reject the other.

75. "We must realize that long-term economic growth in real terms can be achieved not *with* but only *without* inflation." Robert B. Anderson, Secretary of the Treasury, April 20, 1959, in Franklin L. Burdette, *Readings for Republicans* (New York: Oceana, 1960), p. 93. This view is typical, and subsequent Republican presidents and candidates have not deviated significantly from this position, with the possible exception of the first Nixon administration in the 1970–71 period.

76. "We are unalterably opposed to unwarranted growth of Federal power. We shall carry forward the worthy effort of the Kestenbaum Commission on Intergovernmental Affairs to clarify Federal relationships and strengthen State and local government. We shall continue to dispense with Federal activities wrongfully competing with private enterprise, and take other sound measures to reduce the cost of government." Republican Platform of 1956, in Kirk H. Porter and Donald B. Johnson, eds., *National Party Platforms, 1840–1965* (Urbana: University of Illinois Press, 1956), p. 553.

77. In fact the government deficit has been greater under Republican than Democratic administrations. The average annual deficit in deflated 1972 dollars for all levels of government was $3.23 billion under the Eisenhower administration and $12.36 billion under the Nixon-Ford administration. In contrast there was a $9.97 surplus under the Truman administration, a deficit of $5.00 billion under the Kennedy-Johnson administration and a deficit of $6.38 billion under the Carter administration. These figures are however somewhat misleading as they are largely due to the effects of the automatic stabilizers built into the tax and expenditure structure. If we look at the budgets of the various administrations using the full employment surplus concept, with full employment at 4 percent, the Republicans have only had deficits in 1954, 1972 and 1975. For a more detailed comparison of budgeting deficits under the full employment surplus concept see Perry, "Stabilization Policy."

78. This tendency was manifest in the Eisenhower administration's emphasis on monetary policy. "It was the first period in which monetary policy was free to play the role of partner to fiscal policy which the postwar consensus prescribed for it. Moreover, and this was the main element in the test, the country had its first Republican administration in twenty years." Herbert Stein, *The Fiscal Revolution in America* (Chicago: University of Chicago Press, 1969), p. 281. As chairman of the CEA under Nixon, Stein placed heavy emphasis on the role of monetary policy in the policy mix.

79. In this the Reagan administration is following Republican tradition rather than being innovative. Despite this bias, federal government spending in real terms has in fact grown during all the postwar Republican administrations, though no more than under Democratic administrations. It must be remembered however that this was in a period of worldwide expansion in the governmental sector and that only in the 1952–1954 period was there a Republican administration and a Republican Congress.

80. An examination of figures 8 and 9 shows that although the Phillips curve trade-off between inflation and unemployment was not markedly different from that of other industrial countries, unemployment, even under Democratic administrations, has been higher than in other industrial countries and inflation has been lower. The Democrats during the 1960s regarded 4 percent unemployed as the "full employment point" at a time when British governments saw full employment as around 2 percent unemployed.

81. In the period 1948–1975 average unemployment rates under Democratic administrations were 4.6 percent. Under Republican administrations they were 5.2 percent. If one allows for lagged effects of change of regime as does Douglas Hibbs in "Political Parties," then the party differences are even greater.

82. Only under President Nixon have the Republicans tried to implement a wage-price policy and even then it was only after considerable pressure from a Democratic Congress.

83. This is clearly manifested in the debate over the substance of the economic stimulus package for 1977. While not succumbing to labor's insistence on manpower policy emphasis, the Democrats did include it in a relatively minor role, complementary to their other preferences such as the income tax rebate, income tax reform and the business tax credit.

84. It should be noted that the Roosevelt and Truman administrations hardly used monetary policy at all. Only after the 1951 agreement between the Federal Reserve and the Treasury did a systematic monetary policy become possible.

85. This was particularly well exhibited in the 1961–65 period when tax cuts and expenditure increases were applied concomitantly with great success until Vietnam intervened. Heller calls this "the classic example of modern fiscal policy and multiplier economic at work." Heller, *New Dimensions*, p. 72. It was also described as a "triumph of high test Keynesian economic therapy." Dexter Keezer, "Business and Government—Do They Speak the Same Language?" *Saturday Review*, March 5, 1966, p. 23.

86. During the 1960s, as well as most of the 1950s, Democrats saw 4 percent unemployment as the "full employment" mark, although at the end of the 1960s there was some willingness to look at a lower figure. See Heller, *New Dimensions*, p. 64. In the 1970s however the combination of higher inflation and unemployment with structural changes in the composition of the labor force led to some upward revisions toward a 5–5½ percent figure. The Republicans have generally thought an unemployment rate 1 to 2 percent above that favored by the Democrats to be more realistic.

87. As has been pointed out by many commentators this is almost certainly due in part to the low rates of unionization in the South and the fact that the constituencies of many southern congressmen were more rural than those of northern congressmen.

88. This is illustrated by the Ways and Means Committee scores on support for a larger federal role. In the two years before their appointment, the eleven Republicans appointed to the committee in the 1957–1966 period voted for bills that enlarged the federal economic role 19 percent of the time on average. This compares with scores of 79 percent for the seven southern Democrats and 91 percent for the nine northern Democrats appointed during this period. Though the scores for the Ways and Means Committee members understate somewhat the differences between northern and southern Democrats more generally, it is reasonable to conclude that southern Democrats vote more like northern Democrats than Republicans on spending issues. Furthermore the Ways and Means Committee shaped much of the economic legislation during the 1947–1975 period. For further discussion see Manley, *Politics of Finance*, especially pp. 31 and 41. However, in the early 1980s, as the South moved from a one- to a two-party region, and as economic issues became more visible, southern Democrats came under increasing pressure from the right and their voting patterns moved closer to those of their Republican counterparts.

89. Looking at what he calls the "government management" dimension, Aage Clausen finds only about 5 percent of the variation in policy positions of congressmen in the 85th and 86th House is explained by their region or state, whereas 84 percent is explained by their party affiliation. This compares with 55 percent explained by region and party and 5 percent explained party affiliation for civil liberties policies. For further information see Aage R. Clausen, *How Congressmen Decide: A Policy Focus* (New York: St. Martin's Press, 1973), p. 168.

90. Pomper with Lederman, *Elections in America*, p. 164.

91. An example is the much vaunted Reagan tax cut proposal, which though advertised by Republicans as a major reduction in the tax burden, and by the Democrats as the height of fiscal irresponsibility, was actually intended to leave 1984 federal revenues at the same level as 1981 in real terms.

92. For example President Johnson is often thought of as having greatly and permanently expanded the role of government in the economy. However in 1963 federal budget outlays

were 19.3 percent of GNP. In 1969 they were 20.4 percent. Total government spending, including state and local spending, was 31 percent of GNP in 1963 and 32.7 percent in 1969. All other developed nations except Japan spent even more, with the average being about 5 percent higher than in the United States. Further, most of these countries expanded the percent of GNP going to government even faster than the United States in the 1963–1969 period.

93. Many important organizations, such as the Business Roundtable and the Business Council, operate in considerable secrecy and their influence is hard to prove. For a good attempt to deal with such organizations see McConnell, *Private Power*, chap. 8.

94. The reasons have to do in part with the looseness of the parties and the fact that most Republican presidents in the postwar period have had to face Democratic Congresses and in part with more general explanations. See Paul Peretz, "Who Gets What, How and Why: The Economic Effects of Party Change," paper presented at the American Political Science Convention, New York, September 4, 1979.

95. An objection could be made that this is because policy is constrained in the long run by the natural rate. It can be answered that, even if there is a natural rate, one would expect powerful Democratic presidents to choose a low short-term rate, thereby unloading higher short-term rates onto their Republican successors.

96. These figures are consistent with time series analyses by Hibbs and Beck, though more so with Beck, who argues for a smaller party effect on unemployment than Hibbs. See Hibbs, "Political Parties," and Nathaniel Beck, "Parties, Administrations and American Macro-economic Outcomes," *American Political Science Review* 76 (March 1982): 83–93.

97. Nordhaus, "Political Business Cycle"; MacRae, "Political Model."

98. Assar Lindbeck, "Stabilization Policy in Open Economics with Endogenous Politicians," *American Economic Review* 66 (March 1976): 1–19.

99. Bruno S. Frey and H.J. Ramser, "The Political Business Cycle: A Comment," *Review of Economic Studies* 43 (October 1976): 553–55.

100. Bennett T. McCallum, "The Political Business Cycle: An Empirical Test," *Southern Economic Journal* 44 (January 1978): 504–15.

101. Nordhaus was in fact a member of President Carter's Council of Economic Advisers.

102. Tufte, *Political Control*.

103. Ibid., pp. 101–102.

104. Ibid., p. 27.

105. There is a possible way out of the contradiction. It is conceivable that disposable income could increase even when the economy was being slowed. This does not appear to be the case. Per capita disposable income grew faster, or declined less, than per capita GNP in four of the postwar presidential election years, but grew more slowly in five others. Of the two theories the stimulation hypothesis fits better. However even here it is worth noting that per capita GNP grew more slowly than its postwar average in four of the nine presidential election years. See Winters et al., "Political Behavior," for a careful and skeptical analysis of Tufte's evidence.

106. Hibbs, "Political Parties"; Tufte, *Political Control*.

107. Although the figures vary over time, in 1976 around 52 percent of blue-collar workers were Democrats and around 16 percent were Republicans. This compares with around 38 percent Democrats and around 28 percent Republicans among professionals and executives. See Everett Carl Ladd with Charles D. Hadley, *Transformations of the American Party System*, 2d ed. (New York: Norton, 1978), pp. 296–97, for a complete breakdown of party identification by various categories of stratification.

108. Schlozman and Verba show that in 1972 37 percent of those employed failed to vote compared to 47 percent of the unemployed. They attribute this primarily to the socio-economic characteristics of the poor and to lower registration by those more likely to be unemployed. Rosenstone finds that short-term unemployment causes reduced turnout net of other characteristics of the unemployed, something he attributes to higher participation costs. Feldman's thesis that the unemployed blame themselves rather than the system for their predicament seems however a more useful explanation. See Kay L. Schlozman and Sidney Verba, *Injury to Insult: Unemployment, Class and Political Response* (Cambridge, Mass.: Harvard University Press, 1979), chap. 9; Rosenstone, "Economic Adversity;

Feldman, "Economic Self-Interest." For figures on non-voting in 1976 see William J. Crotty and Gary C. Jacobson, *American Political Parties in Decline* (Boston: Little, Brown, 1980), pp. 14–16. The presented figures should be multiplied by around 1.78 to allow for the tendency to claim one has voted when one has not. For data on non-participation see Sidney Verba and Norman Nie, *Participation in America: Political Democracy and Social Equality* (New York: Harper & Row, 1972). An extensive bibliography on non-voting can be found in Gary King, "Non-Voting, 1969–1979," *News for Teachers of Political Science* no. 29 (Spring 1981): 10–15.

109. Schlozman and Verba, *Injury to Insult,* chap. 11.

110. Frank Sorauf, *Party Politics in America*, 4th ed. (Boston: Little, Brown, 1980), pp. 155–56. It will be recalled that we examined the attitudes of those in the different parties in chapter 5. They appear to fit, at best, only roughly with official party ideologies.

111. This is however almost certainly an artifact of the class composition of the two parties and the disproportionate Democratic party identification of blue-collar workers and union members.

Index

DATE DUE			
GAYLORD			PRINTED IN U.S.A.